JUDAISM AND
CHRISTIANITY

essays by

LEO BAECK

translated with an introduction
by Walter Kaufmann

JUDAISM AND

CHRISTIANITY

The Jewish Publication Society of America

Philadelphia 1958 · 5719

The publication of this book was made possible through a bequest by Sidney Neumann, of Philadelphia, at one time a trustee of the Jewish Publication Society.

The Society gratefully dedicates this volume to his memory.

A NOTE TO THE READER

Dr. Leo Baeck was still among the living when the Jewish Publication Society decided to make available to the English reading public some of his writings bearing on Judaism and the origins of Christianity. Dr. Baeck graciously agreed to this plan. He chose the essays to be included in the volume and picked Dr. Walter Kaufmann as the translator.

We are grateful to Dr. Kaufmann for his willingness to give so much of his time and energy to this task.

Dr. Baeck also suggested the inclusion in this volume of the essay, "The Faith of Paul," which appeared in the *Journal of Jewish Studies,* published in England, vol. III (1952), no. 3. We are grateful to the *Journal* and its editors for their courtesy.

Unfortunately, circumstances made it necessary for us to postpone the publication of the volume until now. In the meantime, Dr. Baeck passed on to the Academy on High. May the thought and scholarship which he bequeathed to us serve to deepen our understanding of the faith and strengthen our loyalties to the tradition which he exemplified so nobly in his life.

THE JEWISH PUBLICATION SOCIETY
OF AMERICA

LEO BAECK: *A Biographical Introduction
by Walter Kaufmann*   3

1 THE SON OF MAN   23

2 THE GOSPEL AS A DOCUMENT OF
THE HISTORY OF THE JEWISH FAITH   41

3 THE FAITH OF PAUL   139

4 MYSTERY AND COMMANDMENT   171

5 ROMANTIC RELIGION   189

LEO BAECK: *A Biographical Introduction
by Walter Kaufmann*

When Leo Baeck died in 1956, he was widely hailed as one of the most saintly men of our time; but few indeed realized that he was the author of one of the most important polemics ever launched against Christianity—and very probably the most interesting one written from the point of view of another religion. Unlike Kierkegaard, in his *Attack on Christendom,* Baeck did not merely criticize the millions of indifferent Christians, but the Christian religion itself. And unlike other critics, he did not attack religion in general but only what he called "romantic religion."

A few days before publication, in 1938, Baeck's critique of "Romantic Religion," and the whole book of essays of which it formed a part, was destroyed by the secret police of the Nazi state. Less than ten copies survived. Soon after, World War II broke out. And Baeck survived it. He resolved that his essay should be translated and published in English, along with the other essays in the present volume, which he himself selected. In time to come, he may well be remembered as much for this book as for anything else.

2

To use one of his own favorite expressions, "there is something twofold about" Leo Baeck. Although his ideas may well have their greatest effect still ahead of them, he himself belongs to a past chapter of Jewish history, no less than Maimonides. It was a proud chapter: there have been few periods in history when so small a group has made as many major contributions to literature and music, art and science, philosophy and religion, as did German Jewry.

Still flourishing in the nineteen-twenties, it is dead today. To give some idea of its many-sided genius, it is best to enumerate at least a few names: Felix Mendelssohn and Jacques Offenbach, Gustav Mahler and Arnold Schönberg; Marx, Lassalle, and Rathenau; Ehrlich, Einstein, and Freud, and August von Wassermann, Otto Meyerhof, and James Franck; Börne and Borchardt, Wolfskehl and Mombert, Arnold and Stefan Zweig; Ludwig Borchardt, the Egyptologist; Husserl and Cassirer. If a few of these men were Jews in spite of themselves, and still others—like Adolf von Baeyer and Hugo von Hofmannsthal, Heinrich Hertz and Gustav Hertz, and Ludwig Wittgenstein—were only of partly Jewish descent, the Jews of Germany and Austria also made major contributions to Jewish history and Jewish studies; for example, Leopold Zunz and Michael Sachs, Abraham Geiger and Samson Raphael Hirsch, Gabriel Riesser, Graetz, and Herzl.

Though this necrology includes names of the first rank, the most distinctive contribution of German Jewry lies elsewhere. In the areas considered so far American Jewry bids fair to continue where German Jewry left off. But there were also some German-speaking Jews who somehow straddled German and

A Biographical Introduction

Jewish literature and thought—rather more so than any of those named so far. Most famous among these are Heine and Kafka; but alongside them there is a line of others who accented Judaism even more. It opens with Moses Mendelssohn, includes Moritz Lazarus and Heymann Steinthal and Hermann Cohen, and ends with Franz Rosenzweig, Martin Buber—and Leo Baeck.

Baeck was equally at home in Aristotle and in the Talmud, in the Bible and in German literature: he was the heir of the best the world could offer him—and a rabbi. The way in which he fused this multifarious heritage was inimitably his own; but the ability and the resolve to effect such a fusion he shared with Moses Mendelssohn and his other heirs.

In these men Judaism lost the narrowness of the ghetto and recovered the scope it had always had when it was free—without ceasing to be Jewish. The major reason for the wide appeal of these men and their impact was that they were not eclectics, nor primarily apologists.

There was something serene and irenic about Baeck, and no man could have been more polite than he could be. But he had fire and originality and was at heart an iconoclast. He never preached a sermon that did not sparkle with new ideas, and every conversation with him and almost every letter from him was memorable. He was sometimes wrong, but always wise and never dull.

It is entirely fitting that his essays on *Judaism and Christianity* should be published as his last major work. For his first major work was his book on *The Essence of Judaism,* his reply to Harnack's classic on *The Essence of Christianity.* In English, this point, which no German reader could miss, has been lost because Harnack's book was translated under the title *What is*

Christianity? Baeck's thought was polemical from the beginning, and the central theme from beginning to end is his polemic against Christianity.

It might be fashionable to slur over this truth and to misrepresent the facts ever so slightly by saying that he wanted to reopen a dialogue between Judaism and Christianity, as if he had wanted to restore Judaism to the role of an equal partner. With his staggering politeness, he might even have put the matter that way himself. It is told that in his homiletics class he would often begin his comments on a trial sermon: "It was wonderful." But after some generous compliments he would proceed, "If I may say just one thing"—and rip the sermon to shreds.

Baeck's point was not that Judaism was not inferior to Christianity but rather that Judaism was distinctly superior. It is one of the oddities of our time that this view is scarcely ever discussed in public. Yet it would be very strange if it were not shared by most Jews; and Christian theologians must surely take for granted that this is at the very least the position of practically all rabbis. Most Christians are convinced of the immeasurable superiority of Christianity over all other religions, and quite especially over Judaism; but it is polite to grant that the Jew, of course, considers his religion the equal of Christianity; and it is the acme of liberalism to grant that, theoretically at least, he might be right. The view, however, that Christianity is inferior to Judaism is simply ignored.

The Essence of Judaism could still be read as primarily a work of apologetics. The essays in the present volume are thoroughly militant in spirit, though so polite that those who merely browse in them might miss that fact. It would be a pity if they did. For whether

6

one agrees with Baeck on particular points or not, what he here tries to do needs doing so badly.

Serious Christians should care to know in what respects one of the outstanding Jewish thinkers of our time considered their religion to be open to objections: not just Catholicism or Luther, or some few beliefs or excesses, but the very core of Christianity. Religion tends to become repulsive when it is not under attack, and it is often at its best when it is persecuted. German Judaism was a case in point; so, specifically, are Baeck's essays. As Kierkegaard well knew, though his contemporary admirers seem to have forgotten it, Christianity needs less apologetics and more criticism. Serious Christians should therefore welcome Baeck's *Judaism and Christianity.*

Readers who consider themselves neither Jews nor Christians may find these essays fascinating in two ways. First, they may view them as unusually interesting contributions to the history of ideas. Secondly, adopting the perspective suggested here, they may concentrate on the manner in which so proud and wise a man responded to a hostile world, and particularly to the challenge of Christianity: Baeck's response differs not only from Heine's and Kafka's but also from Rosenzweig's and Buber's.

And Jewish readers? There is no danger that any of Baeck's writings will make them complacent: like the prophets, Baeck stresses the central importance of the challenge in Judaism rather more than his contemporaries. And he himself lived true to this challenge and exemplified what he taught, unlike some of the most outstanding German philosophers and theologians who before 1933 had talked, and after 1945 went right on talking, with a cracked existential pathos—cracked by the rift between life and thought or, as Baeck might have said, between "mystery and commandment," or, in one word, by their "romanticism." Baeck was a great man, and he may yet lead Jewish readers to reflect on dimensions of their own religion of which they had never been aware.

In sum, this is a signally important work for anyone seriously concerned with Judaism or Christianity. It may prove to be a seminal work. No doubt, it has faults —in the original, too—but a lack of nobility is not one of them.

3

Baeck's style was legendary even among his devotees in Germany. Nobody questioned that it was highly peculiar, but nobody minded seriously. It seemed natural that a man of Baeck's originality should express himself in unconventional ways.

One of his more frequent idioms was, *"Es ist ein zwiefaches"*—"It is something twofold." This phrase was generally followed by a prolonged contrast. Two good examples of this mode of thought may be found in the present volume, in the juxtaposition of "Mystery and Commandment" and of "Classical" and "Romantic Religion."

Whether one finds the roots of this dialectic in German philosophy or in the Talmud, this way of thinking is relatively rare in the English-speaking world. Baeck's thinking revolves around substantive concepts; and he does not explain these by placing them in the context of some experience until they become mere labels for something that could also be spelled out in greater detail. Rather he discusses them as if they were entities: he explains them not functionally but antithetically, by playing them off against some counter-concept.

In this way, his contrasts tend to become too neat and might even become entirely abstract and untrue to experience if it were not for his unusual fund of historical knowledge. He is never at a loss for illustrations that are not only pertinent but so important that they require us to reconsider our preconceptions.

Baeck's erudition is never second-hand, never a matter of being able to cite some dubious tract that comes in handy, never an obtrusively learned way of saying what we knew anyway. He read the Hebrew Scriptures in Hebrew, the New Testament and the Greek philosophers in Greek, Tertullian and Augustine and some of Luther in Latin, and, of course, German literature in German; and instead of producing convenient but questionable excerpts, he used quotations that came to him from an intimate knowledge of the sources. Since he always made his own translations, which occasionally involved new interpretations, the translations in the present volume often had to deviate from the standard versions.

One feature of Baeck's style that may strike some readers as more teutonic than talmudic is that in a sense it is deeply uncritical. Possible objections are scarcely ever considered, and when they are introduced it is often merely as foils for neat retorts. Baeck is the preacher and he is "telling us"—even in the long essay in which he criticizes the "romantic" conceptions of the finished man and of finished truth while upholding the ideals of search, quest, and step-by-step approximation. He seems to write as if he had the truth and merely faced the problem of communicating it. But what he does tell us is so profoundly opposed to traditional ideas about Judaism and Christianity that he simply did not have to worry lest the reader might be taken in before considering the matter fully. There was no danger whatsoever that his suggestions might be accepted as new dogmas. Obviously, Baeck was not trying to say the last word and to settle issues definitively. He wanted to make us reconsider unquestioned dogmas, unquestioned assumptions, unquestioned attitudes; he wanted to open up discussion of issues that are still held widely to be settled once and for all.

"There is something twofold about" his thinking: the voice is often the voice of a preacher—sometimes dogmatic, always serene and peaceable and polite—but the soul is the soul of a revolutionary who craves open horizons and is willing to tear down old walls of prejudice and preconception. Something of this contrast was obvious to all who knew him.

Less than a year before his death, he was invited to speak at the University of Frankfurt, in Germany, in February 1956. Academic speeches were read off by way of introducing him. Then Baeck spoke. He was in his eighties: tall, commanding, venerable. He did not use any notes at all—he never did. His speech, as always, was urgent and exciting—the speech of a young man who is full of ideas, some of them perhaps a little wild, and alive! His imagination had caught fire and he had something to say. He spoke about the idea of rebirth—and one could hardly help feeling that, in spite of her economic recovery, Germany was spiritually dead compared to this old man who, having come back from the grave of Theresienstadt, seemed so much younger than any other philosopher or theologian who had survived World War II in Germany. Unlike all the rest, he knew the meaning of rebirth.

4

About the art of translation people have very different ideas. The German tradition of translating Homer

A Biographical Introduction

into dactylic hexameters (Voss), Shakespeare, with every pun intact, into iambic pentameters (Schlegel), and every author in accordance with his own peculiar style, has never won wide acceptance in the English-speaking world.

In Germany, translating is respected as one of the fine arts, and the best German poets have added to the rich store of fine translations—from Goethe and Hölderlin to Stefan George and Rilke. In the United States, a translator is widely considered a writer manqué who, unable to write anything worthwhile himself, uses the content furnished by a foreign writer and imposes on it —not his own style which, alas, he lacks, but rather what his publisher considers currently acceptable English. Where Schlegel's translation of Shakespeare, and Voss's of Homer, are more or less definitive and need not be brought up to date any more than the originals, it is a common axiom in the English-speaking world— and follows from what has been said—that every generation must in turn make new translations of the same texts—assuming that public interest has survived the initial mutilation, which rarely happens.

Naturally, there are some fine English translations and many bad German translations; and the translator himself is the very last person who should discuss the quality of his own work. If he has any sense at all, then, having exposed himself rather more thoroughly to the original than almost anybody else, he should realize most clearly how inadequate his translation is. But he is not likely to find this inadequacy where others find it—and he may even find himself asked by his publisher to explain at least briefly what he has been trying to do.

It was during the winter 1950/51, after he had read my *Nietzsche: Philosopher, Psychologist, Antichrist,*

11

that Baeck asked me to translate his essays. He was enthusiastic about my translations because he found them so faithful. Feeling that my English versions of Nietzsche still sounded like Nietzsche, he expected that my English versions of Baeck would still sound like Baeck. To accede to his request and then to render his prose into ordinary English, void of any peculiarity, would have constituted a betrayal.

In this case, duty and inclination coincided. The Baeck translations were made in 1953 while I was also translating Nietzsche for a volume in The Viking Portable Library, and it was a welcome challenge to keep their idioms distinct. Later, when I translated Rilke and Heidegger, it seemed imperative not to flatten out their differences in style, either by making Heidegger sound like Rilke or, forbid, Rilke like Heidegger.

It should go without saying that a translator generally does not agree with all the ideas in the texts he translates, that he does not think the way his author does—and that he does not write the way his author does. But once he undertakes the translation, he is on his honor not to retouch the ideas, however slightly, to bring them closer to his own—and not to impute his own style to his author either. In the present volume, only a few obvious misprints in the references have been corrected. A few very minor departures from the original in "Mystery and Commandment" are due to Baeck himself. Any reader who cares to know what the translator thinks about some of the questions discussed in this book may turn to my *Critique of Religion and Philosophy* (Harper & Brothers). In the present volume, the voice is the voice of Baeck.

Long sentences, to be sure, have often been broken up in translation, and every effort has been made to produce a readable English text. But as this is Baeck's last book and some of the original texts are all but inaccessible, it is generally more important that the book should be exceedingly faithful to Baeck's intentions than that the reader should find it much smoother and easier than the German text ever was for German readers. What matters most is that he should find himself addressed by Leo Baeck.

5

Baeck is not nearly as well known in America as he ought to be. Therefore, at least a brief sketch of his life and major publications seems called for.

Baeck was born in Lissa, Posen, then a part of Prussia, on May 23, 1873. He studied in Breslau, Silesia, then also a part of Prussia, and in Berlin. It was in Berlin that he received his Ph.D. from the University and his rabbinical diploma from the *Lehranstalt für die Wissenschaft des Judentums,* to which he later returned as a teacher.

In 1905, when he was a rabbi in Oppeln, Silesia, he published *Das Wesen des Judentums.* For the second edition, in 1922, he revised the book thoroughly and expanded it from 167 pages to over 300. By 1932 the book had reached its sixth edition. In 1936 an English translation appeared in London; in 1948, a revision of that translation was brought out by Schocken Books in New York. *The Essence of Judaism* is the book for which its author was best known during his lifetime.

In 1912 Baeck accepted a call to Berlin. Two years later, World War I broke out. He volunteered as an army chaplain and served on both the Western and the Eastern fronts. After the war he resumed his work as a rabbi and a teacher at the *Lehranstalt.* He kept publishing, and a bibliography of "The Writings of Leo Baeck," compiled by Theodore Wiener and published by the Library of Hebrew Union College—Jewish Institute of Religion, Cincinnati, Ohio, in June, 1954, lists over 400 publications. But between the two World Wars he never found time for more than essays and reviews, and two volumes of collected essays.

The first such volume came out in 1933: *Wege im Judentum: Aufsätze und Reden*—i.e., "Paths in Judaism: Essays and Lectures." It was divided into six parts: Of Faith, Ties and Paths, History and Struggle, Goal and Conflict, Men and Destinies, *Hochschule* and Academy. Many of the essays in the first four parts also featured that characteristic "and." One of these, "Mystery and Commandment," originally published in *Der Leuchter* 1921/22, was selected by Baeck for inclusion in the present volume.

The second volume of collected essays bore the title *Aus drei Jahrtausenden: Wissenchaftliche Untersuchungen und Abhandlungen zur Geschichte des jüdischen Glaubens*—i.e., "Out of Three Thousand Years: Scholarly Inquiries and Essays concerning the History of the Jewish Faith." This book was printed but never published. The Gestapo destroyed almost the entire edition before publication. Less than ten copies were saved: one may be found in the New York Public Library, another in the library of Hebrew Union College in Cincinnati.

As this volume is all but lost, at least a list of its contents should be given here. It contains 24 essays which may be numbered here to facilitate references: 1. Does Traditional Judaism Possess Dogmas? 2. Theology and History. 3. Romantic Religion. 4. Judaism in the Church. 5. Greek and Jewish Preaching. 6. Two Examples of Midrashic Preaching. 7. The Ancient Opposition to the Haggadah. 8. The Pharisees: A Chapter of Jewish History. 9. The Gospel as a Document of the

History of the Jewish Faith. 10. The Son of Man. 11.
Simon Kefa. 12. Three Ancient Songs. 13. Just Men and
Angels. 14. Secharja ben Berachja. 15. The Third Gen-
eration. 16. Faith. 17. The Kingdom of God. 18 "He
That Dwelleth in the Bush." 19. The Origin of Jewish
Mysticism. 20. Sefer Yezira. 21. Sefer Habahir. 22.
Popular Philosophy in the Middle Ages. 23. The De-
velopment into an Ethical Personality. 24. Religious
Education.

All this may sound "scholarly" enough, as the subtitle says; even academic and innocuous. Why, then,
was the book destroyed by the secret police? There may
have been any number of reasons, but one of them was
probably that the book, far from being innocuous,
represented a rare act of courage—as any reader of the
present volume may judge for himself.

Four of these essays (numbers 4, 5, 8, and 19) have
been translated and included, along with two other
essays and a brief selection from number 9, in *The
Pharisees and Other Essays,* published in 1947 by
Schocken Books in New York. Three others, including
the two longest and most important essays Baeck
ever wrote, are included in the present book: numbers
3, 9, and 10. Any reader who turns to the essay on
"Romantic Religion" to look at the last two paragraphs
in the section on "Humanity" may form some notion of
one reason why the book was suppressed. He will also
realize quickly that the book, however scholarly, is far
from "academic." Indeed, it is more scholarly and less
academic than almost the entire religious and theological literature of our time.

An earlier version of the essay on "Romantic Religion" appeared in the *Festschrift* for the fiftieth an-
niversary of the *Hochschule (alias, Lehranstalt) für
die Wissenschaft des Judentums,* in 1922. It was then

intended as the first section of a larger work on "Classical and Romantic Religion." Unmistakably it represented one of Baeck's most important efforts. Later he revised and expanded it for inclusion in *Aus drei Jahrtausenden*. It is the final version of the text that has been translated for the present volume.

The essay on "The Gospel" was not only included in *Aus drei Jahrtausenden* but also appeared separately as a small volume in the so-called *Bücherei des Schocken Verlags*—a wonderful series of little volumes on Jewish subjects—in Berlin in 1938.

"The Son of Man" appeared originally in *Monatsschrift für Geschichte und Wissenschaft des Judentums,* in 1937, while "Mystery and Commandment," originally published in 1921/22, as mentioned above, is from *Wege im Judentum.*

The remaining essay, on "The Faith of Paul," was not translated by me. It appeared originally in *The Journal of Jewish Studies* in London in 1952 and was based on a lecture delivered to the "Society for Jewish Study" in London.

Before the Gestapo destroyed Baeck's book, he had become the acknowledged leader of German Jewry. After Hitler had come to power in 1933, a small committee had been formed to represent the Jews of Germany vis-à-vis the government, and Baeck had been elected chairman of this so-called *Reichsvertretung der Juden in Deutschland.*

The members had many opportunities to emigrate but stayed to alleviate as far as possible the lot of the remaining Jews and to help as many as possible to emigrate. Their negotiations sometimes took the members of the committee into foreign lands, but although they managed to evacuate their families from Germany, they themselves returned again and again into the lions' den—not because they trusted that God would deliver them but because they hoped to be able to deliver a few of their brothers. One by one, they gave up their lives in concentration camps. Baeck's own tribute "In Memory of Two of Our Dead"—Otto Hirsch and Julius Seligsohn—may be found in the first *Yearbook* of the Leo Baeck Institute of Jews from Germany, published by the East and West Library in London in 1956. The same volume contains many other essays on "Jewish Organization and Spiritual Resistance During the Hitler Epoch," on "Jewish Thought and Its Re-Orientation," and on the history of German Jewry.

In 1943 Baeck himself was deported to Theresienstadt where he continued to exert himself to keep up the morale of his fellow inmates. Because of his poor eyesight he had trained himself early to preach and teach without notes; now he taught philosophy as well as religious subjects without any books. Owing to a fortunate mistake, he escaped liquidation and survived until the Russian army arrived and liberated the prisoners at Theresienstadt. Immediately, he used his influence to help prevent any revenge.

He was then in his seventies, but anything but an old and broken man. His wife had died in Germany, his daughter was living in London. For years to come, he spent half the year in London with his daughter, the other half at the Hebrew Union College in Cincinnati, teaching. Indefatigably he commuted across the ocean. Nor was he content to rest in England for six months at a time. He traveled widely and gave occasional lectures in Israel, and also in Germany. And he continued to write.

In 1952 he published an essay on "Israel und das deutsche Volk" in the German periodical, *Merkur*. The response to this article, which is as completely honest as it is free from resentment, touched him more deeply than the reception of his steady flow of scholarly essays in English publications. In 1955 the Europäische Verlagsanstalt in Frankfurt am Main published a short book which Baeck had written during the Hitler years and dedicated "To the Life and Memory of My Wife!" *Dieses Volk: Jüdische Existenz*—i.e., "This People: Jewish Existence." One gathers that this little volume with its less than 200 pages was really read, read with the heart, by simple German people and by ministers— Baeck was moved by the letters that came to him from Germany—and even by reviewers.

Three reviews may be quoted here. The first appeared in *Die Kultur:* "When the two poets, Thomas Mann and Bertolt Brecht, died, Germany knew that two great men had left the realm of the living. Who knows it in the case of Leo Baeck, the 'poet on a higher plane,' who died November 2, 1956, in London? Germany may think today that it suffices morally to have Martin Buber's books on one's shelves. Buber's reputation should not be contested. No less important for humanistic German literature is the lifework of the rabbi, Leo Baeck—for a literature, that is, which rises above the merely aesthetic and places men's thinking at the center of their reflections." *Merkur* said: "The day will come when this book, probably the last great Jewish message in the German language, will be prized as an important testimony of Jewish teaching in this age and, no less, as the enduring legacy of a Jew from Germany to the German people." Finally, a sentence from *Deutsche Rundschau:* "In its beauty, intensity, simplicity, and greatness, his language becomes as plain as that of the Biblical patriarchs, as if it came from far away, and yet it welled up in the direst distress in our own midst."

A Biographical Introduction

After the War, Baeck wrote a sequel of almost twice the length of the original volume. He gave it the same title and subtitle; merely added "A Second Part." The book is no epitaph; the chapters are entitled: I. Growth and Rebirth. II. Way and Comfort. III. Praying and Learning. IV. The Kingdom of God. V. Hope. When the book appeared in 1957, Baeck was dead.

He needs no eulogy. He only needs to be read.

1

THE "SON OF MAN"

The question of the meaning of the words "son of man,"
ben adam, bar enash, has long been an important topic
in the history of religion. There is an almost insuper-
able opposition between that which this term originally
signified in its Hebrew and Aramaic form, and that
which it later came to mean in the Greek Gospels. For
the attempt, which has often been made, to establish
a relation between them by contending that the term
assumed a new significance in the Book of Enoch and in
the Fourth Book of Ezra, does not stand up under examination. Nor can it by any means be conceded under
these circumstances, however popular the idea may be
in some quarters, that the language and teachings of
Judaism in the century before the destruction of the
second temple used the expression to designate the expected messiah.[1]

1. For the multifarious answers which have been given to this
question, compare the following works: C. G. Montefiore, *The
Synoptic Gospels* I (2), pp. 64-80; H. Weinel, *Biblische Theologie
des Neuen Testaments,* § 34; Bousset-Gressmann, *Die Religion*

The phrase is of ancient biblical origin. It belongs to elevated, poetic style and, through the individual, designates the species. Often it is used alternately with the other collective names for man: *ish, enosh, geber.* In the Pentateuch it occurs once, in Balaam's speech; in Joshua, Judges, Samuel, and Kings it does not occur at all. The first part of the Book of Isaiah does not contain it, probably owing to mere chance; but we do encounter it in the second part of this Book as well as in Jeremiah, Psalms, and Job. Without exception, it designates man in general, as opposed either to God or to the animals; it denotes the human race, the human kind.[2]

In the Book of Ezekiel, the phrase has a special character; it is used by God, often together with the pronoun "thou," to address the prophet. Here the prophetic style shows its manifoldness. Like Abraham and Moses before them, Samuel and Elijah, too, had heard God address them by their names; likewise, Amos and Jeremiah—both after having been asked by God, "what seest thou?" The other prophets did not experience the call in the same way, not even Isaiah when he heard his

---

des Judentums im spät-hellenistischen Zeitalter, pp. 262ff.; G. F. Moore, *Judaism in the First Century,* II, pp. 333ff.; Wellhausen, *Evangelium Marci,* pp. 14f. and 66ff.; J. Klausner, *Jeshu hanozri,* pp. 266ff.; H. Junker, *Untersuchungen über literarische und exegetische Probleme des Buches Daniel*; and the literature listed in the second edition of *Religion in Geschichte und Gegenwart,* in the article "Menschensohn." For the general character of the pseudepigraphic literature, compare Travers Herford, *Talmud and Apocrypha,* pp. 171ff. and 211ff.; and for the more general bearing of this question on the history of religion, compare Rudolf Otto, *Menschensohn und Gottesreich.*
2. Numbers 23.19; Jeremiah 49.18 and 49.33, 50.40, 51.43; Isaiah 51.12, 56.2; Job 16.21, 25.6; Psalms 8.5, 80.18, 146.3. The Psalms very often employ the plural, *bne adam,* which we also find in Moses' song of farewell, in Joel, in Micah, in Jeremiah, and in Proverbs.

call in a wonderful and entirely personal manner, nor Zechariah when he, too, was asked, "what seest thou?" Only in the Book of Daniel is the prophet again addressed by name by the messenger of God, presumably as a fully intended archaism.

It is entirely in accord with the whole character of Ezekiel that the poetic expression, "son of man," should for this prophet be the way in which the voice of God makes its demands on him; for again and again this prophet feels seized and hurled down by God's sublime omnipotence, and so he must always be called and raised up again—but called not by his name, but with these words, "son of man," which signify to him the whole vast distance between himself and God. The Book of Daniel adopted this phrase from Ezekiel; Daniel, too, when humbled to the ground, is once addressed thus by a messenger from heaven.[3]

But in addition to this, the Book of Daniel lends our words, as well as their synonyms, a special connotation. It tells of beings who belong to the world above, yet look like men. In this it follows the expressions which Ezekiel used to describe his first vision. As Ezekiel says, ". . . . likeness of four living creatures; and this was their appearance: they had the likeness of a man—*demut adam*"; "upon the likeness of the throne was a likeness as the appearance of a man—*demut kemar'e adam*"; Daniel, too, says, "behold, there stood before me as the appearance of a man—*kemar'e gaber*"; "behold, one like the similitude of the sons of men touched

3. Ezekiel 2.1 and often; 2.8 and often; Genesis 22.1; Exodus 3.4; I Samuel 3.10; I Kings 19.9 and 19.11; Amos 7.8 and 8.2; Jeremiah 1.11 and 24.3; Isaiah 6.9; Zechariah 4.2 and 6.2; Daniel 10.11f., 12.4 and 12.9, and 8.17. For man in general, as opposed to the animals, and once also as opposed to God, the Book of Ezekiel employs the word *adam*.

my lips—*kidemut bene adam*"; "there touched me
again one like the appearance of a man—*kemar'e
adam*"; and then finally, in the Aramaic section, the
sentence which was to become so important in the history of religion: "Behold, there came with the clouds
of heaven one like unto a son of man—*kebar enash*."
Here the reference each time is not to a man, but to one
who has the appearance of a man, who looks like a man;
and only after further designations have made this
quite clear, does the text say, more briefly: "man." For
example: "a man clothed in linen, whose loins were
girded with fine gold of Uphaz; his body also was like
the beryl; and his face as the appearance of lightning";
or "the voice of a man between the banks of Ulai"; or,
when the name can be given, still more briefly, "the
man Gabriel." Always a being from above is meant, one
of those with human appearance dwelling up there. It
is not God, and it is not a human being, but yet is compared with what is human. In the place where after
"the great beasts, which are four," "there came with
the clouds of heaven one like unto a son of man," something human may vibrate in the phrase: that in which
the bestial manifests its power is here opposed by that
in which the human shows what is highest in it.[4]

The style of the Book of Daniel became decisive for
all subsequent apocalypses. We see this first of all in the
so-called image speeches of the Book of Enoch, which
are really nothing but an old midrash for the Book of
Daniel. The Book of Daniel is here presupposed everywhere and its words, which can be understood only by
referring back to Daniel, are used throughout. Just as
there, God is spoken of here, too, in an image: "the

4. Ezekiel 1.5, 1.10, 1.26; Daniel 8.15, 10.16, 10.18, 7.13, 10.5,
8.16, 12.6, and 12.7.

ancient of days" and "the hair of his head like pure wool"; and here, too, we read of the "son of man" and encounter references to him. And what is said about him is also the same as in Daniel. As the Book of Daniel says of him that he appears after thrones have been put there and God has sat down amid his myriads for judgment, after the books have been opened and the power been taken away from the beasts, that he may now be granted lasting dominion, so the Book of Enoch, too, says: "There I saw him who has the head of an old man, and his head was white as wool, and with him was one whose face was as that of a man"; "to him, to this son of man, the conclusion of the judgment was entrusted, and he made the sinners and seducers of this world disappear from the earth and perish"; and we then encounter reference after reference to him who is "as a son of man."

It is much the same in the Fourth Book of Ezra. Even as the vision of Daniel begins with this apparition: "Behold, the four winds of the heaven broke forth upon the great sea; and four great beasts came up from the sea," and then reaches its most astonishing point in the image, "there came with the clouds of heaven one like unto a son of man," the Fourth Book of Ezra says: "A tremendous gale rose up from the sea and stirred up all its waves. I beheld how the gale brought one out of the heart of the sea who had the likeness of a man. I beheld how this man flew with the clouds of heaven." It is the same, finally, in the Apocalypse of John, The Revelation of St. John the Divine. Daniel had seen one "clothed in linen, whose loins were girded with fine gold . . . , his eyes as torches of fire, and his arms and his feet like in color to burnished brass, and the voice of his words like a tremendous roaring"; and John envisages "one like unto a son of man, clothed with a garment

27

down to the feet, and girt about the breasts with a golden girdle . . . , his eyes were as a flame of fire and his feet like unto burnished brass . . . and his voice as the roaring of many waters"; and like Daniel, he, too, sees "a bright cloud, and sitting upon the cloud one like unto a son of man."[5]

The images and words of the Book of Daniel still speak in all these books, either by being simply repeated or haggadically elaborated; nowhere is anything essential and new added to the conceptions of the Book of Daniel. It is nothing less than the apocalypse *par excellence;* and one of its important elements is the apparition of him "who is like unto a son of man and comes with the clouds of heaven and steps before God."

·

5. Enoch 46.1ff., 71.10ff., 42.2ff., 48.2, 69.26ff., 70.1, 71.17. Note also 60.10 where Enoch is addressed, after the manner of Ezekiel, "thou son of man," and 71.14 where Enoch is called the son of man who has been born for justice; here "son of man" designates simply man, after the ancient biblical manner. On the other hand, compare with this, both in the same and in the preceding chapter, 71.17 and 70.1, "that son of man" which designates, in the manner usual in this book, the one with the appearance of a man in the Book of Daniel. The only original terminology in Enoch is: son of the mother of all the living (compare the compilation in Beer, note on 46.1), *i.e.,* son of Havvah, Eve, after Genesis 3.20; *ben havvah* corresponds to *ben adam.* The expression of Eleazar ha-Kappar, in the middle of the second century, in the *Yalkut* for Numbers 23.7, after *Midrash Yelamdenu,* may be apocryphal: "He foresaw that a man, son of a woman, would rise and make himself God and try to confuse the whole world." Else it already mirrors the Christian dogma. In the Fourth Book of Ezra, compare 13.2f., after Daniel 7.2f.; and note here "this man" and, in 13, verses 5, 32, and 51: "the man risen out of the sea." This throws further light on the references in the Book of Enoch: "this son of man," "that son of man." In The Revelation, see 1.13f., after Daniel 10.5 and 7.9; compare also Revelation 1.7. For the style, compare also 5.6: "as though it had been slain." For the Fourth Book of Ezra, compare A. Kaminka in *Monatsschrift zur Geschichte und Wissenschaft des Judentums,* 1932, pp. 121ff.

Wherever in later works "that son of man," "this son of man," or "the son of man" is mentioned, it is the quotation from Daniel that is speaking.

In the Gospels, too, we see this clearly wherever they contain fragments out of apocalypses. When it is said here: "they shall see the son of man coming in the clouds of heaven with power and great glory," and "ye shall see the son of man sitting on the right hand of power, and coming in the clouds of heaven," one cannot fail to see that it is sentences from apocalypses, similar to that of John, that speak here, using, no less than The Revelation of St. John, the quotation from Daniel.[6]

Yet these two sentences, in which the old meaning is still evident, are overshadowed by the many others which show time and again that the word has received a new sense in the Gospels and has become a very specific term. It is no longer the ancient apocalyptic image that appears in it; it has become an independent theological concept; it no longer serves as a parable, as testimony of a vision, but to designate something specific. It is now the phrase which unequivocally denotes the Christ of the Church; used by him, too, to designate himself.[7]

The time when this decisive change took place can be determined. It was the time after the Apocalypse of John; for here the word occurs only as a quotation from Daniel. It was the time after Paul's epistles; for these do not contain this phrase at all—of course not as a quotation, seeing that they do not contain anything really apocalyptic, but also not as a designation of the Christ, although it would have to occur here in this

6. Matthew 24.30 = Mark 13.26 = Luke 21.27; cf. I Thessalonians 4.15f.; Matthew 26.64 = Mark 14.62; cf. Acts 8.56.
7. Compare the synopsis of all relevant verses in Weinel, *op. cit.*, 191ff.

29

sense if it had by that time come to be an accepted designation for him. It was the time after the Barnabas epistle; for when this epistle declares with almost impassioned brevity, "Jesus, not son of man but son of God," it is again clear that this phrase cannot yet have been an unequivocal designation for the Christ.[8] But it was the time before the epistles of Ignatius; for when he writes to the Ephesians—and this sounds like a very emphatic objection to this sentence of Barnabas— "Jesus Christ, the son of man and son of God,"[9] then the phrase has evidently become the new concept which is to designate the essence and the name of the Christ. Thus the change in meaning clearly took place at the turn from the first to the second century. What a fixed term this expression then became quite generally, appears also from a sentence in which Rabbi Abbahu, a younger contemporary of Origen who also lived in Caesarea, turns against the Christology of the Church. When he is able to say, "If anyone says to you, 'I am God,' then he lies; 'I am the son of man,' then he will regret it; 'I shall ascend to heaven,' then he has spoken, but will not achieve it,"[10] then it is quite clear that by that time the term "son of man" referred so unequivocally to the Christ of the Church, and only to him, that in a religious controversy it could serve as the mark of recognition. The sphere, too, can be determined where this change came about. Inasmuch as in the Judaism of that time, as we know from the Targumim and the old talmudic and midrashic writings, the words "son of man" were used only for man in general and not as a

8. The Epistle of Barnabas 12.10.
9. Ignatius, Ephesians 20.2.
10. Jer. Taanit II, 1 end, p. 65b near the bottom, with reference to Numbers 23.19. Compare also the sentence of Eleazar ha-Kappar, cited in note 5, above.

name for the messiah,[11] it can have acquired its new significance only in the Church; and this is also implied by the polemical twist of Abbahu's statement.

The long development up to this point is quite clear. Again it begins with the Book of Daniel. This book above all has such vast significance for the history of religion because we here encounter an essential change in the messianic idea. In the thinking and the aspirations of the prophets, this idea meant a tension between the present and the future; between what existed and was still there now, and that which was becoming and yet to be. In the Book of Daniel, however, the idea signifies an opposition between the here below and the there above, between this world and the beyond. What is "to come" is here no longer a day toward which one is drawn by hope—*jammim ba'im*—but a world which opens up before one's visionary powers—*olam ha-ba'*. There the expected one, the object of longing, is a scion of the house of David who will fulfill history; here he has become the supernatural being who descends from the heavenly heights to end history. There, in the prophetic world, the line of longing is horizontal; here —and this is the essence of the apocalyptic orientation —it is vertical. Yet it is noteworthy that in the course of time the later attitude did not suppress or supplant the earlier one in the soul of the Jewish people. Both retained their place and direction, though at times they fought with each other: the son of David and the one

11.   Of the many examples, the following may be cited as especially characteristic: a sentence of Abbahu in Jer. Joma V, 3, p. 42c = *Pessikta de-Rav Kahana*, p. 178a, "not a man—*bar nash*—but God"; further a sentence of R. Jehuda, in the middle of the second century, *Pessikta de-Rav Kahana*, 190b = Shebuot 39b, "if one lets anybody—*bar nash*—swear"; finally the anonymous haggadic interpretation *Wayikra Rabba* for 1.2, that the meaning of *ben adam* should be "son of the just and pious."

like unto a man on the clouds of heaven. In the New Testament, too, we see how they stand next to, and opposed to, each other. While the apocalyptic orientation always gratified that impatience which wanted not to wait but to experience, as well as the desire for the miracle, the prophetic-messianic attitude derived its perennial power from the historical consciousness of the people, from its will to find the past again through the future.[12]

It is hard to say how far the beginnings of the apocalyptic idea, this intensification of the messianic idea into something supernatural, reach back. It is, however, noteworthy that this opposition of above and below is characteristic of the Alexandrian-Greek philosophy of revelation, and that the Book of Daniel, which is the first document of Palestinian-Jewish thinking to exhibit it, was written only after Palestine had for over a century been part of the Egyptian sphere of influence and culture. But whether this change in outlook had already taken place within Judaism and thus made Jewish thinking receptive for the Alexandrian philosophy of revelation, or whether, conversely, it was only the Alexandrian influence which made possible the change, can scarcely be determined now. But however this may have been, this change has had a tremendous effect on Jewish thought: the notion of "the world to come" has ever since been a decisive idea. Everything of first-rate value is now assigned its primary and permanent place beyond this world. The Holy Scripture and the sanctuary, the people of Israel, its patriarchs and its messiah, now belong with their beginnings and their continuance to the other world, to the ideal realm.

12.   Compare the Psalms of Solomon 17; Philo, *de praemiis et poenis* 16. Compare also L. Baeck's article, "Messias," in *Religion in Geschichte und Gegenwart*, second edition.

Thus they, like every idea, are something original that was created by God before the world of becoming. They are expressly conceded pre-existence, now poetically, now conceptually. The messiah, too, now becomes he that was from the beginning. To be sure, the old messianic faith retains a goal insofar as he who is from the beginning shall appear on a day in time as the scion of David; and the particular teaching about the ideal pre-existence of the messiah—his pre-existence in "the thoughts of God," and about his hidden name which shall one day be revealed—still leaves some room for the historical orientation; nevertheless, the messiah has now become pre-existent, an ideal being, he that has always been with God.[13]

With this, however, he moved close to another figure, to another idea—so close that both could merge, even had to merge. The people of Israel, too, has its pre-existence like the messiah; it, too, belongs to the other world. And in this supernatural world, messiah and people really have no separate content, no different meaning. What else are both of them here but the genius of Israel, the ideal Israel? The dividing line which two separate words wanted to indicate disappears in the ideal realm; and in Jewish thought and poetry they often did become one. How this could come about is shown already by the seventh chapter of the Book of Daniel. Is he that "is like unto a son of man and comes with the clouds of heaven and may step before the Lord" the messiah or the people of Israel, "the people of the saints of the Most High"? Thus it is here said of him who "came with the clouds of heaven"— using words which recall the old prophesies of the mes-

13. *Bereshit Rabba* I, 4, ed. Theodor, p. 6; XIV, 6, ed. Theodor, p. 130; and the many passages cited by Strack-Billerbeck, *Kommentar zum Neuen Testament* III, 700ff.

siah—"and there was given him dominion, and glory, and a kingdom, that all the peoples, nations, and languages should serve him; his dominion is an everlasting dominion, which shall not pass away, and his kingdom that which shall not be destroyed"; and afterwards the same is here also said of the people of Israel: "the kingdom and the dominion, and the greatness of the kingdoms under the whole heaven, shall be given to the people of the saints of the Most High; their kingdom is an everlasting kingdom, and all dominions shall serve and obey them." Have not the features and traits of both merged even here? The ideal Israel or, in Daniel's language, the *sar*, the archon, the aeon of Israel has become the messiah; and the messiah, the ideal Israel. This is almost clearer still in the Book of Enoch. Here we encounter references to "the anointed," and he is also often called "the chosen"; and this same word is just as often used for the people of Israel. Similarly, he is called "the just," and the people of Israel likewise, only using the plural. The king of the end of time and the people of the end of time stand there with the same predicates; and this also makes it understandable how it could later be similar in the realm of the Church with the Christ and the Church.[14] The roots, however, out of

.

14. Daniel 7.9, 7.21, 22, 27; Enoch 52.4 (the anointed); 48.6ff., 49.2, 50.1, 51.3ff., 52.6ff., 53.6, 55.4, 56.6, 58.1ff., 61.8ff., 62.1ff.; cf. also the so-called Sixth Book of Ezra 1.53 and 1.56 (the chosen); Enoch 38.1ff., 46.3ff., 47.1, 61.13, 62.2, 71.19; cf. 60.2 (the just). Cf. Isaiah 60.21 and Psalms 37.29, as well as Sanhedrin X,1; *Tanhuma*, "*Hayye Sara*," end. For "my son," Fourth Book of Ezra 13.32; cf. Exodus 4.22 and Psalms 2.7. An apocalyptic *haggada* of R. Meir is characteristic—*Tanhuma* "Wayyetze" II; here Jacob appears as the *sar* of the people of Israel as opposed to the *sarim* of Babel, Media, Javan, and Edom. It should also be recalled that in Philo, *de prof.* 20, *de somniis* II, 28 and 34, it is sometimes the Logos and sometimes Michael that is designated as the "high priest."

which all this developed, reach back still further, into
the time before the Book of Daniel. Already the Isaiah
of the exile used the same name, "the chosen of the
Lord"—this old attribute of the anointed—both for the
people of Israel and for the "servant of the Lord." Nor
can the old question what these words, "servant of the
Lord," mean in the speeches of this prophet, be answered in any other way: already here both the people
and the man who represents the people's worth and
dignity—now it is the prophet and now the messiah—
coincide in meaning.[15]

Here it should be noted how in the religious realm the
attempt to express oneself becomes almost a wrestling
for expressions. Everything conceptual comes only
gradually. The word "messiah" in its definite and conceptual sense thus belongs only to a later age; only the
pseudepigrapha, the New Testament, the Targum, and
the Mishnah have it. When the old prophesies want to
speak of the ruler of the future, of the house of David
in which justice will dwell and remain, then they can
only proclaim this king of days to come in ever new
images and comparisons: as the shoot out of the stock
of Jesse, the twig out of his roots upon whom the spirit
of the Lord shall rest; as the child born unto us, upon
whose shoulders the government will be and whose
name will be called prince of peace; as the son whose
name his father shall call Immanuel, that is With-us-is-

15. II Samuel 6.21 and 21.6; I Kings 11.34; Psalms 89.3 and
106.23; Isaiah 43.10 and 43.20, 44.1, 45.4, 65.9, 65.15, 65.22;
52.13ff., 61.1. It is noteworthy that the Septuagint generally
translated the "servant of God" with the word παῖς, which also
means "child" (Isaiah 42.1, 49.6, 50.10, 52.13), and rarely with
the word δοῦλος (49.3 and 49.5). It should also be noted how the
Gospel according to Luke and the Book of Acts use the word παῖς
to designate Jesus (Acts 3.13, 4.27 and 4.30) as well as David
(Luke 1.69) and the ideal Israel (Luke 1.54).

God; as the righteous shoot who shall execute justice
and righteousness in the land; as the one shepherd who
shall feed them and be their shepherd.[16] Even of the
man who belonged to a future which would come to pass
in the way of this world, one could speak only in parables. How much more did this have to be so when it was
a matter of speaking of him who belonged to the beyond,
to the other world, who, as the genius of the people or
the messianic liberator, was full of the most abundant
significance. No single word, no single designation could
name him; only the image could point to him: with the
clouds of heaven one had come like unto a son of man
and had stepped before God. This image, in its completeness or abbreviated, as a quotation from, or as an
allusion to, the Book of Daniel henceforth served to
speak of him.

The sentence which provided this image entered the
Greek world and the Greek language of the Church.
But here the words "son of man" were no longer, as in
Hebrew, a compound for simply designating a human
being; here one was confronted with two words, and
they meant: a son of a human being. And that which
these two Greek words thus articulated soon gained a
significance in the development of the Church which led
to a parting of opinions and, eventually, of convictions.
The teaching of the new faith had combined the two
ideas which lived among the Jewish people—the prophetic idea of the son of David and the apocalyptic one
of an otherworldly being—into the doctrine of the heavenly and the human origin of the messiah, the doctrine
of the son of God who is born as a human child. But
against this human birth, against this son of a human
being, there now rose a radical Gnostic and Marcionite

16. Isaiah 11.1ff., 9.5f., 7.14f.; Jeremiah 23.5; Ezekiel 34.23.

opposition. And the Church had to turn against this. As it had emphasized the conception of the son of God against Judaism, it now stressed the idea of the son of man against Gnosticism—the more emphatically the more violent the opposition grew. In this controversy, the son of man became the watchword that prevailed. Where the Epistle of Barnabas still had been able to venture the sentence, "Jesus, not son of a man but son of God," Ignatius now writes to the Ephesians: "Jesus Christ, the son of a man and God." In the words of Irenaeus which follow this example, *"filius dei filius hominis factus,"* the Catholic Church recognized its definitive doctrine. The "son of man" thus turned from an image into a firm concept and became an essential part of the dogma. The Hellenization of our word was accomplished.[17]

In this fight against Gnosticism, which was a fight about the son of man, the Church attained self-confidence and became the Catholic Church. To prevail, it created the canon of the New Testament. In the Gospels of the canon[18] the term "son of man" was accorded its place; and one may now understand why this phrase

17. If the Epistle of Barnabas should have to be dated later, and if 16.3f. should have to be interpreted in such a way that one would have to relegate the epistle to the time of Hadrian, then the above-quoted sentence would represent a final protest against the ecclesiastical doctrine of the son of man. The Epistle to the Hebrews could already interpret the "son of man" in Psalms 8.5 as referring to the messiah; cf. I Corinthians 15.27 and Ephesians 1.22. For Irenaeus and the ecclesiastical dogma, compare Harnack, *Dogmengeschichte*, I (4), pp. 596f. and 606f. note. When Harnack finds in Gnosticism an "acute Hellenization," one may point out how it was above all a Hellenization of our word that proved influential.

18. The Gospel according to Mark, too, belongs, in its canonical form, only to the last part of the first century. An interesting chronological pointer has now been added by E. Bickermann in his essay, "Les Hérodiens," in *Revue Biblique*, 1938, pp. 195f.

2

THE GOSPEL AS A
DOCUMENT OF THE HISTORY
OF THE JEWISH FAITH

The question how the Gospels in the New Testament could have developed out of the ancient message of Jesus the messiah has been much disputed. But like the question of the original meaning of these tidings, it can really be approached in one way only: by way of the sphere in which all those events took shape. Only in terms of its own space and time will everything become clear to us. We must understand the nature of oral tradition as it was then alive in Palestinian Judaism. We must penetrate its very soul and grasp the essentially poetic manner in which tradition in those days was handed down and apprehended. Only then will harmony and discrepancy in our Gospels be grasped, too. For the Gospels must be understood, not in terms of textual sources out of which they might have been composed, but in terms of the tradition out of which they originated. In the following pages, an attempt has been made to point up the channels of this tradition.

Following them, we can get back to the original

ancient message. At the same time, the channels of this tradition provide the only approach to the beginnings of Christianity. A life of Jesus can be written, if at all, only after one has determined what the first generation after Jesus related and handed down. The further attempt has here been made to recover this earliest tradition.

Our conclusion was not summoned; it appeared: the Gospel emerges as a piece, not inconsiderable, of Jewish history—a testimony of Jewish faith.

TRADITIONS

The Tradition of the Gospel—Since the beginning of the third century, twenty-seven scriptures, written in Greek, are recognized in the Church as apostolic and canonical. They are accepted by the Church as the scriptures of the "new covenant," the "New Testament"; and as such they are added to the books of the "old covenant." They are called apostolic—which means that they are derived from the circle of Jesus' apostles. They are of canonical character—which means that they are valid and binding for the whole Church and are meant to be read at religious services.

The beginning is made up of four Gospels—or, as Justin, the defender of the Church in the middle of the second century, wanted to translate this word more precisely: "memorabilia of the apostles which are called Gospels." Their titles: The Gospel according to Matthew, according to Mark, according to Luke, according to John. They are called "gospel" or "evangel" (good tidings) after a biblical, prophetic word which at that time, however, also formed part of the Hellenistic language; for they wanted to proclaim Jesus as the Messiah, "the Christ." They are four in number—accord-

ing to the interpretation of Irenaeus of Lyon, in the
second half of the second century—even as north, east,
south, and west, as well as the strangely shaped animals which Ezekiel had seen on the firmament, are four.

All four are alike designated as Gospels. But compared to the fourth, that of John, the first three somehow have a common character. In spite of manifold
differences, these three agree in essential parts and features and thus make possible a common perspective, a
"synopsis." Therefore they have been called the "synoptic Gospels" ever since Johann Jakob Griesbach
(1745-1812). That they antedate the fourth Gospel is
proved by every comparison of their language and contents. But they, too, in their present form, belong to a
relatively late time—a time separated by several generations and catastrophes from the time which they
seek to describe.

The historical material in these three Gospels does,
to be sure, contain earlier elements. For these Gospels
depend on an originally oral tradition which had been
handed down by disciples. All ancient testimonies agree
in this. The Gospel according to Luke begins with a
prefatory sentence, distinctly literary in nature—the
only sentence of this kind in any of the Gospels. It says
that ". . . many have taken in hand to draw up a narrative concerning those matters which have been fulfilled
among us, even as they delivered them unto us, which
from the beginning were eyewitnesses and ministers of
the word." Two things are here asserted: first, that
there was a tradition going back to Jesus' contemporaries; and secondly, that several attempts had been
made to base literary works on this tradition. Paul, too,
appeals to this tradition; he declares: "For I received
of the Lord that which also I delivered unto you"; "For
I delivered unto you . . . that which I also received"

43

(I Cor. 11.23 and 15.3). The Second Epistle to the Thessalonians, too, speaks of this oral tradition: "... hold to the traditions which ye were taught, whether by word or by our epistle" (2.15).

What that sentence in Luke refers to is described even more definitely and with more detail by the Phrygian bishop Papias, in the second third of the second century. He says of himself: "Unlike the many who delight in those who tell many things, I prefer those who teach the truth. ... Whenever a pupil of the elders appeared, I inquired after the words of the elders: what did Andrew say, or Peter, or Philip, or Thomas, or James, or John, or Matthew, or any of the rest of the Lord's disciples; or what does Aristion say, or John the elder, the disciples of the Lord? For I always think that what is gleaned from books will not profit me as much as what comes from the living and enduring voice." Then he relates in the name of John the elder that Mark, "after he had become an interpreter for Peter, wrote down exactly, though in no particular order, as much as he could remember of the words or deeds of the Lord. Mark himself never heard or followed the Lord; he only heard and followed Peter who preached whenever it seemed called for." Concerning Matthew, too, Papias has something to tell: he "collected the sayings (*Logia*) in the Hebrew vernacular, and everybody then translated them as best he could." (*Die Apostolischen Väter,* edited by Bihlmeyer, pp. 134 and 136)

What Papias tells us makes it possible for us within certain limits to gain a clear picture. This is what it shows: In Papias' time, more than a century after the death of Jesus, there were written versions of the Gospel; but a living oral tradition still existed alongside of them even at that time. This tradition, no less than the written records, comprised two elements: the

44

sayings and the deeds of Jesus. Matthew, to be sure, had put down only the sayings of Jesus, which he had collected in the language of Jesus, in "the Hebrew vernacular"—in other words, in Aramaic—and his work was then repeatedly and variously translated into Greek. The reliability of the tradition, no less than its standards, was by no means always the same. Sometimes it tried to be careful and exact, sometimes it took pleasure in extravagance. It was the latter manner that achieved greater popularity: many liked to tell and hear many things, regardless of their reliability. Papias deplored this tendency, and yet he himself did not remain entirely free from it, as is proved by the following fact: there are a number of sentences in the Apocalypse of Baruch, an apocryphal writing composed after the destruction of the Second Temple, which Papias cites as sayings of Jesus "which the elders remember having heard from his disciple John." (Bihlmeyer, *op. cit.*, p. 133)

We are now in a position to recognize the road which began with the apostolate of Jesus' disciples and led up to the canonical Gospels. It started from oral tradition, and it led through oral tradition. Here and there in its course this tradition was crystallized in writing, always embodying the author's peculiarities. Eventually, a number of these books were declared to be canonical and became, as it were, a dam that stopped the tradition's flood forever.

Tradition in Judaism—Even if we did not possess these ancient testimonies in which the primitive Church itself reports on its oral tradition, the spirit of the people among whom the Gospel originated would still point in the same direction. The specific nature of

Jewish spiritual and religious life at that time was determined by a characteristic and continuous tradition.
First and foremost, this tradition was embodied in the
books of the Bible. The holy scriptures had been committed to writing, and every scroll, every sentence—indeed, every letter—was guarded with the most scru-
pulous care. The Bible was among the Jewish people, in
the words of the Torah, "an inheritance of the congregation of Jacob"; and one was ever decidedly and
gratefully conscious of this inheritance and its value.
At the same time, however, there was real concern lest
one become a mere custodian of an heirloom—nothing
but an epigone of a possession. The words of a teacher
of the first century are characteristic: Jose the Priest
said, in direct opposition to the written word, "*Learn
the Torah, for it is no* inheritance." He only said ex-
plicitly what the possession of the Bible had for a long
time meant to the people. It was the book beside which
there should really be no other; hence it was much more
than a mere book or whatever else had been written
down. Hence it was also quite insufficient merely to read
and know it; it had to be discovered again and again,
word for word: one always had to take possession of it
anew. Out of the idea of the spiritual inheritance there
developed the commandment of seeking and searching
in the Bible so that it might never cease really to speak
and to show things. One sought and searched what the
written word might proclaim and mean (*maggid ha-
katub, melammed ha-katub*). The word one read could
never be a merely written and finished word: it always
spoke, moved, and progressed. It always had something
new to say. Thus the Bible had really two different
aspects: it was a written work, the "written teaching"
which was read and copied again and again; and it was
also a work disclosed and preached by men—the "oral

46

teaching" which was proclaimed and grasped and handed on perpetually. The tradition which lived in the Bible never ceased and never fell silent.

When a religious word had been disclosed, as it were, out of the Bible and been presented by a true teacher, it became almost a revelation from God. Did it not come out of the word of God? And had not a master, one of the pious and wise, uncovered it? Everybody had to hear of it and preserve it. Above all, the loyalty of the disciple should preserve it; and his desire to carry it abroad should spread it and guarantee its survival. It was an oral word; and yet in a sense it was to be written down, too—inscribed in the disciple's memory. A spiritual tie bound the disciple to the teacher and extended to every succeeding generation: thus arose the "chain of the tradition" which depended on reverence and a kind of piety. A sacred obligation found expression in the fact that the same word which the Bible had used to designate the prophets' "hearing" (*shemua'*) was also applied to what the disciple had heard from his teacher. In the idiom of that time, every disciple was to be his teacher's "witness"—able to bear pure and true testimony to his master's words. In his disciples the teacher was to live on, and—to cite another saying of that time—"his lips should still speak from the grave." The history of religion among the people of Israel appeared as a grand tradition that extended through the centuries: "Moses received the Torah from Sinai and delivered it to Joshua, and Joshua to the elders, and the elders to the prophets, and the prophets delivered it to the men of the great assembly." When Paul says, "I received that which also I delivered unto you," it is not accidentally that he uses the very same words which we encounter in this sentence at the beginning of the Chapters of the Fathers. Paul is here appealing to tra-

and dubious tends gradually to disappear out of the master's words and ways. This will happen especially when the tradition touches the ultimate questions of life, for then it has a deeply personal significance for the pupil and will be colored by his most decisive feelings and convictions. What he has experienced deeply, what has become truth and faith for his soul, the master, too, must surely have known and proclaimed. Knowing and handing on these matters becomes a question of life and death.

Moreover, a pious imagination does its work, too. Involuntarily poetic and creative, it adds ever new features and details, supplies ever new colors and ever new splendor and wealth. Everywhere the human spirit knows the urge to connect ideas and associate pictures; and this urge was particularly strong in Jewish thought at that time, and wove its fabric. As the days and generations pass, popular proverbs and sayings, events, deeds, and miracles related of men who lived long ago, enter the image of the beloved master and become permanent elements of it; for nothing elevated or beautiful should be denied him.

Scripture itself afforded many openings for this process. It was read in a peculiar manner. On the one hand, there was the wish to place everything in a particular time and situation. Even where the Bible itself did not refer to any particular person or event, the poetic imagination supplied the situations. Confronted with a nameless prayer in the Psalms or with a proverb, one would ask who might have said this, or of whom the text was speaking; and then one might answer: it was Adam, or Abraham, or perhaps Jacob, or Moses. As one read the Bible, one looked for individual and entirely personal references. But this is only one aspect of a truly remarkable paradox. For on the other hand, there

was the tendency to raise the words of Scripture above
the particular incident and above any specific time to
which they might belong: they were lifted into the
realm of timeless being, even into the sphere of the
pre-existent and ideal. Where the Bible spoke of what
had occurred to a definite person in a definite hour, the
reader understood it to speak of what occurs always.
All biblical history did not only tell something, it also
meant something. It did not relate what had been once
upon a time and had come and gone, but it proclaimed
something permanent and enduring—something which
happened long ago, but also happens again and again
and is, for all the changes in place and detail, always the
same. A particular story reveals, as it were, a grandiose
drama which is performed over and over again; the
masks are changed, but the protagonists and their opponents are always the same.

The division between the ages and the differences
between the times sank out of sight: past and present
began to coalesce. All the pressures and experiences of
the day, the cares and troubles of one's own life, the
fears and hopes of one's own mind were fused with
what had happened formerly, with the fortunes of former generations of which the tradition spoke. A person
who had lived long ago and in a day of the distant past
began to speak of the reader and his suffering and
longing. And the other way around, the reader's inmost experiences, his inmost struggles, expectations,
and anxiety, gave flesh and blood and shape and color
to the events of the past. The ancient tidings took the
shape of today, and what the Bible related or what was
handed down by former generations gained meaning
and definition through the current hour. Past became
present, present became past, the centuries were
bridged. The ideas and men of former times merged

50

with those of today, and those of today with those of former times. Above all, in times of grief and suffering, when the present could only seem senseless and godless, it was, as it were, annulled in order to let the ever abiding, which is beyond all change, emerge in its place. Faith perfected what imagination had begun.

Biblical Reality—All this was made possible by the commanding position which the Bible held among the Jewish people. For the Bible was the supreme court of all understanding and knowledge. It was not a work written by men, but the revelation of the living God. As the word of God, it could never fail to be relevant to the present and valid for the future; here must be the answer for today and tomorrow. For "the word of our God shall stand for ever." In relation to every single day or question, the words of the Bible were compelling. Whatever happened or was said must be understood in terms of the Bible. By this criterion it was measured, determined, and shown to be genuine or spurious. The words of the Bible alone could show what had really and truly happened. Not what the eye had seen or not seen, not what men had related or contested could furnish a decisive answer, but only what the word of God had proclaimed and what preaching and tradition said it meant. One did not only think and hope in terms of the Scripture, but experience and knowledge, too, were molded by it, often decisively. Therefore we find that in the Gospels the final sentence which is meant to embrace everything is so often: "that it might be fulfilled which was spoken by the Lord through the prophet." Or consider the article of faith which is to Paul's mind fundamental and supports everything else, that of the sacrificial death and resurrection of Jesus:

the sole and complete proof of it which decides and determines everything is contained in the single emphatic phrase, "according to the scriptures": "I delivered unto you . . . that Christ died for our sins *according to the scriptures,* and that he was buried, and that he was raised up on the third day *according to the scriptures"* (I Cor. 15.3-4). The words of the Bible had become the ultimate criterion of all reality and all history.

This helps us to understand how contemporary figures could be read so personally and so vividly into the figures of the Bible. Friends and foes of bygone ages simply became friends and foes of today, while those of today merged with those of former times. It is by no means sufficient to remark that the names of biblical characters were in times of danger used as code names which those on the inside would readily recognize. The reader of the Bible was really impressed with an underlying and essential identity. He read about Esau or Edom and felt quite certain that Rome was meant; he did not merely think so, he did not merely believe that this might be an insinuation—he knew that it was so. He read about Balaam and knew that everything, word for word, referred to the cunning adviser of his own enemies, the false prophet outside his own gates. In the Apocalypse or Revelation of St. John, it is said to the community in Pergamum: "thou hast there some that hold the teaching of Balaam" (2.14) ; and The Second Epistle General of Peter warns: "forsaking the right way, they have gone astray, following the way of Balaam" (2.15). Surely, the men who wrote this, and whoever read it in those days, were quite certain that it was the old Balaam who had now appeared again to lead astray. Or one heard of the destruction of the first temple and knew that the story referred also, and no less, to the destruction of the second temple; and when one heard of Nebuchadnezzar, one knew that one was also hearing of Titus. The words of the prophets were a part of living experience, for they did not only speak *about* the present, they also spoke *in* the present situation. They proclaimed and explained what had really happened now and what these events meant.

Elaboration of the Bible—All the events of the day that were then handed on were similarly determined by the words of Scripture which molded all knowledge and preaching. But beyond all this, the poetic imagination found ways of penetrating the Bible itself, and this led to further developments. Even as the Bible had time and again fashioned stories, such stories were now frequently introduced into the Bible. Where there seemed to be gaps, one wanted to fill them lest Scripture lack anything. And where the requirements of contemporary longings were not satisfied, additions were envisaged to make the Bible more complete. Where something might lack clarity, one wanted to clarify and explain. After all, the Bible did not only mean everything, it must also contain everything. This is aptly suggested by the admonition of Ben Bagbag who lived in that time of change: "Study it from every angle, for everything is contained in it." So it almost became necessary to let Scripture say still more. As generation after generation found its own new experiences in the Scriptures or traditions, it was always tempted to develop them further and refashion them, to continue them and then to hand them on in a way which would ensure that its own new experiences would henceforth always be understood exactly and in every detail. As it pursued its course through the generations, the Bible reflected their thinking and poetic imagination.

53

The same had happened to the biblical narrative even within the canon of the Holy Scriptures. One need only compare the Books of Samuel and Kings with the Chronicles to see how the old stories were almost irresistibly refashioned. As a single example, consider what the Second Book of Samuel and the First Book of Chronicles have to tell of David's wish to build a sanctuary for the Lord:

II Sam. 7.8-14	*I Chron. 22.8-10*
Thus saith the Lord of hosts: . . . When thy days are fulfilled, and thou shalt sleep with thy fathers, I will set up thy seed after thee, that shall proceed out of thy body, and I will establish his kingdom. He shall build a house for My name, and I will establish the throne of his kingdom for ever. I will be to him for a father, and he shall be to me for a son.	The word of the Lord came to me, saying: Thou hast shed blood abundantly, and hast made great wars; thou shalt not build a house unto My name, because thou hast shed much blood upon the earth in My sight. Behold, a son shall be born to thee, who shall be a man of rest; and I will give him rest from all his enemies round about; for his name shall be Solomon (man of peace), and I will give peace and quietness unto Israel in his days. He shall build a house for My name; and he shall be to Me for a son, and I will be to him for a father; and I will establish the throne of his kingdom over Israel for ever.

The intentions of the later narrator in this case are clear. Where his predecessor had merely related a fact, he asked about the reason and wanted to make it plain: David was not allowed to build the temple because he had shed blood; Solomon was allowed to build it because he was a man of peace. What happens here is typical: the retelling involves the completion and explanation of the story. Those who retold the story, developed it further.

The ancient talmudic tradition, the so-called oral doctrine, contains even more numerous and manifold examples of substantially the same process. Again one example may serve in place of many. Besides the Pirke Avoth, the Chapters of the Fathers, we also possess the Avoth of Rabbi Nathan, a tradition which contains important parts of the same material and is ascribed to Rabbi Nathan who lived during the second half of the second century. The parallel existence of these two books is in many ways similar to that of the Gospels and therefore throws considerable light on them. Let us compare these two traditions, using a sentence already mentioned once before. Only we shall omit the many quotations from Scripture adduced in the second tradition as evidence:

Avoth I.1	*Avoth de-Rabbi Nathan I.2-3*
Moses received the Torah from Sinai and delivered it to Joshua, and Joshua to the elders, and the elders to the prophets, and the prophets, deliv-	Moses was consecrated by the cloud of the divine presence and received the Torah from Sinai. Through Moses the Torah was given from Sinai. The Torah which the Holy One, blessed be he, gave to Israel was given only through Moses; it was given to Moses to be the messenger between the children of

<table>
<tr><td>ered it to the men of the great assembly.</td><td>Israel and the Omnipresent. Joshua received from Moses; the elders received from Joshua; the judges received from the elders; the prophets received from the judges; Haggai, Zechariah, and Malachi received from the prophets; the men of the great assembly received from Haggai, Zechariah, and Malachi.</td></tr>
</table>

The trend here is similar to that illustrated by the passage from Chronicles: in the Avoth, too, those who hand on the tradition feel the wish to explain and instruct. The man transmitting the tradition has become a commentator: the incomparable significance of Moses is stressed most emphatically in solemn repetition; the judges, who had really been Joshua's successors without, however, having been mentioned in the earlier tradition, are now assigned a place between the elders and the prophets; and among the prophets, finally, the break marked by the Babylonian Exile is now indicated, and the three prophets who lived after this are assigned a separate role in the transmission of the tradition.

There is still another literature in which we encounter many peculiar variations of this process of continual creation and elaboration: the Apocrypha and Pseudepigrapha which are intermediary between the Bible and the oral doctrine. Here the reflective and poetic imagination, which was constantly attracted by the Bible and revolved around it, has fashioned many new stories and books. A few examples may illustrate this point. The Second Book of Chronicles had related (33.18-19) how the sinful king Manasseh had humbled himself and ruefully prayed to God, and how all this had been recorded in ancient historical works. It is easy to see that the search which was ever centered in the Bible had to ask before long what Manasseh may have said when he entreated God; and then a man of a later generation elaborated the sentences of Chronicles and wrote a "Prayer of Manasseh." In the Book of Jeremiah (29.1) a letter is mentioned which the prophet is said to have sent from Jerusalem to the exiles in Babylon, and his words of admonition and comfort are recorded. But a question arose nevertheless: would not Jeremiah have warned the exiles against the idolatry which surrounded them so seductively—even though the book of the prophet does not record this? And so a "Letter of Jeremiah" was written which contained what the pious reader had previously missed. Moreover, the Book of Jeremiah frequently refers to Baruch ben Neriah, the trusted disciple of the prophet. Should not this man, who was so close to the prophet, have tried to counter the disasters of his time by offering his people his own instruction and comfort? Reflective readers filled such gaps, and various works of Baruch originated.

This post-biblical literature also shows something else: it was in the most serious and threatening times that the words of the Holy Scriptures were felt to be most urgent and moving; and it was then, too, that one felt the strongest urge, if not a real compulsion, to continue the process of creation. Disaster was in the air and many an hour suggested that a great turning point was ahead. One looked back into the remote past searching for some answer, studied what had happened and what had been said long ago, and sought a message for today and tomorrow: naturally it was presupposed that what was happening now, or about to happen, had been known to the ancient men of God, and this belief spelt assurance and comfort. They simply must have foreseen it, it must have been revealed to them. Before the Flood, there had been Enoch "who had walked with God and been taken by God"—must he not also have known of the new Flood which was approaching now? Baruch had seen the events leading up to the destruction of the first temple, and he had witnessed the catastrophe—surely, his prophetic spirit must have foreseen another destruction of Jerusalem, another burning of the temple. Ezra had lived through a great change from destruction to a new beginning—how could he have failed to know of the new catastrophe and the new destiny of the people? Surely, these men must have grasped the future in their present, and they must have prophesied the meaning of all time, the whole development from the beginning to the end of time. This was the origin of all those apocalypses which comprise such a large portion of post-biblical literature: they were books of revelation ascribed to biblical characters, strange poetic creations which relate the fortunes of different generations in distant times and places, the ups and downs of events, the end and the Last Judgment. Everything that might have been insinuated by dark passages in Scripture which seemed to conceal or to suggest something, everything that had long lived among the people as a tradition or a legend that dealt with origins or ends, and whatever else there was of longing and of hope, was here collected. The tone was one of most profound conviction: through dreams, visions, and ecstasies, everything mysterious had become quite real for the authors of the books. Therefore the images always outweigh the sentences, and what has been beheld predominates over what is merely known.

The Style and Logic of the Tradition—It was above all the Bible itself, but later also the literature that had followed in its wake, that furnished the pattern for all these varied expressions of the poetic imagination: from here came not only certain forms and conventions but also some of the contours and embellishments. There was, for example, the story of the miraculous life with its temptations and its steadfastness, its ailments and its cures: the stories of Daniel, Judith, and Tobit served as examples. There were the stories of martyrdom in the Book of Daniel and the Second Maccabees. There were the lists of ancestors and of successive generations in Chronicles. There were the collections of proverbs, not only in the Book of Proverbs, but also in the Books of Ecclesiastes and Sirach; and in the Psalms one possessed prayers, hymns, and songs of praise devoted to the words of God and wisdom. Then there were parables and brief sentences which epitomized basic concepts of the Bible; and the people knew these and had become accustomed to them through the oral tradition. The arrangement and style of short prayers was familiar to all, and so was the apocalyptic image, the picture of the events expected in the end, for which the Book of Daniel served as the prime model. Whatever was said or written was, in spite of all peculiarities and distinctions, presented in terms of a traditional genre, within the outlines of some ancient model. The style was fixed.

No less, and even more, the content was in a sense

predetermined. All the really decisive conceptions, thoughts, and hopes which might be awakened by a new day were, so to say, children of the Bible. The essentials were long settled. The Holy Scriptures had spoken once and for all, and every generation knew what would be the course from the creation to the final days; how beginning and end were related to each other; what was involved in the proclamation and the fulfillment of the divine will; what suffering and martyrdom, temptations and tests could mean, and how they could give a changeful human life eternal significance; what the life and suffering, the endurance and the triumph of the Messiah would be like when he would come one day; what fortunes the last days would bring; and what it would be like when the world above would enter into our world below, and the realm of miracles would with its messengers descend to this earth. Age after age could only repeat this, whatever details they might reveal or present with lines and colors of their own. It was possible to pronounce the answer, to describe and embellish, and perhaps even to interpret it, but one lacked the ability and the authority to *give* the answer: it confronted man as something ancient and definitive. The contents of faith, certainty, and hope had been clearly written down once and for all and transmitted by tradition as something fixed and final. Every day and every experience had to be placed in this context, and everything in the present that seemed peculiar or new had to be fitted into it. Never, however, could the events of the present determine the abiding content. Whatever the day might show or not show—what was that compared to what the word of God had revealed? Here were only the things that one thought one recognized or wanted to refute; there, what the Eternal One had ordained from the beginning that it might remain valid for ever: was any comparison even possible? How could one add to what the Holy Scriptures had said, or subtract from it? If there was any history, it could only be the fulfillment of the words of Scripture. The Bible, together with the tradition that emanated from it and led back to it, molded the meaning and knowledge of all that took place and determined the course of whatever was said to the people about God, man, and world.

The Holy Scriptures were the cosmos which contained all meaning, and every particular had its meaningful place in it; hence there developed a special way of intellectual searching and finding—one might almost say, a special logic. The form of thought here was determined neither by explication alone, and hence analytic, nor only by composition, and thus synthetic; it was juxtaposition that predominated and associative thinking: similarity and analogy became decisive. Psychologically, it was recognition that became fundamental: by an experience one was reminded of a biblical verse, and by one such verse of another. Ideas, words, and events which seemed to lie far apart were in this way brought together and entered an association; and inferences were drawn from here to there. A human being with whom one was confronted and an event in which he figured were all at once shaped decisively by a biblical passage to which they seemed close. A similarity gave way to an immediacy, an identity: "For this is he that was spoken of . . ." (Matt. 3.3).

Profound experiences of recognition recurred constantly as one discovered connections between one biblical passage and another and ways that led from the world to the Bible. For one was convinced that nothing in the Holy Scriptures was merely accidental: everything had a meaning and value. The principle here was the same which Aristotle used to justify inferences by analogy: "God and nature do nothing in vain." This principle of sufficient reason is here applied to the Bible: it contains the revelation of God, and God has said nothing in vain, without meaning or purpose, not even the smallest detail. One is dealing with the word of God, and every word is profound and contains a mystery. Relations between such words, or to them, are therefore connections in the sphere of ultimate insight. Finding the men and events of this life in the Bible and placing the becoming of this world alongside the being of Scripture had here become the way to reality. Such recognition became a task and content of the tradition. The tradition was meant to offer everything that mattered, a totality, and therefore had to demonstrate the fortunes and the history which it related in the Bible. So it happened that whatever was transmitted was first placed within the Bible.

The Special Characteristics of the Gospel Tradition— The old Gospel tradition belongs in this Jewish cultural environment with all its peculiarities, and it has to be understood in terms of these special features of Jewish tradition. It partakes fully of all these characteristics, for it is really nothing but a part of this tradition. Its course and its fortunes become comprehensible only in this context in which it took shape. Here, too, the beginning is that pupils have heard the words of their teacher—for it is as a teacher that Jesus appears first of all—and experienced his deeds and his passion. To hand on what they had heard and seen would have been required of them in any case, as a pious obligation which they owed their master. Here, too, the tradition

The Gospel as a Document of History

comprehended words and events; and here, too, everything was placed in the traditionally fixed forms and frame. Here, too, the tradition was handed down by individuals and invariably reflected their individuality: every disciple, and every disciple's disciple, had his own ears and his own mind, his own worries and his own longings, his own temptation and his own struggle. Here, too, the imagination saw and created, and the will to give form explained and supplemented. These men, too, experienced everything in terms of the Bible, and the words of Scripture directed, commanded, and exerted an inner compulsion. For these men, too, a fixed content, a fixed religious doctrine, was there to begin with and was most vividly real and the whole truth. For them, too, and for those who received the tradition from them, their master's lot and fate had long been revealed and always preordained. They, too, were convinced that this ancient prophecy and promise meant even far more than all that human eyes had seen or not seen: every great event was nothing but an answer given long ago and the fulfillment of a prophecy. The tradition of the Gospel is, first of all, in every one of these respects, simply a part of the Jewish tradition of that time.

Only a single example shall be given here: it shows how the elaboration and modification characteristic of the oral tradition was so prominent in the Christian community, too, that it affected even sentences of which one should suppose that the tradition would have stipulated a precise and unchangeable text. Consider the so-called Lord's Prayer: we know it in three different forms—two in the two Synoptic Gospels which have it (the Gospels according to Mark and John do not contain it at all) and a third one in the Gospel according to Marcion. They are here juxtaposed:

Matt. 6.9ff.	*Luke 11.2ff.*	*Marcion*
O u r F a t h e r which a r t in h e a v e n , h a l - lowed be thy name. Thy king- dom come. Thy will be done in earth, as it is in heaven. Give us this d a y o u r d a i l y b r e a d And forgive us our debts, as we f o r g i v e o u r debtors. A n d bring us not into temptation, but deliver us from the evil. (For thine is the kingdom a n d the power and the glory for ever.)	Father, hal- lowed be thy name. Thy king- dom come. Give us day by day our daily bread. And forgive us our sins; for we ourselves also forgive every one that is in- debted to us. And bring us not into tempta- tion.	Father, Thy H o l y S p i r i t come upon us and purify us. Thy kingdom come. Give us day by day our daily bread. And forgive us our sins. And let us not be brought into temptation. *(Harnack's edi- tion, p. 189)*

The transformations which took place here as the tradition developed are clearly recognizable. Apart from minor deviations which are probably due to dif- ferences in the Greek translation, the following points stand out. In the Gospel according to Matthew the prayer has three features lacking in the Gospel accord- ing to Luke: the clause in the beginning, "which art in heaven," and the third and the seventh entreaty. The

64

final sentence—the doxology, or praise of God—is still missing in the earliest manuscripts of this Gospel. It was probably from the liturgy of the religious services that it found its way into the prayer. And this must have happened very early, for a Christian catechism dating from the first half of the second century—the so-called Teachings of the Apostles—in which we find the Lord's Prayer with minor deviations, contains this conclusion (8.2). Finally there is Marcion's version of the prayer in the middle of the second century, and this is also encountered in some later works. On the whole, this version agrees with Luke's; but it lacks the opening sentence, "hallowed be thy name," and says instead: "thy Holy Spirit come upon us and purify us." This change is surely due to Marcion's Gnostic striving for faith. The Lord's Prayer which was so important even to the early Christians has thus found a place in only two of the canonical Gospels, and each of these offers a different version, while still further deviations appear in another, non-canonical Gospel, of the second century.

The point illustrated by this example does not distinguish the Christian tradition from the general character of the Jewish one. In addition to all these common elements, however, there is something distinctive that belongs to the Christian tradition alone and which had a decisive influence on its growth—something that accounts for the fact that it developed in its own way. To begin with, it was this: the man whose life and words the tradition wanted to report had early ceased, in his disciples' faith, to be a mere teacher—and when they believed in him, he eventually came to believe himself to be the messiah, the *Christos*. The Christian community was firmly convinced that he had been the messiah. So his image had to be embellished to an ever greater extent with everything that the Bible and the reflections of centuries had seen in the anointed of the Lord, the son of David, upon whom the spirit of God will rest, the helper and liberator—and with everything that had been prophesied concerning him. Out of the suffering of the time a poem of his passion had developed, and out of its longing and ideals a vision of his power and his deeds—and all this, too, had to become part of his image. Moreover, unfaltering faith had long raised the figure of the messiah beyond all human limitations into a supra-historical, supra-terrestrial sphere. He was endowed with the radiance of the heavens and transfigured above the earth. The apocalypses in particular had related how he had been chosen by God from the beginning and dwelt in another world, from which he would eventually descend when his time came. His growth was surrounded by miracles. Of all this the people felt sure; this much was known. And this meant that the tradition of Jesus' life had to be fitted into this mysterious image in which the world beneath and the world above were blended. It was this image that supplied the outlines and the texture. The events of his earthly existence could not and must not be solely decisive for the tradition or furnish its exclusive contents.

Satan and the Second Coming—In the faith of the pious, this conception of the beyond went hand in hand with a gloomy image. It was from beneath, out of the abysses of baseness and evil, that it arose to enter human reflections and inquiries. This was the background against which one understood the appearance and activities of the messiah. Behind and against the messiah, popular phantasy had long projected the image of his opponent and adversary: the depraved spirit, the tempter and "accuser"—the "satan": he was the anti-messiah, the Antichrist. Many even thought that they had felt his presence in the hours of temptation. For in those days people, and particularly simple folk, did not live in a world inhabited only by human beings, some friendly and some hostile: one felt that one was no less surrounded by spirits, some of them good and others, perhaps even more numerous, who were evil, wicked, and ruled by Satan. To fight Satan, to overcome his lures, and to vanquish him forever— that, too, was part of the messiah's mission. If Jesus was the messiah, then this great drama between the world beneath and the world above must have had its place in his life. His triumph over the dark, impure powers must form an essential part of faith in him— and it is noteworthy that the New Testament makes more of these powers than of the angels. Faith in him therefore introduced all this into the tradition. Whatever these people had seen or whatever had been related to them received its ultimate significance and its full content from elsewhere: they knew or had to be told at the same time what was behind all this—how the messiah invisibly fought the battle that was to lead to the triumph of humanity and its liberation from those threatening it.

Altogether, everything that the tradition here included pointed far beyond this life. What these people heard and what their souls craved was to them no mere event of the day, however large the day might loom, nor a word of the present hour, however serious. It was a matter of ultimate issues, of the meaning and goal of all life. Salvation, redemption was at stake: that which would come and then be final—the kingdom of God. Yet the inner certainty concerning the events of the future when the days would be fulfilled could be based only on what had happened now, what had occurred in the historic days when the messiah had walked through the Jewish land. Therefore it became important to know in detail what had happened and what it signified, what had been done and said, and what it meant if one related all this and clung to it. Those who told it as well as those who heard it felt the full responsibility for truths upon which everything depended: their salvation or destruction, eternal life or eternal death. So the tradition had to be more than only tradition; it had to become a password, an affirmation of faith, a creed, even an obligation to lead others on the right path. Every error, whatever its origin, had to be averted; every doubt, whoever might entertain it, must be repulsed.

Patience was out of place here, for people were living in the certain expectation of a day which might possibly appear tomorrow like lightning and confirm everything that had happened. It was a newly-awakened and emotionally aroused congregation that nourished the earliest tradition and handed it on. They lived under a tension: without rest but full of faith, watching eagerly and confidently, they waited for the Last Judgment when he that had come before would return to judge all men. The expectation of the Second Coming, the return of the messiah, never relaxed; questions and ideas about it occupied every mind. Though the day was slow in arriving, one did not doubt its coming. One did not hesitate to give away one's possessions: what did possessions matter now that everything was to be changed! Without wavering, people turned their backs on their land, their houses, their fields: what did a home matter now that everything was soon to be transformed! This longing and this faith also guided and formed the tradition. People were deeply convinced that many of the things that had happened or been said must have had reference to the Second Coming and must have prophesied a "beginning of travail" (Mark 13.8), the beginning of the end. An apocalyptic tone or twist was now added to many things, and everything apocalyptic invites further reflection and is a spur to the poetic imagination. The atmosphere was oppressive and heralded a storm: surely, the messiah's soul must have sensed this and it must be possible to find it in his words.

All agreed in this great expectation, in this certainty that Jesus had gone through his brief life as the "son of David," as the messiah, and that his Second Coming was imminent. But there were differences in degree and color in what they had been told of this and so remembered, and in what was now discussed among them. Jesus had had disciples, but not all had been equally close to him. There was the inner and the outer circle. Some of them had joined him sooner and some later and followed him around, while others—a very few whom one knew by name—had always been close to him and were known as the confidants of his spirit and heart. Even among these, however, there were differences in gifts and ability as well as differences in affection and prestige. It is quite clear in the ancient scriptures how one of these disciples is placed in the foreground here and another there: here it is Peter, there John, and there James, the brother of Jesus. It could not have been otherwise. Each told of the master in his own language, prompted by his own love and loyalty and faith; here it was the language and convictions of the one that won the ears and hearts of men, there those of another. Thus each found those who surrounded him and joined him, and these in turn found those who liked to hear their version.

Even in early Christianity various groups and sects were formed in this manner: congregations within the congregation of the expectant. Each possessed its own living tradition which was its treasured possession; for them this was the truth which they were determined to protect from all harm and distortion, resisting any encroachment. Before long, therefore, the tradition developed into traditions and the Gospel into the gospels of the different congregations; and this also accounts for the number and the peculiarities of the Gospels. The longer the "Lord delayed his coming" (Luke 12. 45) and the day that would set an end to all opinions failed to arrive, the more these opinions could grow in rigidity, separate, and oppose each other.

Paul—The second generation was to witness a new and remarkable answer to the question of the Second Coming. A man out of the Greco-Oriental world of Asia Minor had entered the circle of those in Jewish lands who were expecting the return of the messiah: Saul from Tarsus whose Roman name was Paul. In Asia Minor, East and West had been fused in mysticism and Gnosticism, in the miraculous conceptions of a mystery and sacraments—the mystery of the god who had died young and been resurrected and the sacraments of water and blood, bread and wine; and these sacraments were said to unify with this god all those who, having faith, received them, thus granting the recipients eternal, divine life. With all this the young Paul had been acquainted in his homeland, and he could not have forgotten it when he went to the land of Israel to study there. Now he could feel, not only the hopes of the Jews, but also the yearning for what had been promised in these mysterious realms, for this triumph over death,

70

and for this endowment with divine powers. Even before the messiah would return, faith in him might well grant everything that the mysteries wanted to offer the initiated: through a sacrament that would unite the believer with him, faith might penetrate beyond mere waiting and expectancy, and the believer might experience a kind of ownership and possession, a salvation this very hour—the here and now of the sacrament and its miracle.

Could it not be that conceptions from here and from there were really pointing toward each other? The pagan mysteries proclaimed one who had passed away in the bloom of life and risen to new life. Did not the tradition of the congregation also tell of him who had died young on the cross? And was it not part of the Jewish faith that the dead would be awakened again? And did not the word of the prophet speak of a resurrection on the third day? And did not the word of the prophet possess more truth and reality and certainty than all that the eye could see or the senses behold? The pagan sacrament with the sacred nourishment of bread and wine and the sacred baptism of water and blood promised a consecration and eternal life—a deification. Were not baptism with water, a blood covenant, and the consecration of bread and wine also among the ancient and venerable customs of Judaism? Did not Judaism and paganism meet at this point? Might not the presence of the savior, the Second Coming for which people were waiting, be granted in the hour of faith when the mysterious sacrament was received? And did not this mean a gift which all the commandments of the Bible could never give: the attainment of the ultimate goal, salvation, grace?

It does not greatly matter here to which generation we attribute the several letters which are ascribed to

Paul. Whatever may be said about that, there is no
doubt about this: one day, this man, Paul from Tarsus,
joined the congregation of Jesus' adherents; and one
day he began to preach and spread his own new faith
and a new theology which was designed to furnish a
biblical foundation for his faith; and he preached this
theology zealously, eloquently, and impatiently alongside of and against the older one; and eventually the
letters which bear his name were canonized in the New
Testament as scriptures propounding the faith of the
Church. And it is unmistakable that these letters proclaim something quite different from what the Gospels
wanted to tell, something entirely distinct from what
Jesus had, according to this tradition, said or done.
What found its place here was not the doctrine of Jesus
but a doctrine about him, not his own faith which he
had communicated to his disciples but faith in him.
What is central here and determines everything is not
the commandment or the comfort which Jesus had offered the distressed, the suffering, and those who had
gone astray, but the sacrament that the believer is to
receive in his name; not his life and work and passion
but his incarnation, his death and resurrection; not
his divine service to men, his preaching of the kingdom
of God, but a salvation which is the share of those that
believe in him; not a task and a confidence but a grace
that is fulfilled; not a demanding faith but a doctrine
of salvation.

Whatever judgment one may form concerning details,
this was something quite different from the tradition
which is still clearly evident in the Gospels: the reports about and the preaching of Jesus, the messiah, as
those who had loyally followed him had preserved them
and handed them down that one might be prepared for
his return. It was something new and necessarily had

to arouse contention in the original congregation and among the congregations. When it began to prevail and stood alongside the earlier teaching, it had to influence the tradition of the Gospel and effect its ideas and words, whether this was wanted and intended or not. The peculiar dialectic which characterizes the proofs in the Pauline epistles obviously did not find its way into the reports of the Gospels, for these scriptures, of course, did not want to offer proofs but wanted to relate and proclaim. Nevertheless, the Pauline faith did affect the tradition and the eventual written versions of the Gospels. Again and again we readily recognize its dogmatic imprint.

The Greco-Roman World—But a transforming influence was also felt from still another quarter. The glad tidings of Jesus, the messiah, had at first been meant primarily for the Jews: it was to his own people that he was said to have been sent as the liberator. But the Jewish people had their spiritual sphere, their congregations which extended far beyond the borders of the land of Israel, above all throughout the Roman Empire of which Israel had been made a part; and these congregations, particularly those in the east and west, had become centers of religious expansion. Strong and constant missionary activity aimed to lead human beings out of all nations to Judaism, or even into Judaism. The Jewish religion was ready at that time to spread out its arms to welcome proselytes; and the ancient biblical word that God loves the stranger (Deut. 10.18) was often interpreted to mean also: God loves the proselyte. Particularly around the Mediterranean, in the lands with Hellenistic-Roman culture, many

73

minds had been attracted and won over by the teaching of Judaism.

The development of Greco-Roman thought and feeling had in many ways facilitated a meeting of minds. The tendency toward a conception of the divine as one and spiritual, the development of a social conscience, and the aspiration to understand everything human meant so many approaches to Judaism. This is what then seemed to be the meaning of the ancient blessing of Noah that "Japheth shall dwell in the tents of Shem": this prophecy seemed near fulfillment. As it progressed, this Jewish missionary activity had self-confidently utilized old forms and aids and also devised new ones. There were those sent forth—which is what "apostles" means—while the Greek translation of the Bible, the so-called Septuagint, functioned like a chief apostle; methods were devised, catechisms and instructional books came into being, and a particular mode of presentation was developed—as it were, a special language for missionary purposes. Many documents as well as the works of Philo and Josephus (which were after all in a sense also missionary writings) show how the attempt was made to translate Jewish insights into Greek thought. The Bible appears as the book of the most universal wisdom, the prophets as the ideal thinkers, the teachers of Judaism as philosophers, the revelation of God in man as the Logos, and piety as the possession of the highest virtue. Those educated in Greco-Roman culture were to be helped to find themselves again in Judaism.

It was this setup of Jewish ways and expressions and pagan open-mindedness that was inherited by Christian missionaries who went abroad to proclaim the messiah. Without this inheritance their preaching would not have been possible; and in its general appearance this preaching scarcely added anything at first. But for its special new message, the tidings of the appearance and return of the messiah, the pagan people to whom it was addressed were somehow prepared. When the apostle spoke of the messiah to Greeks and Romans, he had the advantage, whether he knew and wanted this or not, of being able to speak in their own language and in terms of their own conceptions: he could tell them as something new, prompted by his faith, what could be found in their spiritual and religious world, too. This, however, led to a reciprocal influence. Even in the properly Jewish missions it had happened at times that concepts from here and there were fused, and what had been genuinely Jewish was changed and infringed. This happened even more to the preaching of the *Christos* when it was carried into the Greco-Roman world. Its form and expression received much from this new environment. What one had to offer was influenced by Greco-Roman conceptions and images and acquired a new tone and eventually even new content. The pupil became the teacher.

In particular, this was the fate of the idea of the savior, and even more of the word itself. The disciples of Jesus were familiar with this from the Bible; God, and he alone, is here the savior. Yet there was a way that led from here into the Greco-Roman world. Consider an inscription dating from the year 9 B.C.E.: it proclaims the resolve of the Greek cities in Asia Minor to adopt the Julian calendar and to have the year begin on the birthday of Augustus, and it refers to this emperor in these words: "Providence which determines everything in human life . . . has given us the sublime one whom it has, for the salvation of men, endowed with perfection; it has sent him to us and those after us as savior (*Soter*), and he will end all war and order all things. . . . The day of his birth has brought the world the glad tidings (evangels) which will be realized through him." On a memorial stone in Halicarnassus, dating from the year 2 B.C.E., the emperor is called "Savior of the whole human race whose works have not only fulfilled the prayers of all but surpassed them." Now consider, for example, how Jesus is, in the Gospel according to Luke, proclaimed as the savior (*Soter*) : "There is born to you this day the Savior." Here a predicate which the Bible ascribes to God alone has been attributed to the messiah, and it is unmistakably a concept and form of expression out of the cult of the emperor that asserts itself: the Greco-Roman ideas did not only meet those of Judaism, they were able to mold them. Greco-Roman notions excited the poetic imagination and easily moved it to transform and imitate; it was tempting to slant things toward the Greeks and Romans.

The stories of the holy miracle-worker which were then quite common in the Mediterranean world were similarly attractive. The many portraits of Apollonius of Tyana furnish a wealth of illustrations. He lived during the second half of the first century and was a much praised Pythagorean. Even before he is born, Apollonius is announced by a heavenly apparition as a "divine man." His first hours on earth are accompanied by miraculous events. As a youth he likes to go to the temple of the god where his words amaze everybody. He goes from place to place as a teacher, proclaiming words of wisdom and commandments in terse maxims which often only intimate what might be meant. Trusted disciples surround him. He prophesies, drives out demons, cures the sick and awakens the dead; he repudiates bloody sacrifices and praises true justice, and he practices and demands self-denial. There are so many parallels to the Gospels that it was at one time supposed that the story of Apollonius must have been written as a kind of polemic with the Gospels in mind. In fact, it merely shows what complexes of ideas and wish phantasies were then prominent in the Greco-Roman world and moved from place to place. As the missionary preaching of the "divine man," the *Christos*, was carried abroad, it could easily be influenced by all this, quite involuntarily; and it could no less easily be approximated to all this deliberately. The missionary slogan, "to the Greeks a Greek," could at times be realized in a sense not originally intended.

The Fate of the People—Thus the world one wanted to win over and convert soon won over and penetrated thought and speech in many ways. Even more important and decisive, however, were the events and experiences of a grave and serious time. The years of Jesus' life and the decades after his death—these years in which the country of the Jews had become a dependency of Rome—were now oppressive and now exciting. Some were overcome with a feeling of helplessness; resistance, and for that matter any activity at all, seemed senseless to them. Others wanted to be defiant and fight. But both experienced the present as a time of transition. Things simply could not remain as they were: clearly, one era had come to an end and another, a promised era, must be about to commence. The vacillating sense of the merely provisional took hold of many minds. Every day seemed to be speaking of the messiah—telling some that he was about to come while saying to others, who believed that they had beheld or experienced him in the person of Jesus, that he would soon return. Such days with their constant ups and downs all but compel reflection and poetic fiction; and this will be especially true of those who concentrate on what has already happened and been begun, those whose thoughts dwell constantly on the life, works, and death of a man who means everything to them. This time, heavy with mystery and full of "signs" (Matt. 24.3), has again and again molded and transformed the tradition of the Gospel, projecting into it its own character.

Most decisive of all, however, was the effect of a great historic event, the destruction of the temple in the year 70. Those living in the Jewish world were deeply shaken by it. For them it was not only a major catastrophe but, as can be readily imagined, no less an apocalyptic event. It seemed to represent an intrusion from the beyond and a challenging, frightening question which demanded an answer. And for the congregation to which nothing was more certain than that in Jesus the messiah had been seen and heard, only one answer was possible. The ruins of the temple had to be understood as the great proof of their faith. If the temple, the sanctuary of God, had gone up in flames, then God Himself must have spoken. Roman hands had hurled the torches, but they had been instruments only. God had passed judgment: by means of the consuming fire he had demonstrated to everybody that time had come to an end and the great turning point had been reached. He had passed sentence over those who had refused to realize this. God had made His decision in a way which every eye must see and every ear hear, and He had decided against all those who had refused to see and hear the messiah when he had still lived among them, those who had not believed when they had been confronted with the tidings.

This made a deep impression on the tradition of the Gospel—so deep that it affected the past: everything that had happened and been related was now, *ex post facto,* related to this catastrophe. This was almost a psychological necessity for the believer. For what God had caused to happen now must surely have been known by the messiah. More than anything else, a word about the destruction of the temple must have passed his lips. So it happened that sentences which were put into Jesus' mouth only later, found their way into the tradition: "Your house will be left unto you desolate" (Matt. 23.38). "Seest thou these great buildings? there shall not be left here one stone upon another, which shall not be thrown down" (Mark 13.2). "But when ye see Jerusalem compassed with armies, then know that her desolation is at hand" (Luke 21.20). In the apocalyptic atmosphere of those days, the Now and the Once could be fused easily.

Above all, one idea was now projected into the past. With this catastrophe God had proclaimed his judgment over the Jewish people who had refused to believe. This word must surely have come out of the mouth of the messiah himself—this rejection of the Jews, of the mass, the majority who had refused to recognize him and had denied him. Surely it must have been that way: after the words of admonition and comfort he must soon have spoken words of condemnation. The motif of the guilt incurred by the Jewish people now enters into the tradition. The story of the messiah must now also include an accusation against the "evil generation" (Matt. 12.45) who had opposed the anointed of the Lord and been his adversary. That God had now turned his back on the Jewish people became an article of faith for the new congregation. There is a story preserved in the Talmud (Hagiga 5 b) in which Rabbi Jehoshua ben Hanania, a teacher of the generation that lived immediately after the destruction of the

79

temple, meets a Christian who tells him solemnly that the Jewish people has now become "the people from whom the Lord has turned away his face." It is in line with this that a later age could claim that the congregation of Jesus had left Jerusalem even before the siege, to emigrate to Pella on the other side of the Jordan (Eusebius, *Hist.* III, 52ff.). The old congregation of Christ's disciples was assumed to have detached itself from the Jewish people even at that time, and to have been brought to safety before the catastrophe.

The Separation from Judaism—Many people wanted to differentiate themselves from Judaism no less than from the Jewish people. The final step proposed by the radical Gnostic movement which relegated the faith of the Old Testament to the realm of evil was, of course, decisively repudiated by the Church, and its resistance proved successful. But although the Church did not accept it into the canon, it still recognizes the Epistle of Barnabas which was composed in the time of Hadrian and in effect sets aside the Old Testament by allegorizing it. The author wants to differentiate himself completely from the Jews. For him the covenant between God and the Jews has long ceased to exist (4.6f., 14. 1f.) ; he refers to them with the disapproving word "those," which automatically establishes a distance (2.9, 3.6, 4.6, 8.7, 13.1) ; and he characterizes them with epithets which were in those days reserved for pagans. A similar attitude toward Judaism is evident in the canonical Epistle to the Hebrews, which was written after the destruction of the temple. The Law of Judaism here becomes only a "word spoken through angels" (2.2) ; its commandments are merely "carnal" and cannot really consecrate (7.16ff.) ; the Jewish priesthood has come to an end and the true high priest has appeared only in Jesus (5.5ff., 7.11f.) ; he alone has proclaimed salvation and the true word of God (2.3ff.) ; and when the believer is required in the end to "go forth without the camp" (13.13), the meaning is clear. The same tone out of the same time, the tone of this wish for separation, is heard in the Gospel according to John. Only it is still harsher here, even hostile, though at one point one finds the statement that "salvation is from the Jews" (4.22). The "Law" here becomes in the mouth of Jesus "your law" (8.17, 10.34) — precisely as Pontius Pilate, the Roman governor, also speaks of it here (18.31) — or even "their law" (15.25). The Jews are spoken of as a foreign people; the usual expression for them is "the Jews" (1.19, 2.6 and 18ff., 5.10 and 15f., and often elsewhere). They are so completely separate that an angry accusation against them can say: "Ye are of your father the devil" (8.44). It is no longer a question of the place of Jesus within the Jewish people or of something new in Judaism, as it had been in the old tradition of the congregation; one is concerned exclusively with something new that is opposed to Judaism, with the position of Jesus in opposition to the Jewish people.

The vast difference from the earlier attitude and the profound change marked by the year 70 become clear as soon as we compare all these verses in the Gospel according to John with what Paul had still said to the pagans about the Jews, in his Epistle to the Romans: "Did God cast off his people? God forbid. For I also am an Israelite, of the seed of Abraham, of the tribe of Benjamin. God did not cast off his people which he foreknew. . . . If the root is holy, so are the branches. But if some of the branches were broken off, and thou, being a wild olive, wast grafted in among them, and didst become partaker with them of the root and the fatness of the olive tree, glory not over the branches: but even if thou gloriest, it is not thou that bearest the root, but the root thee. . . . For I would not, brethren, have you ignorant of this mystery, lest ye be wise in your own conceits: a hardening in part hath befallen Israel, until the fulness of the Gentiles be come in. And so all Israel shall be saved, even as it is written (Isaiah 59.20f.) : 'There shall come out of Zion the Deliverer; he shall turn away ungodliness from Jacob; and this is my covenant unto them, that I shall take away their sins' " (Romans 11.1 and 16f. and 25f.). The whole vast change in thought and feeling becomes clear when one reads these sentences and then turns to those others which speak of "the Jews." One realizes what a complete change in the attitude toward Jews and Judaism took place during the period which lies between the Epistle to the Romans and the Gospel according to John. The congregation of the old apostles had wanted to be, and had been, a congregation within the Jewish people, and the tidings which they proclaimed had been tidings within Judaism, within it and by no means only alongside it—and this sense of belonging together had also been reciprocated. Now, however, the congregation and tradition stand thoroughly opposed to the Jewish people and to Judaism, and by no means only alongside it. It is easy to see how these facts, coupled with a corresponding sense of opposition which was thus engendered among the Jews, had to exert a steady influence on the tradition, changing and refashioning it until it was finally written down.

This tendency toward separation was then still further strengthened and continued by certain political factors. The suppression of the rebellion was followed

82

by special measures which the Romans took against the Jews. Until then, the Jews had had the same rights as other peoples in the Roman Empire, and even a number of additional privileges; now oppressive and discriminatory decrees were passed against them. For the Christians—and especially for those living outside Palestine—it could, and even had to become a political question, too, and at times even a question of their civil status, whether they were to be considered Jews or not. And this question immediately and inexorably led to the further question whether they were to side with Rome. All the reflections suggested by the developments of that time indicated that the answer had to be affirmative. The majority therefore opted for Rome and against the Jewish people. To the author of the so-called Revelation of St. John, who lived at the time of the destruction of the temple, such an answer would still have seemed satanic. But for subsequent generations it became a matter of course, the more so because the Jewish people were then still further oppressed with additional decrees which one wanted to escape. And this separation could be justified also by pointing to the opposition to the new congregations which had by then developed in Judaism. The anti-Jewish, pro-Roman attitude now becomes part of the tradition. And for the final version of the fate and words of Jesus and the written form of the Gospels it became decisive.

As a consequence, the tradition was now presented and intended almost exclusively for the pagans. Now they appear as the neighbors and the righteous and are to be won over, while the Jews are moved into the distance or even become a target. Every proclamation and scripture now testifies to this change. All hopes and wishes are directed toward the vast Roman world. All opportunities are concentrated here. For in the second third of the second century, after the ill-fated rebellion of Bar Kokhba, Judaism withdrew from all missionary activity, and the Christians were confronted with this vast and no longer disputed sphere which invited attempts at conversion. One wanted peace with this world, with its state, and with its people, for one wanted to be able to reach them. Therefore one liked to speak of them always with unmistakable sympathy. Particularly in relating the death of Jesus, one wanted to exculpate them in order to establish the culpability of the Jews. The clearest illustration of this tendency, which had by then been notable for some time, is furnished by the apocryphal Epistle of Pilate which was probably composed toward the end of the second century. Here Pontius Pilate, the judge of Jesus, appears almost as a disciple of Jesus and an apostle to the pagans. But these signposts of the time can be quite clearly recognized even in the Gospels. In the Gospel according to Matthew, Pilate is pictured almost as one of the pious and pure of the Bible: he washes his hands in innocence, and for Pilate's wife Jesus is the "just man" (27.19ff.). The decisive motif is fixed. And the Gospels received their final form along this line.

The Canonical Gospels—When the Gospel was finally put into writing—a little earlier here, a little later there—many versions were in existence. This multiplicity corresponds to that of the communities in different countries and among different peoples and to the manifold peculiarities both of the circumstances surrounding such composition and of the faith prompting it here and there. Through the Church fathers and through papyrus finds, we know of numerous gospels:

there are those of the Ebionites, the Nazarenes, the Hebrews, and the Egyptians, as well as the Gospels of Peter and Thomas and the first Gospel of James. As far as we can see, the abilities of those who fashioned and composed these gospels differed greatly in quantity and quality, and so did their influence. Undoubtedly, however, each had its own circle of believers for whom it was the true tradition and revelation—and surely also its opponents for whom it represented error and distortion, if not outright lies. In many places, the gospels stood opposed to each other. One only has to listen to the voices of those days to recognize this. The Epistle of Polycarp, written during the first half of the second century, complains that some men "falsify the sayings (*logia*) of the Lord in accordance with their own wishes" (VII.1, ed. Bihlmeyer, p. 117). The Epistles of Timothy in the New Testament, which belong to approximately the same period, say the same thing. Here we find the admonition: "Hold fast the form of sound words (*logia*), which thou hast heard of me" (II.1.13) ; we find a warning against him that "teacheth a different doctrine, and consenteth not to the sound words of our Lord Jesus Christ, and to the doctrine which is commanded by reverence" (I.6.3) ; and there is a reference to the fact that "they do not endure the sound doctrine, but after their own lusts heap to themselves teachers, having itching ears; and they turn away their ears from the truth and turn unto fables." (II.4.3f.) The assumption seems justified that the other side adopted much the same tone. But if such sharp words were possible, then it is clear to what extent the multiplicity of traditions had in the end led to mutual opposition. Undoubtedly, it could threaten the unity of the communities and the unity of the faith.

Such a unity had gradually been approximated.

Where the circumstances had made this possible and various personalities had determined it, many communities had begun to follow a general course which could be considered the standard. There had developed a consciousness of the essential common ground, a "catholic" conviction. A Church-forming power began to assert itself. Now it became necessary, and also possible, to decide on a canon of the new holy scriptures and to determine the form of the New Testament as a whole as well as the gospel tradition in particular. The general outline was clear now. On the one hand, the Church had to define itself against Judaism, out of which it had developed, by establishing what was historically and doctrinally new and distinctive; and on the other hand, it had to distinguish itself from doctrines which, though derived from the Church, seemed heretical and dangerous to it: particularly, the teachings of Marcion and radical Gnosticism. It was the right faith, the "sound doctrine," that required the canon. It required a Bible that could be placed alongside that of the Jews, alongside "the Scriptures." Like the Church itself, the canon, too, must of course represent a compromise, a mean. It was such a compromise, both regarding the contents and the number, that four Gospels, those according to Matthew, Mark, Luke, and John, were declared to be accredited, true, and genuine.

Certainly none of them was written down in the form in which these four Gospels confront us today, earlier than in the generation after the destruction of the temple. Two of them even point to a still later period, in the second century. Old traditions are clearly and recognizably preserved in them; but what each of them exhibits primarily in its over-all contents is nevertheless not what Jesus had said, hoped, and experienced. What each of the Gospels, taken as a whole, presents to us is rather what was believed, thought, wished, and desired by Christian communities under the guidance of authoritative teachers at the turn from the first to the second century. It is what they confidently considered the truth concerning the life and words of Jesus, all their opponents notwithstanding. What is foremost and clearest in our Gospels is not so much the religion and fate of Jesus as the conviction and course of the communities of that time. It was not first of all, and certainly not alone, a tradition that determined and guided them, but at least as much a purpose. Men envisaged the past in the perspective of their own days and painted it in the light of their own experiences, coloring it with their own hopes and concepts. The men who wrote down these Gospels wanted to bear true and enduring witness of themselves, of that which the Christ meant to them and should henceforth always mean to everybody, of that which should to the exclusion of all else be valid in preaching and instruction—their own faith. The Gospels were meant to be a didactic work for the community which would preserve and spread the right and "sound" faith.

The Peculiarities—Although the synoptic Gospels belong together in many ways, both regarding content and language, these common features do not preclude that within this over-all character each has its own clearly marked peculiarities. Of these three, the Gospel according to Mark is now generally conceded to be the earliest. It probably belongs to the years following the destruction of the temple. The violent change which this catastrophe brought about in the Christian community may well have furnished the decisive impulse for the first attempt to fix the tradition in writing. Such a development would have a parallel in the fact that the oral tradition in Judaism was first committed to writing after the Bar-Kokhba war. The author of the Gospel according to Mark has his eye on the pagan world. He addresses himself to those pagans who have become Christians and wants to edify them and strengthen their faith—but also to those who stand before the gates, for he wants to lead them in and convert them. In its aim, this Gospel is already directed against the Jewish people and against Judaism. The Jewish people here are hard of heart and therefore rejected by the savior; the time of Judaism is over; the words of Jesus have passed sentence on its law and its teachers. This in itself reveals a Pauline influence. But even beyond this, Pauline ideas have again and again become decisive in this Gospel. Jesus is here elevated into the supernatural sphere: he is not so much the messiah as the mediator of the new covenant, or testament, which he has instituted by shedding his blood (10.45; 14.24). A new temple has been erected by him—the temple of those believing in him. He stands revealed as the son of God by the miracles of his life, which are not human but divine miracles, as well as by the miracles of his death, his transfiguration and resurrection. The foremost meaning of his life is not found in what he said and did, but in that which touched him from above, not in his earthly course but in his death and resurrection. It is for this reason that miracle after miracle is related here. The Gospel according to Mark is really the miracle Gospel which, after all, was fitting for the Greco-Roman world which wanted to hear this kind of evidence for what was great and liberating. All this is told in artless sentences, in the Greek language of the simple folk of the East; but the manner of presentation is vivid and at times excited. One can see how the author feels that he is bearing witness of the salvation of the world.

The Gospel according to Luke, probably written down early in the second century, is a book with an entirely different style. The author writes it as an educated man and addresses himself to educated people, such as the "most excellent Theophilus" to whom he dedicates it. He possesses literary skill, and beyond that we can detect an artistic bent. He has the poet's pleasure in telling a story and enjoys painting and embellishing each detail. He is familiar with the language of the Greek Bible translation, the Septuagint, and he even knows how to use it to recreate prayers in soft, warm tones, after biblical models and with biblical sentences. But he knows no less how to use what was then the religious language of the Greeks, and he likes to employ it particularly when speaking of the savior. If the style is accepted as proof, he must also have written parts of The Acts of the Apostles. In his literary intentions, he is essentially an apologist and polemicist: he wants to defend and to fight, to edify and to convert. He, too, addresses the Greco-Roman world; he has his eye on it as he writes and often shows special consideration for it. He wants to put the nature, history, and development of his faith into the right light before the Greco-Roman world and demonstrate to it the legitimacy and reliability of the new community. He has turned his back on the Jews: they are evil and do not want to hear or see. The pagans, on the other hand, are here presented as the righteous who please God (4.25ff.). The new faith has, according to this interpreter, been aimed at them from the beginning: seventy missionaries, in accordance with the "seventy nations" of the pagans, have been sent forth by Jesus himself (10.1ff.). For these people for whom he writes, the author of this Gospel, too, clothes everything in miracles. In particular, he has taken such birth stories and legends, as had for a long time migrated from the East to the West, and woven them into his narrative. In this, and in all other respects, too, he has elevated the figure of Jesus into the beyond even more than Mark. The great world which the messiah fights and overcomes is that of Satan and the demons; and in order to fight the evil spirits everywhere, seventy disciples are here sent forth where only twelve are sent forth in Mark. It is in the supernatural spheres that the life of the savior has its true origin and province. Corresponding to this, a certain pessimistic and ascetic line, not uncharacteristic of Hellenistic thought at just that time, appears in the judgment on *this* world, in the preaching to men.

Compared to the poetic touch of Luke's work, the Gospel according to Matthew is more prosaic. But there is in its manner something pleasantly plain, something that has popular appeal. And in the course of the centuries it has probably been the Gospel read most and liked best. In the sequence of the synoptic Gospels it is presented as the first, but according to the date of its origin it is very probably the last. What is most characteristic of it is this: it represents an attempt, less to offer another version of the Gospel, than to bring together the traditions accumulated over a period of time, in the past and in the present, which had formed and crystallized in different places. It is the Church, becoming conscious of its catholic task and beginning to take shape, that speaks here—the Church and the beginning of its dogma which would bring together and reconcile the contradictions: these contradictions of the son of David and the son of God, of the old and the new law, of the kingdom of God and the Church (16.18; 18.17), of the enthusiasm of the expectant and the morality of the contented, of the twelve disciples of the master and the chosen successors to whom the keys are given which lock and unlock. Everything has its place in this Gospel: the earlier as well as the later, that which has been as well as that which has developed, and therefore also both what is friendly and what is hostile to the Jews. This Gospel likes to say—both. This is its most striking characteristic: it is the mediating Gospel and, as it were, wants to represent a harmony of the Gospels. It wants to effect a balance, not by melting down diversity into a historic or dogmatic unity, but by presenting together what stands opposed or was consecutive. It is thus ruled by the same principle which created the canon of the New Testament, and this may explain why it was placed at the beginning. Although it is the youngest of the synoptic Gospels, it contains in its own way more than a little of the oldest traditions.

It is questionable whether any early traditions are also contained in the fourth Gospel, that named after John. Probably it was written down after the Hadrianic war, at a time when the Christian community wanted less than ever to be confused with Judaism. Properly speaking, the fourth Gospel is no real Gospel at all, but, even much more than the others, a didactic work. In solemn monotony, now in allegories and abstract concepts, now in a wondrous ethical mysticism, this book wants to proclaim to educated Greeks that the messiah, the Christ, the "only begotten son of God" has existed from the beginning as a mediator of the creation, as the life and light of the world, and that this divine logos has become flesh in Jesus and truly dwelt in him. In his actions and speeches, this Gospel likes to give the human Jesus something of the character and deportment of a Greek sage, of a ruler in the sphere of the true and the good. It is a characteristic example of this tendency that Jesus here engages in a dialogue with his

91

and recover its parts and pieces which are still recognizable underneath.

At times, the layers can be determined quite easily and unequivocally. The Gospels according to Matthew and Luke, to give an example, contain a great condemnation of "the Pharisees and scribes" which culminates in a cry of woe unto Jerusalem. Here retribution is proclaimed to "this generation"—"that upon you may come all the righteous blood shed upon the earth, from the blood of righteous Abel unto the blood of Zacharias son of Barachias, whom ye slew between the temple and the altar" (Matt. 23.35; Luke 11.50). Now it is related in Flavius Josephus' *Jewish War* (IV.5.1f.) how this Zacharias son of Bariskaios—that is the Hellenized form of Barachias (really Berachya) used here—was stabbed and killed by the zealots between the temple and the altar, in the year 68: so it is clear to what time these sentences of the great cry of condemnation and woe belong. They could not have been spoken by Jesus, but were put into his mouth. They can have come only from the Christian community which had witnessed the destruction of the temple and considered this the great sign. Thus they do not reflect the character and intentions of Jesus, but attitudes and purposes encountered in the Christian community at this, far later, date.

Or consider another example: in the Gospels according to Matthew and Mark, Jesus' disciples ask him about the signs of his second coming and of the end of the world which is to be ushered in with this event; and he replies: "When ye shall see the abomination of desolation, spoken of by Daniel the prophet, stand in the holy place (whoso readeth, let him understand): Then let them which be in Judaea flee into the mountains" (Matt. 24.15f.; Mark 13.14). Again it is clear that these words could not belong in the time of Jesus. They must owe their origin—and the parenthesis "whoso readeth let him understand" is significant—to the anxieties and reflections of a time in which another "abomination of desolation" was to be erected in the sanctuary. For it is of such an outrage by Antiochus Epiphanes that the Book of Daniel (11.31 and 12.11) had spoken to the people. But the time when this was to be done again is known and fixed historically: it was the time of the mad Caligula who wanted to put up his statue in the temple in Jerusalem, too. That this is the event referred to becomes still clearer when we turn to another text; for the same event is alluded to in similar words and still more plainly in a later book of the New Testament: the Second Epistle to the Thessalonians which is ascribed to Paul. Here, too, the signs of the "coming of our Lord Jesus Christ" are discussed and the first of these is described as "the adversary who exalteth himself above all that is called God (Daniel 11.36), or that is worshiped; so that he as a god sitteth in the temple of God, representing himself to be a god" (II Thess. 2.4). Thus it is a definite and historically fixed event that is referred to in both in the Epistle to the Thessalonians and in the Gospel. From historical records we know how deeply the threat of the emperor's intention excited the people, what anxiety it caused, and what determination to resistance it evoked among the Jews. Surely it made the Christian communities feel that the end of time was now at hand. We may even suppose that at that time, in the year 40, an apocalypse in the manner of the Book of Daniel was passed around to reassure and strengthen everybody, and that this is the source of the sentences which were later accepted both into The Second Epistle to the Thessalonians and into two of the Gospels. In any case, these are not words spoken by Jesus to his disciples, but words of an unknown writer of a later generation.

The Transposition into an Earlier Time—These two examples of younger layers in the Gospels are at the same time characteristic illustrations of a *vaticinium ex eventu*—that is, the way in which something that has occurred or is about to occur is transformed into a prophecy belonging to a former age. The fulfilment of the future is projected back into the past as if it had been preached and prophesied in advance. In the Gospels this happens not infrequently. We encounter an example near the beginning, where John's baptism of Jesus is to be related. Of John it is there said: "And he preached, saying, There cometh one mightier than I after me, the latchet of whose shoes I am not worthy to stoop down and unloose" (Mark 1.7; similarly, Matt. 3.11 and Luke 3.16). Considering that John the Baptist died before Jesus commenced his career, it seems clear that something which a later age wanted to hear from history has here been put into his mouth. All those in whose faith Jesus was not only the Christ, but also the son of God, had to assume that John had not said anything of his own and that he had not even been an independent figure in his own right. The old tradition which is still quite recognizable had considered him a major figure: Elijah whom the Lord, according to the word of Malachi, the last prophet, would send "before the coming of the great and terrible day of the Lord, to turn the heart of the fathers to the children" (3.23f.; Luke 1.17 and Matt. 11.14). The old tradition had believed that he was the man of whom Isaiah had prophesied (40.3) that he would prepare the way and make a path (Matt. 3.3; Mark 1.2; Luke 3.4); and that is why it had been considered right and proper that the Gospels should begin with him. As the Gospel developed, however, he became a figure that only barely appears. And this is understandable enough; for the son of God who descends to the earth from the heavenly sphere by virtue of a miracle, and to be himself a miracle, cannot have had a precursor nor anyone who opened men's hearts before him and for him. There is no longer any place for this work of John. He becomes merely one of the believers. He exists, as it were, merely to stretch out his arm to point at him who exists now and evermore. According to the old tradition, Jesus had come from Galilee to be baptized by John (Matt. 3.13; Mark 1.9) and to follow him (Mark 1.14); but now John is made to say to Jesus: "I have need to be baptized of thee, and comest thou to me?" (Matt. 3.14). To the community for which Jesus was the "Lord," John could not have more than this relatively small significance.

The same story of John also shows how the expressions and patterns of a far later faith were projected into earlier times: it shows how the earlier age is embellished with Christian features. Thus Mark (1.8), and similarly each of the other two synoptic Gospels, lets John say with reference to him that is to come after him: "I indeed have baptized you with water: but he shall baptize you with the Holy Spirit." Clearly, Christian words of a later age have here been put into his mouth. For John's reference here to a baptism with the Holy Spirit is in the religious style of Paul. That those redeemed by the Christ are granted a supernatural life in the spirit, only Paul taught; and the fourth Gospel later took up this theme. For Paul and those after him, this spirit is the guarantee of eternal life, the power of God in the believer; it is the strength of the world to come and a heavenly gift which is granted with the sacrament of baptism. And the Gospel here lets John the Baptist already proclaim this doctrine.

Matthew (3.11) and Luke (3.16) then even add another word, that of fire: "He shall baptize you with the Holy Spirit and fire." Here the experience of the old community of the expectant finds expression alongside the Pauline theology. This community had expected the confirmation of its messianic claims through being granted what Joel had prophesied long ago (3.1f. and Acts 2.16ff.): "And it shall come to pass afterward, that I will pour out My spirit upon all flesh; and your sons and your daughters shall prophesy, your old men shall dream dreams, your young men shall see visions; and also upon the servants and upon the handmaidens in those days will I pour out My spirit." That is how the Whitsun story in the Acts of the Apostles, this first story of the community, relates it. This spirit from God, this Holy Spirit, or Ghost, or, as it was also called in the Judaism of that period, the spirit of prophecy, has often been pictured in Jewish poetry with the image of fire. And that is how the Whitsun story, too, relates it: "And suddenly there came a sound from heaven as of a rushing mighty wind, and it filled all the house where they were sitting. And there appeared unto them cloven tongues like as of fire, and it sat upon each of them. And they were all filled with the Holy Spirit" (Acts 2.2ff.). When the Gospels according to Matthew and Luke speak of the baptism with the Holy Spirit and fire, they also carry the experience of the first Christian community into the figure of John the Baptist. They let him speak as one who participated in this Whitsunday, the community's day of revelation.

When the doctrine of the Holy Spirit thus entered into the old story of Jesus' baptism, it also introduced

97

something further. As Jesus is baptized, it is said:
"And straightway coming up out of the water, he saw
the heavens opened, and the Spirit like a dove descend-
ing upon him: And there came a voice from heaven,
Thou art my beloved Son, in whom I am well pleased"
(Mark 1.10; Matt. 3.16; Luke 3.22). It is highly prob-
able that an old tradition finds expression here, a
miraculous story of the disciples. For them the baptism meant the beginning of Jesus' messianic mission—
his mission to become the helper and liberator of the
people of Israel. The dove, in Greek folklore the bird
of the soul, was in the Jewish poetry of those days a
symbol and sign representing the community of Israel.
Therefore, it hovers over the man who commences his
way to deliver the people, and the voice from heaven
says: "My son in whom I am well pleased." For in the
poetic language of the prophets, both the people of
Israel and he in whom the people is personified, its king,
its messiah, are called the chosen one of God and his
son. For the later age which was further removed from
Judaism, this symbol was no longer acceptable in this
way. So it was transformed into something which it
had never been in the Jewish world in which Jesus had
lived: as an image of the Holy Spirit it was introduced
into the Christian sphere and given a place among
Christian concepts.

The Original Tradition—It is not always as easy as
this to recognize the upper layers which cover up the
earlier strata. At times, the tradition has given way
completely to later stories. This happened especially
where occasions and situations were invented to connect the "sayings" or *logia* of Jesus with his life and
"deeds." Again and again, the Gospels resemble a

palimpsest: new things have, as it were, been written over the old tidings. But on the whole it is nevertheless possible to get back to the original tradition. If one notes the special characteristics of each of the three authors and, so to say, eliminates them, the procedure and method to be followed after that can be shown quite clearly. All of the following are indicative of later strata: first of all, whatever accords only with the experiences, hopes, wishes, ideas, and the faith and the images of the faith of a later generation; then, events which were clearly begotten in the image either of biblical verses or of the gradually developing dogma and its symbolism; also, whatever is related or spoken with an eye on the Greco-Roman world or the Roman authorities, any obvious attempt to curry favor with them as well as anything prompted by the desire not to be confounded by them with the Jewish people; moreover, whatever is in the Hellenistic style, modeled after Hellenistic prophets and miracle-workers; and finally all that reflects the age of the catastrophe, the age after the conquest of Jerusalem and the destruction of the temple. All this belongs to the history of the faith of the Church, but is not part of the old Gospel. The following, on the other hand, must be part of the old and original tradition: whatever is completely different from the tendencies and purposes of the generations which came after the first generation of disciples; whatever contradicts the tenets which later became part of the faith; whatever is different from, or even opposed to, the intellectual, psychic, and political climate in which these later generations gradually found themselves; whatever, in other words, exemplifies the way of life and the social structure, the climate of thought and feeling, the way of speaking and the style of Jesus' own environment and time. In all this we are confronted with the words and deeds of Jesus.

In this way—but indeed only in this way—we uncover something which is truly a unity, a distinctive whole—something that bears witness to a personality and a life. We are confronted with something that accords fully with the words in which the Peter of the Acts of the Apostles tries to summarize briefly what was the old tradition of the life and death of Jesus. In these words, incidentally, the phrase "Holy Spirit" is still used in its old Jewish meaning, in the sense of "spirit of inspiration" or "spirit of prophecy."

"That word ye know, which was published throughout all Judaea, and began from Galilee, after the baptism which John preached, about Jesus of Nazareth, namely, how 'God anointed him with holy spirit' and with power (Isaiah 61.1), so he went about doing good, and healing all that were oppressed of Satan; for God was with him. And we are witnesses of all things which he did both in the land of the Jews and in Jerusalem; whom they slew and hanged on a tree: him God 'raised up on the third day' (Hosea 6.2) and showed him openly; not to all the people, but unto witnesses chosen before of God, even to us, who did eat and drink with him after he rose from the dead" (Acts 10.37ff.). For the disciples, this had been the content of the life and death of their master.

In the old Gospel which is thus opened up before us, we encounter a man with noble features who lived in the land of the Jews in tense and excited times and helped and labored and suffered and died: a man out of the Jewish people who walked on Jewish paths with Jewish faith and hopes. His spirit was at home in the Holy Scriptures, and his imagination and thought were anchored there; and he proclaimed and taught the word

100

ᲕᲘ2550

of God because God had given it to him to hear and to preach. We are confronted by a man who won his disciples among his people: men who had been looking for the messiah, the son of David, who had been promised; men who then found him and clung to him and believed in him until he finally began to believe in himself and thus entered into the mission and destiny of his age and indeed into the history of mankind. These disciples he found here, among his people, and they believed in him even after his death, until there was nothing of which they felt more certain than that he had been, according to the words of the prophet, "on the third day raised from the dead." In this old tradition we behold a man who is Jewish in every feature and trait of his character, manifesting in every particular what is pure and good in Judaism. This man could have developed as he came to be only on the soil of Judaism; and only on this soil, too, could he find his disciples and followers as they were. Here alone, in this Jewish sphere, in this Jewish atmosphere of trust and longing, could this man live his life and meet his death—a Jew among Jews. Jewish history and Jewish reflection may not pass him by nor ignore him. Since he was, no time has been without him; nor has there been a time which was not challenged by the epoch that would consider him its starting point.

When this old tradition confronts us in this manner, then the Gospel, which was originally something Jewish, becomes a book—and certainly not a minor work—within Jewish literature. This is not because, or not only because, it contains sentences which also appear in the same or a similar form in the Jewish works of that time. Nor is it such—in fact, it is even less so—because the Hebrew or Aramaic breaks again and again through the word forms and sentence formations of the

Greek translation. Rather it is a Jewish book because—
by all means and entirely because—the pure air of
which it is full and which it breathes is that of the Holy
Scriptures; because a Jewish spirit, and none other,
lives in it; because Jewish faith and Jewish hope,
Jewish suffering and Jewish distress, Jewish knowledge and Jewish expectations, and these alone, resound
through it—a Jewish book in the midst of Jewish books.
Judaism may not pass it by, nor mistake it, nor wish to
give up all claims here. Here, too, Judaism should comprehend and take note of what is its own.

THE EVENTS

John the Baptist and Jesus—This is what is written in
the book of Malachi the prophet and the book of Isaiah
the prophet: "Behold, I send My messenger, and he
shall clear the way before Me; and the Lord, whom ye
seek, will suddenly come to His temple; and the messenger of the covenant, whom ye delight in, behold, he
cometh, saith the Lord of hosts." "A voice calleth:
'Clear ye in the wilderness the way of the Lord, make
plain in the desert a highway for our God. Every valley
shall be lifted up, and every mountain and hill shall be
made low; and the rugged shall be made level, and the
rough places a plain; and the glory of the Lord shall be
revealed, and all flesh shall see the salvation of God;
for the mouth of the Lord hath spoken it.'" Thus it
happened that John (Johanan), the son of Zechariah
(Secharya), baptized himself and preached baptism
and repentance in the wilderness of Judaea. He said:
"Repent ye: for the kingdom of God is at hand." John
had his raiment of camel's hair, and a leather girdle
about his loins; and his nourishment was locusts and
wild honey. Then went out to him Jerusalem and all

Judaea, and they baptized themselves before him in the Jordan, confessing their sins.[1]

And it came to pass in those days, that Jesus came from Nazareth of Galilee and baptized himself in John's presence in the Jordan. And straightway, as he came up out of the water, one saw the heavens open, and the shape of a dove descended and was over him, and there came a voice from heaven: "Behold My servant, whom I uphold; Mine elect, in whom I am well pleased; I have put My spirit upon him, he shall make the right go forth to the nations."[2]

Now Jesus was "full of the spirit" of God. He remained there in the wilderness many days.[3]

1. Matt. 3.1-7; Mk. 1.2-7; Luke 3.1-7. Luke also offers a miraculous birth story about the Baptist, in the manner of Greek birth legends.—The Hebrew word *tawol*, which was translated into Greek as *baptizein*, is intransitive and means immersing oneself or baptizing oneself. The believers "baptized themselves": the adherents of John did it in his presence, at his bidding. A correct reading, *enopion*, has been preserved in Luke 3.7. Matthew and Luke also have at this point a philippic against the Jews; and all three Gospels add a reference to him who is to come after John; cf. above, the section on "The Transposition into an Earlier Time." The baptism "for the remission of sins," to which our Gospels refer here, is a later addition of Pauline times.—The two verses from Scripture which are cited here are Malachi 3.1 and Isaiah 40.3ff., the last verse in the old reading of the Septuagint.

2. Matt. 3.13ff.; Mk. 1.9ff.; Luke 3.21f. In the scriptural verse which is cited here (Isaiah 42.1), the first words of the voice from heaven have been omitted in our Gospels, and a reference to the sonship of God has been substituted in their place. The verse is one of the old messianic sentences. Cf. above, the end of the section on "The Transposition into an Earlier Time."

3. Matt. 4.1-12; Mk. 1.12f.; Luke 4.1-14. Cf. Deuteronomy 34.9. This passage furnishes a characteristic example of the manner in which the tradition elaborated and embellished. The old tradition had said that Jesus, after he had baptized himself in John's presence, remained there—that is, with John, in the wilderness—forty days. In the language of the Bible, the word

103

Jesus was about thirty years old in the beginning of all these events.

This is the generation of Jesus: David begat Solomon of the wife of Uriah. Solomon begat Rehoboam. Rehoboam begat Abia. Abia begat Asa. Asa begat Jehoshaphat. Jehoshaphat begat Joram. Joram begat Uzziah. Uzziah begat Jotham. Jotham begat Ahaz. Ahaz begat Hezekiah. Hezekiah begat Manasseh. Manasseh begat Amon. Amon begat Josiah. Josiah begat Jechoniah and his brethren, about the time of the Babylonian captivity. After the Babylonian captivity, Jechoniah begat Shealtiel. Shealtiel begat Zerubbabel. Zerubbabel begat Abiud. Abiud begat Eliakim. Eliakim begat Azor. Azor begat Sadoc. Sadoc begat Eliud. Eliud begat Eleazar. Eleazar begat Matthan. Matthan begat Jacob. Jacob begat Joseph, the husband of Mary (Miriam) of whom was born Jesus, who is called Messiah. And when eight days were accomplished for the circumcising of the child, his name was called Jesus (Jeshua), which means "he will help his people from their sins."[4]

"forty" designates an indefinite number. A later age asked itself what Jesus might have done and experienced during this time. Mark related briefly in one sentence: "He was tempted of Satan; and was with the wild beasts; and the angels brought him food"—much as the Bible had related of Elijah (I Kings 17.3ff. and 19.5ff.). Luke and Matthew elaborate the temptation in great detail and let Jesus fast forty days and forty nights, as Moses did on Sinai (Exodus 34.28). The events associated with the lives of the great men of previous times are introduced into the life of Jesus.—In connection with Satan, cf. the section above on "Satan and the Second Coming."
4. Matt. 1.1-21; Luke 2.21 and 3.23-38. In both Gospels a miraculous birth story has been added. The genealogy which is intended to exhibit Jesus as a *ben David*, a progeny of David, has been extended by Matthew back to Abraham to show Jesus as the heir of the promise made to Abraham. Luke even extends it back to Adam to let Jesus appear as the new Adam. Both ideas are Pauline; cf. Galatians 3.16 and Romans 5.14 and I Cor. 15.22. Both birth story and genealogy are lacking in Mark.

After this it happened that Herod the tetrarch laid hold of John, and bound him, and put him in prison for Herodias' sake, his brother's wife, whom he had married. For John had said to Herod: "It is not lawful for thee to have thy brother's wife." And he sent and beheaded John in the prison. And when his disciples heard of it, they came and took up his corpse and laid it in a tomb.[5]

Preaching in Galilee—Now when Jesus heard that John was taken, he departed into Galilee; and leaving Nazareth, he came and dwelt in Capernaum (Kfar Nahum), which is upon the sea coast, in the region of Zebulun and Naphtali: that it might be fulfilled which was spoken by Isaiah the prophet, saying: "The land of Zebulun, and the land of Naphtali, by the way of the sea, beyond the Jordan, Galilee of the nations—the people that walk in darkness have seen a great light; and to them which sat in the region of shadows light is sprung up." From that time Jesus began to preach, saying: "Return, for the time is fulfilled and the kingdom of God is at hand."[6]

As he was walking along the sea of Galilee, he saw Simon and Andrew, the brother of Simon, casting a net into the sea: for they were fishers. And Jesus said unto them: Come over here, after me; and I will make you fishers of men. And they straightway left their nets and followed him. And as he went on a little, he saw

5. Matt. 14.1-13; Mark 6.14 and 17-30; Luke 3.19ff. and 9.7ff. Matthew and Mark embellished the execution of John novelistically.
6. Matt. 4.12-17; Mark 1.14f.; Luke 4.14f.; Isaiah 8.23f. To this preaching of Jesus, which is the same as that of the Baptist, Mark still added at a later time: "Believe in the Gospel."

Jacob, the son of Sabdai, and his brother John, too, in a ship, mending nets; and he called them. And they left their father Sabdai in the ship with the hired servants and went after him.[7]

They went into Capernaum; and straightway on the sabbath he entered into the synagogue and taught. And they were astonished at his doctrine: for he taught them as one to whom it has been given by God, and not as one of the scribes.[8]

And forthwith, when they were come out of the synagogue, he entered into the house of Simon and Andrew, with Jacob and John. But Simon's wife's mother lay sick of a fever, and anon they told him of her. And he came and took her by the hand, and lifted her up; and immediately the fever left her, and she ministered unto them. And at even, when the sun did set, they brought unto him all that were diseased; and he healed many and cast out many evil spirits.[9]

7. Matt. 4.18-23; Mark 1.16-21; Luke 5.1-12. Luke has embellished the story poetically in his characteristic manner. Matthew took up the metaphor of the fisher of men and elaborated it into a separate parable (13.47ff.).

8. Mark 1.21f.; Luke 4.31f. Mark—and then after him Luke, elaborating the story still a little further—adds in the Greek manner how Jesus exorcized an unclean demon out of a man in the synagogue.

9. Matt. 8.14ff.; Mark 1.29-35; Luke 4.38-41. Mark, in his favorite manner, has all the city gather together at the door. He, and Luke and Matthew following him, also elaborate the exorcizing of the demons. In all three Gospels, a series of miraculous cures follows. There can be no doubt that the old tradition told of Jesus' healing power. In a later age, which was influenced by Hellenism, these cures are exalted further—on the one hand, into something perpetual and professional; on the other, into something omnipotent. It is not difficult to distinguish the old tradition from the later additions.—In Mark 2.5, as well as Matt. 9.2 and Luke 5.20, Jesus already appears as the Christ who forgives sins.

106

His fame spread abroad throughout all the region of Galilee.[10]

Some said of him: He is Elijah. And others said: He is one of the prophets.[11]

In the morning, a great while before day, he rose up and went out, and departed into a solitary place, and there prayed. And Simon and they that were with him followed after him. And when they had found him, they said unto him: "All are seeking thee." But he said unto them: "Let us go into the next towns, that I may preach there also: for therefore came I forth." And he preached in the synagogues throughout all Galilee. With many parables he spake to the people in a manner which they could understand.[12]

On this way he came to his home town. And when the Sabbath was come, he began to teach in the synagogue; and the many who heard him were astonished and said: "From whence has he these things? What wisdom is given unto him! Is not this the son of the carpenter, Joseph, and of Mary, and the brother of Jacob and Jose and Judah and Simon; and his sisters, are they not all with us?" And they were offended in him.[13]

10.   Mark 1.28; Luke 4.37. That which is here spoken of is not, as most of the translations have it, "the region round about Galilee" but "the region of Galilee." The Greek word used here was used in the Septuagint already as the usual translation of the Hebrew *kikar*, "region."
11.   Mark 6.15; Luke 9.8.
12.   Mark 1.35-40; Luke 4.42ff.; Matt. 4.23ff., as well as Matt. 13.34 and Mark 4.33. Mark, in his manner, still adds: "and cast out devils." It is noteworthy that Matthew and Mark say, here as elsewhere: "in *their* synagogues." Cf. above, the section on "The Separation from Judaism."
13.   Matt. 13.53ff.; Mark 6.1ff.; Luke 4.16-23. Our Gospels also adduce at this point the Greek proverb: "A prophet is not without honour, save in his own country, and in his own house." On account of the dogma, Mark mentions only the mother.

The Disciples—He went forth again by the sea side; and the multitude from everywhere came unto him, and he taught them. And as he passed by, he saw Mattai, the Levite, the son of Chilfai, sitting at the receipt of custom and said unto him: "Follow me!" And he arose and followed him. And he sat at table in his house, and many publicans, men of guilt, sat together with Jesus and his disciples: for there were many who had followed him. When the Pharisees saw him eat with publicans, men of guilt, they said unto his disciples: "Your teacher eateth with publicans, men of guilt!" When Jesus heard it, he said unto them: "They that are strong have no need of the physician, but they that are weak. I have not come here to call the just but the men of guilt."[14]

They also came over to the other side of the sea, into the country of the Gadarenes, which is opposite Galilee. When Jesus had returned from there, there came unto him one of the leaders of the community, Jair by name; and when he saw him, he fell at his feet, and besought him greatly, saying: "My little daughter lieth at the point of death; do come and lay thy hands on her, that she may be rescued and live. And he went with him. And he took the child by the hand, and said unto her: "*Talitha kumi*"; which is, being interpreted: "Damsel, arise!" And the damsel arose and walked up and down.[15]

14. Matt. 9.9-14; Mark 2.13-18; Luke 5.27-31. In the Gospel according to Matthew, the name Mattai is preserved; in the two others, the tribal name, Levi.—There is no reference here, as our translations have it, to "publicans *and* sinners"; the Hebrew phrase on which the text is based means: "*men* who are publicans and guilty."

15. Matt. 8.28 and 9.18-26; Mark 5.1 and 22-43; Luke 8.26 and 41-56. Matthew, and probably also Luke, has it that the child had already died. Later the story was embellished profusely and interrupted by another miracle story.

He also went about the villages, and he called twelve disciples that they should be with him, and that he might send them forth to preach: Simon, called Kepha; and Andrew, his brother; Jacob, son of Sabdai, and John his brother, whom he called "*Bne regos*—wrathful ones"; Mattai the Levite, the son of Chilfai the publican; and Jacob, his brother; Philip and Bartalmai, Taddai and Tejoma, Simon the Zealot, and Judah of Kerijot who later betrayed him. These twelve Jesus sent forth and commanded them, saying: "Go not into the way of the Gentiles, and into any city of the Samaritans enter ye not: go to the lost sheep of the house of Israel and preach thus: the kingdom of God is at hand."[16]

Afterward, when he went through cities and villages, proclaiming and announcing the kingdom of God, the twelve were with him. And there were also with him certain women, which had been healed of evil spirits and infirmities: Mary, called the one from Magdala; Johanna the wife of Chuza, Herod's steward; Susanna; and others; and they ministered unto him of their substance.[17]

The multitude came together again, so that they could not so much as eat bread. There came also his mother

---

16. Matt. 9.35 and 10.1-8; Mark 6.7 and 3.13-20; Luke 6.13-17. Cf. Acts 1.13. The names of the twelve apostles have been handed down differently. Mattai and Jacob, who are both called "sons of Chilfai," are probably brothers. Lebbaeus probably conceals the name Levi; that is, the Levite. The Zealot, *kannai*, is one who belonged to the group of the Zealots—activists demanding an open fight against Rome. Instead of *ish kerijot*, "the man from Kerijot," one should perhaps read: *siccarius*, the dagger man. The "dagger men" were the most extreme among the Zealots; cf. Acts 21.38.—The genuineness of the last sentence is proved by the fact that it contradicts the later view.

17. Luke 8.1ff. Luke, in his manner, has more to tell of the demons; cf. above, p. 106, note 8.—This passage belongs to the historically important ones related by Luke, which shed some light on the relation to the tetrarch, Herod Antipas. Cf. below, pp. 113 and 119f; Luke 13.31 and 23.12.

and his brothers, who, standing without, sent in unto him, calling him; for there were many sitting about him. And they said unto him: "Thy mother and thy brethren are without and seek thee." And he answered them, saying: "Who is my mother and my brethren?" And he looked round about on them which sat about him, and said: "These are my mother and my brethren!"[18]

From thence he went into the region of Tyre. A woman of Canaan out of that same region, whose daughter had an evil spirit, heard of him. And straightway she came and fell at his feet, and cried: "Lord, help me!" But he answered: "It is not meet to take the children's bread and to cast it unto the dogs." But she said: "Yes, Lord: yet the dogs eat of the crumbs which fall from their master's table." Then he said unto her: "Be it unto thee even as thou wilt." And her daughter was made whole from that very hour.[19]

And again, departing from the region of Tyre, he came unto the sea of Galilee, into the region of the Ten Cities. And they brought unto him one that was deaf and could scarcely speak, and besought him to put his hand upon him. And he took him aside from the multitude, and he put his fingers into his ears, and touched his tongue with spittle, looked up to heaven and sighed deeply, and said: *"Ephata,"* that is, "be opened." And

18. Mark 3.20 and 31-35; Matt. 12.46-50; Luke 8.19ff. In accordance with the later position of the Church, the story is interrupted by an argument with the Pharisees. And at the end of our story, a sentence of commentary has been added: "Whosoever doth the will of God, the same is my brother, and my sister, and mother."—"To eat bread" is a biblical expression for having a meal.
19. Matt. 15.21-28; Mark 7.24-30. In Pauline times it was added later that the woman was helped because her "faith was great." The story is another example of the way in which genuineness is proved by the contradiction to what was believed in later times.

his ears were opened, and the string of his tongue was loosed. He charged them that they should tell no man: but however much he charged them, they published it further and further. Beyond measure they were astonished, so they said: "Thus he hath done all things; he maketh the deaf to hear, and the dumb to speak."[20]

It came to pass, that he went through the corn fields on a Sabbath; and his disciples, as they went, began to pluck the ears of corn. Some Pharisees saw it and said unto him: "Behold, they do on the Sabbath what is not lawful!" And he said unto them: "Have ye not read in the Scripture what David did when he had need and was an hungred, he and they that were with him; how he entered into the house of God, and did eat the shewbread, which is not lawful to eat but for the priests, and gave also to them which were with him? And ye also know that it hath been said: 'The Sabbath was made for man, and not man for the Sabbath.' "[21]

The Messiah—Jesus went out, and his disciples, into the towns of Caesarea Philippi: and on the way he asked his disciples: "Whom do men say that I am?" And they answered: "Elijah—and others, one of the prophets." And he said unto them: "But whom say ye that I am?" And Peter answered and said unto him: "Thou art the Messiah." And he charged them that they should tell no man of him. And they asked him: "Why

20. Mark 7.31-37. A later tradition has then again added further miracles and arguments with the Pharisees.
21. Matt. 12.1-9; Mark 2.23-28; Luke 6.3ff. The final sentence is a quotation of a maxim of the ancient sages; cf. Mechilta for 31.13. The story of David is found in the First Book of Samuel 21.2. Matthew, in accordance with his characteristic manner, adds still further proofs. Our Gospels also add: "The son of man is Lord over the Sabbath"—which annuls the true meaning of the story.

say the scribes that Elijah must first come?" And he answered and told them: "Elijah verily cometh first, and leadeth back all. And Elijah is indeed come, and they have done unto him whatsoever they listed." And then the disciples understood that he spake unto them of John the Baptist.[22]

They departed thence and passed through Galilee; and he would not that any man should know it. And they rose from thence and came into the region of Judaea by the farther side of the Jordan. And they brought young children to him, that he should touch them. But his disciples rebuked those that brought them. But Jesus said: "Suffer the little children to come unto me, and forbid them not: for of such is the kingdom of God." And he put his hands upon them and blessed them.[23]

When he came out into the street, there came one running and asked him: "Master, good one, what shall I do that I may inherit eternal life?" And Jesus said unto him: "Why callest thou me the good one? Dost thou not know what hath been said: 'There is none that is the good one but the one God alone.' And thou knowest the commandments: thou shalt not kill, thou shalt not commit adultery, thou shalt not steal, thou shalt not bear false witness, thou shalt honour thy father and thy

.

22. Matt. 16.13-20 and 17.10-14; Mark 8.27-31 and 9.11-14; Luke 9.18-22. Matthew here says, in accordance with the dogma: "Thou art the Messiah, the son of the living God." And for the doctrine of the Church he also inserts in the first part the story of Peter as the lord of the Church. In accordance with the legend of the death of John (Mark 7.14ff.), the Gospels name not only Elijah and the prophets, but also John; and Matthew further adds Jeremiah. Our Gospels also introduce here prophecies of death, resurrection, and second coming, as well as a transfiguration story.
23. Mark 9.30 and 10.1-13ff.; Matt. 19.13ff.; Luke 18.15ff. There follow some testimonies of later ascetic views.

mother." And he answered and said unto him: "All
these have I observed from my youth." Then Jesus beholding him loved him, and said unto him: "One thing
thou lackest: Go thy way, sell whatsoever thou hast,
and give it to the poor—'and thou shalt have treasure
in heaven'; and then come and follow me." And he was
sad at that saying, and went away grieved: for he had
great possessions. And Jesus looked after him, and then
he said unto his disciples: "How hardly shall they that
have riches enter into the kingdom of God! It is easier
for a camel to go through a needle's eye than for a rich
man to enter into the kingdom of God."[24]

The Road to Jerusalem—During this time there came
certain of the Pharisees, saying unto him: "Go away
and depart hence: for Herod Antipas will kill thee."[25]

As they went on their way, a scribe came, and said
unto him: "Master, I will follow thee whithersoever
thou goest." And Jesus said unto him: "The foxes have
holes, and the birds of the air have nests; but I have not
where to lay my head."[26]

Now they were on the way going up to Jerusalem.[27]

24. Matt. 19.16-28; Mark 10.17-24; Luke 18.18-26. The sentence
"There is none that is the good one but the one God alone" is
another quotation of an old word of wisdom which is mentioned
quite often in the Jewish literature of that time. The same applies to the sentence, "and thou shalt have treasure in heaven"—
and also to the phrase "a camel through a needle's eye."
25. Luke 13.31. Most of the translations here say at the beginning: "In the same hour." The Greek word here, however—
hora—had long been the equivalent of the Hebrew word, *'et*, time,
already in the Septuagint.—This entirely isolated sentence, which
seems very old on many grounds, appears to be connected in
some way with the story (Luke 9.57) with which it has been
linked above. Cf. also p. 109, note 17.
26. Matt. 8.19f.; Luke 9.57f.
27. Mark 10.32; cf. Matt. 20.17 and Luke 18.31. This isolated
sentence is a kind of heading.

On the way they came into a village of the Samaritans; but they did not receive him because he went in the direction of Jerusalem. And when his disciples Jacob and John saw this, they said: "Master, if we may speak, wilt thou not that fire come down from heaven and consume them, even as Elijah did?" But he turned, and rebuked them. And they went to another village.[28]

And it came to pass, that, as he was praying in a certain place, when he ceased, one of his disciples said unto him: "Master, teach us to pray, as John also taught his disciples." And he said unto them: "When ye pray, say: Our father which art in heaven, hallowed be thy name. Thy kingdom come. Thy will be done, as in heaven, so on earth. Give us this day our daily bread. And forgive us our debts, as we also have forgiven our debtors. And bring us not into temptation."[29]

And they came to Jericho: and as he went out of Jericho with his disciples and a great number of people, a blind man sat by the side of the highway begging. And when he heard that it was Jesus of Nazareth, he began to cry out: "Jesus, have mercy on me!" Jesus stood still and said unto him: "What wilt thou that I should do unto thee?" The blind man said: "Rabbuni—which is interpreted, my teacher—that I might receive my sight." And immediately he received his sight, and followed him on his way.[30]

.

28. Luke 9.52ff. This story is preserved only in Luke and somewhat embellished by him in his characteristic manner. The words of the disciples have been translated inexactly everywhere.
29. Matt. 6.9-14; Luke 11.1-5; Mark 11.25. Cf. above, p. 64.
30. Matt. 20.29-34; Mark 10.46-52; Luke 18.35-43. Matthew has this miracle performed on two blind men; Mark adduces a name, Bartimai; Mark and Luke, following the ideas of Paul, also add the sentence: "Go thy way; thy faith hath made thee whole."

114

And when they drew nigh unto Jerusalem, and were come to Bethphage and Bethania, unto the mount of Olives, then sent Jesus two disciples, saying unto them: "Go into the village before you and bring an ass colt." And they brought the colt to Jesus, and laid their cloaks on him; and he sat upon him. And this was done that it might be fulfilled which was spoken by the prophet, saying: "Rejoice greatly, O daughter of Zion, shout, O daughter of Jerusalem; behold, thy king cometh unto thee, he is just and triumphant, meek, and riding upon an ass, even upon a colt, the foal of an ass." And many spread their cloaks in the way; others green leaves which they cut from the fields, and they went before and followed him and cried: "*Hoshia-na*—which is, interpreted: help thou! Blessed is he that cometh in the name of the Lord!" Thus he proceeded into Jerusalem and toward the temple.

When it had become late, he went with the twelve to Bethania, out into the house of Simon the leper. And in the day they went forth from there to Jerusalem. But it was still two days until the Passover sacrifice and the feast of the unleavened bread.[31]

31. Matt. 21.1-10; Mark 11.1-11; Luke 19.29-38; Matt. 12.12; Mark 11.15; Luke 19.45; Matt. 26.1ff.; Mark 14.1; Luke 22.1. Into the story of the ass foal, a miraculous prophetic sign has been introduced. The scriptural verse to which the story refers is Zechariah 9.9. The words of welcome are from Psalms 118.25-26. The spreading of the garments on the way, here mentioned in our Gospels, is an echo of II Kings 9.13. Since Bethphage means "Site of Figs," a miracle story about a fig tree has been added at this point. The visit to the temple is also embellished in line with a decided tendency. Finally, to answer the question what Jesus might have done during these days on his walks, in the temple, and in the house, a number of parables, disputes with Pharisees and Sadducees, and prophecies of the destruction of the temple, a kind of apocalypse, are added.

115

The Last Passover—At the beginning of the feast of
the unleavened bread, on the day when they killed the
passover, his disciples said unto him: "Where wilt thou
that we go and prepare, that thou mayest eat the passover?" And he said unto them: "Go to anybody in the
city." And the disciples did as Jesus had appointed
them; and they made ready the passover.[32]
Now when the even was come, Jesus sat down with
the twelve to eat. And he took a cup and spake the
blessing, and gave it to his disciples, and they drank.
And he took bread and spake the blessing, and brake
it, and gave it to them. After the meal, he again took
the cup and spake the blessing, and they sang the
Psalms of praise.

After this they went out again to the mount of
Olives, and they came unto a place called Gatshemani,
and he said unto his disciples: "Sit ye here, while I go
and pray yonder." But he took with him Peter, and
Jacob and John, the sons of Sabdai. He quivered and
quailed, and he said unto them: "My soul is exceeding
sorrowful, even unto death: tarry ye here and watch
with me." And he went a little farther, and fell on his
face, and prayed, saying: "Abba—which is, interpreted, Father—all things are possible unto thee; let
this cup pass from me: nevertheless, not as I will, but
as thou wilt."[33]

32. Matt. 26.17-20; Mark 14.12-17; Luke 22.7-14. Mark and
Luke add the miracle story of a sign which is to show the place
of the passover meal, similar to the addition to the story of the
foal.—There was a rule in those days that those who lived in
Jerusalem had to offer room to strangers for the passover meal.
33. Matt. 26.20 and 26.26ff. and 26.30 and 26.36ff.; Mark 14.17
and 14.22f. and 14-26 and 14.32ff.; Luke 22.14ff. and 22.39ff. Cf.
also I Cor. 11.23ff. Matthew and Mark insert an episode in which
the traitor is pointed out, and all three Gospels add an interpretation of the last supper as well as a story about the kingdom of
God and a prophecy of the denial of Peter.—The day on which
these events came to pass is designated precisely: it is the day

While he yet spake, Judah, one of the twelve, came, and with him a multitude with swords and staves, from the high priest. Now he that betrayed him had given them a sign, saying: "Whomsoever I shall kiss, that same is he: hold him fast." And as soon as he was come, he went straightway to Jesus, and said: "Rabbi"—which is, interpreted, teacher, or master—and kissed him. And they laid their hands on him, and took him. And one of them that stood by drew a sword, and smote a servant of the high priest, and cut off his ear. And Jesus began and said unto them: "As against a rebel ye are come out, with swords and staves to take me!" And all of his disciples forsook him and fled. And there followed him a certain young man, having a linen cloth cast about his naked body; and they laid hold on him, and he left the linen cloth, and fled from them naked.[34]

---

of preparation for the Passover, the 14th of Nisan, on which the passover was sacrificed at dusk. According to the old tradition, it was a Thursday that year. In the evening, with which the 15th of Nisan begins, the Passover supper is eaten in company. It begins with the blessing of wine and bread and is concluded with another blessing of the wine and the singing of the so-called *Hallel* Psalms. This sequence is still clearly recognizable, although the wine has been placed after the bread in accordance with the formula, "body and blood."

34.   Matt. 26.47-57; Mark 14.43-53; Luke 22.47-53. To represent the solitude of Jesus, an episode has been added, at the beginning, how Jesus prayed and his disciples slept, although he had said to them: "Watch with me." The preceding betrayal of Judah, too, has been elaborated and embellished in many ways, and words of foreknowledge have been put into the mouth of Jesus. The answer of Jesus to the catchpoles has also been elaborated, and Luke has him perform the miracle of healing the ear that has been cut off.—The Greek word *lestes*, which is generally translated "thief," really designates in this context the "rebel," the Zealot. The Septuagint already used it to render the Hebrew *pariz;* and in this sense it even became part of the Hebrew or Aramaic language, and the "zealous" priest Pinchas is thus called *Pinchas Lestes.*—Concerning the high priests of that time, a complaint has been preserved in the Talmud, Pesahim 57a: "Their servants beat the people with staves."

117

The Judgment—And they led Jesus away to Caiapha the high priest, where the scribes and the elders were assembled. And Peter followed him afar off, even into the courtyard of the high priest: and he sat with the servants, and warmed himself at the fire. But the high priest and the Sanhedrin sought for witness against Jesus and found none. For many bare false witness against him, but their witness agreed not together. And as Peter was beneath in the courtyard, there came one of the maids of the high priest: and when she saw Peter warming himself, she looked upon him, and said: "And thou also wast with Jesus of Nazareth." But he denied, saying: "I know not, neither understand I what thou sayest." And he went out and wept bitterly.[35]

Early in the morning, after the high priest and the Sanhedrin had held a consultation, they apprehended Jesus and delivered him to the procurator Pilate. And Pilate asked him: "Art thou the king of the Jews?" And he answered: "Thou sayest it." Then he had Jesus scourged, and delivered him to be crucified.[36]

35.   Matt. 26.57-75; Mark 14.53-72; Luke 22.54-71. The Gospels try to impute the responsibility for the decision of the Sanhedrin to the widest possible circle. Therefore Matthews says, "the scribes and the elders," and Mark, going even beyond this, "all the chief priests and the elders and the scribes"; and then both say, "the chief priests and the Sanhedrin." And then it is the "multitude" and finally even "all the people" that demand the death of Jesus.—The high priest at that time was Joseph ben Caiapha who sided with the Romans. According to Jewish law, a condemnation was possible only on the basis of concurring testimony of two witnesses. Later, the examination was elaborated and embellished in line with the faith and views of a later age, and the "son of God" and the destruction of the temple were introduced as issues. The denial of Peter was embellished, too. —The word here that is usually translated "bind" means only "apprehend" when it stands alone.
36.   Matt. 27.1f., 11f. and 26; Mark 15.1ff. and 15.15; Luke 22.66 and 23.2f. and 23.24. Cf. Josephus, *Jewish War*, II, 149:

Then Judah, which had betrayed him, when he saw that he was condemned, repented himself, and went and hanged himself.[37]

And the same day Herod and Pilate were made friends together.[38]

Then the soldiers of the procurator took Jesus into the courtyard which belongs to the pretorium, and gathered unto him the whole band of soldiers, and they put on him a scarlet robe. And when they had platted a crown of thorns, they put it upon his head, and a reed in his right hand: and they bowed the knee before him, and mocked him: "Hail to thee, king of the Jews!" And they spat upon him, and took the reed, and smote him on the head. And after they had mocked him thus, they took the scarlet robe off from him, and put his own raiment on him, and led him away to crucify him.[39]

The Death and the Tomb—As they went out, they met a man coming out of the country, Simon of Cyrene by name, the father of Alexander and Rufus; him they

---

"The Roman soldiers apprehended many righteous citizens in Jerusalem and brought them before the procurator Florus who had them scourged and then crucified."

37. Matt. 27.3-11. The story was later embellished with the fiction of the thirty pieces of silver to show how a word of one of the prophets (Zechariah 11.12ff) had been fulfilled.

38. Luke 23.12. Cf. above, p. 109, note 17, as well as Acts 4.27: "Herod and Pontius Pilate." In the manner of Luke, this sentence is then amplified into another story. There probably is some historic foundation for this sentence.

39. Matt. 27.27-33; Mark 15.16-21. Before this, a later story of Barabbas has been interpolated. Barabbas was a very common name. The "multitude" or "people" and "the chief priests and elders" are made to demand his liberation even as they insist that Jesus be crucified: this story is meant to exculpate Pilate and inculpate the Jewish people. Cf. above, the end of the section on "The Separation from Judaism," pp. 83f.

compelled to bear his cross. And they brought him unto the place Golgolta, which is, being interpreted, The Place of a Skull. And they gave him to drink wine mingled with myrrh: but he received it not. Then they crucified him. And it was the third hour when they crucified him. And the superscription of his accusation was written over him: "Jesus the King of the Jews." And with him they crucified two rebels; the one on his right hand, and the other on his left.[40]

And around the ninth hour Jesus cried with a loud voice: "Eli, Eli, lama sabachthani?" That is to say: "My God, my God, why hast thou forsaken me?" And some of them that stood there thought that he was calling Elijah. And Jesus, when he had cried again with a loud voice, yielded up the ghost.[41]

.

40. Matt. 27.33-39; Mark 15.21-28; Luke 23.26-32. Our Gospels let those passing by and "the chief priests, the scribes, and the elders" mock; in the end, even those crucified with him join in the mocking. Luke, in his characteristic manner, has embellished everything poetically. To have the words of Psalms 22.19 fulfilled, an episode has also been inserted how the garments of Jesus were parted, casting lots.—To have Psalms 69.22 fulfilled, Matthew has the wine mingled with gall.
41. Matt. 27.45-54; Mark 15.33-39; Luke 23.44-48. Our Gospels enclose everything in miracle stories: before the death, three hours of darkness, with reference to Amos 8.9; after it, the rending of the veil of the temple and, according to Matthew, an earthquake and resurrections from tombs. Matthew also adds mockery by the Jews and a conversion of Roman soldiers.—The last words which are quoted are the Aramaic text of Psalms 22.2. Luke, taking offense at these words, substitutes as an embellishment of his own the words of Psalms 31.6: "Into thy hands I commend my spirit." Furthermore, to add a fulfillment of Psalms 69.22, our Gospels add that a sponge full of vinegar was presented to Jesus on the cross.—The day of the death was the 15th of Nisan, the first day of the Passover—according to the old tradition, a Friday. To humiliate the Jews especially, Pontius Pilate chose this holiday to crucify the "King of the Jews." The entombment occurred on the evening of this day, before sunset, before the Sabbath began.

The Gospel as a Document of History

There were also women looking on afar off: among whom was Mary of Magdala, and Mary the mother of Jacob the less and of Jose, and Salome, who, when he was in Galilee, had followed Jesus; and many other women who had come up with him unto Jerusalem.[42]

And now when the even was come, because it was the preparation, that is, the time before the Sabbath, Joseph of Ramatajim, a respected counsellor, who also waited for the kingdom of God, came, and went in boldly unto Pilate, and asked for the body of Jesus. Then Pilate commanded the body be delivered unto him. And when Joseph had taken the body, he wrapped it in a clean linen cloth, and laid it in his own sepulchre which was hewn out in the rock: and he had a stone rolled before the door of the sepulchre. And Mary of Magdala and the other Mary beheld where he was laid.[43]

When the Sabbath was passed, Mary of Magdala and the other Mary and Salome bought sweet smelling spices, that they might come and anoint him. And very early in the morning the first day of the week, they came unto the sepulchre at the rising of the sun. And when they looked, they saw that the stone was rolled away: but it was very great. And entering into the sepulchre, they saw a young man sitting on the right

42. Matt. 27.55f.; Mark 15.40f.; Luke 23.49. The first two have it that the three women also ministered, performed "diakone," unto Jesus: thus the later institutions of the community are projected into an earlier time. Cf. also Luke 8.3.
43. Matt. 27.57-61; Mark 15.42-47; Luke 23.50-56. Matthew describes Joseph of Ramatayim as a disciple of Jesus. Luke adds that he did not participate in the decision of the Sanhedrin. Matthew lets the "chief priests and Pharisees" secure a guard for the sepulchre, and he has them seal the stone, "lest the disciples steal the body and say unto the people: He is risen from the dead."

side, clothed in a long white garment; and they were affrighted. But he said unto them: "Be not affrighted: ye seek Jesus of Nazareth, who was crucified: he is risen; he is not here: behold the place where they laid him." And they went out quickly, and fled from the sepulchre; for they trembled and were amazed: neither said they any thing to any man; for they were afraid.[44]

He was raised on the third day, and he appeared unto Simon.[45]

THE SAYINGS AND THE PARABLES

The Torah and the Prophets—Which is the first commandment of all in the Torah? The first is: "Hear, O Israel: the Lord our God, the Lord is one. And thou shalt love the Lord thy God with all thy heart, and with all thy soul, and with all that is in you." And this is second: "Thou shalt love thy neighbour as thyself." There is none other commandment greater than these.[46]

44. Matt. 28.1-10; Mark 16.1-8; Luke 24.1-11. Following a biblical story—Genesis 29.8—Mark has the women ask whether they shall be able to roll away the stone; and then he also lets the youth say to the women: "But go your way, tell his disciples and Peter: he goeth before you into Galilee: there shall ye see him, as he said unto you"; but the conclusion, "neither said they any thing to any man," contradicts this. Matthew has an angel descend from heaven while the earth quakes, and lets the angel roll away the stone while the guards are frightened unconscious by the sight. Luke has two men appear. In the Gospel according to Matthew, Jesus then appears to the women and later to the disciples. And the chief priests and the elders here bribe the guards to spread the story that the disciples stole the body. Luke offers an elaborate poetic embellishment of the reappearance. Something similar was later appended to the Gospel according to Mark.
45. Luke 24.34. Cf. I Cor. 15.5.
46. Matt. 22.36ff.; Mark 12.28ff.; Luke 10.25ff. To fit the sayings into the narrative, they have been set in poetically contrived situations—and very often they appear as answers to

122

"All things whatsoever ye would that men should do
to you, do ye even so to them"—for this is the Torah
and the Prophets.[47]

Think not that I want to deduct from the Torah or
the Prophets. I will "not deduct" and I will "not add."
For I say unto you: till heaven and earth pass, one jot
and one tittle shall in no wise pass from the Torah.
Whosoever therefore shall break one of these least commandments, and shall teach men so, he shall be called
the least in the kingdom of God. But whosoever shall
"do and teach," the same shall be called great in the
kingdom of God.[48]

---

questions which have been addressed to Jesus by Pharisees or
Sadducees. Two tendencies can here be distinguishd in the tradition: one which is older and exhibits the common ground of
Jesus and the Jews, and one which is later and would illustrate
an opposition between them.—The two biblical sentences cited
here are found in Deuteronomy 6.4f. and Leviticus 19.18. In the
first of these, Matthew and Luke followed the Hebrew text; and
when they came to the preposition *b'*, which can mean "in" no
less than "with," they translated it quite literally, "*in* all thy
heart, etc." Mark, on the other hand, followed the Greek *ek
kardias*, in line with the Septuagint, and translated, "*from* all
your heart." The final word, the Hebrew *meodecha*, is rendered
in Greek as *dianoia* which had been used in the Septuagint to
render the Hebrew *kerew*, "inside." A scholarly copyist of the
Gospel according to Mark later added, in order to give the usual
translation as well, "from all your power."—Luke inserts the
story of the good Samaritan at this point—probably a piece of
Jewish folklore. How artificial this addition is becomes plain
when we consider that "the neighbour" in this story is the subject and not, as in the biblical verse which it is supposed to
explain, the object.
47. Matt. 7.12; Luke 6.31. The sentence, "All things whatsoever ye would, etc.," this "Golden Rule" is a quotation which is
encountered again and again in the Apocrypha and ancient
talmudic literature.
48. Matt. 5.17ff. and Luke 16.17; cf. Matt. 24.35; Mark 13.31;
Luke 21.33. The first sentence is preserved in the Talmud, Shabbath 116b, where it appears in its more precise old Aramaic
form and is expressly designated as a quotation from the Gospel.

The Jewish People—Ye are the salt of the earth. "But if the salt have lost his savour, wherewith shall one salt?" Ye are the light of the world. So your light shall shine before men.[49]

Give not that which is holy unto the dogs, neither cast ye your pearls before swine, lest they trample them under their feet, and turn again and rend you.[50]

Cf. Deuteronomy 13.1. In accordance with the later doctrine, the sentence was changed later: "not destroy but fulfil." The initial phrase, which is usually translated "I have come," is really the Aramaic *ateti* which, coupled with an infinitive, means only "will." To verse 18, a Pauline addition was made later: "till all be fulfilled." This means, until the Messiah comes; for according to the Pauline doctrine, his advent annuls the "Law," the Torah. In line with this, another verse—verse 20—was added to introduce the Pauline superior justice. In accordance with this, another correction was also added later in Luke 16.16 and Matthew 11.13: "The Law and the Prophets were until John; since that time, the glad tidings of the kingdom of God is preached."— The phrase "do and teach" is another quotation, a commonplace of that time.

49. Matt. 5.13ff.; Mark 9.50; Luke 14.34f. This saying, like the one that follows, is addressed to the Jewish people and not, as the commentators think, to the disciples. In the literature of that time, the Jewish people is sometimes compared with salt, and the prophets already called it the light of the world. The words, "But if the salt have lost his savour etc." were proverbial in those days; cf. Bechoroth 8b. A later tradition interpolated some further sentences as a kind of commentary which was perhaps intended in part to strike at the Jewish people.

50. Matt. 7.6. In the language of the time, and like other sayings of those days, this sentence warns the Jews against setting forth their teachings to the pagans. The word "pearl" which, in its Greek form, entered into the Hebrew and Aramaic vernacular, designates a religious saying. The hypothesis that the original word here was not *kadosh*, "holy," but, parallel to the word "pearl," the Aramaic *kadasha*, "earring," misses the point of this saying. It is possible that the word "swine" refers to the Romans; in the Haggada, Rome is compared to the swine, the beast of Mars.

The Eternal and the Temporal—Blessed are the poor: for theirs is the kingdom of God. Blessed are they that mourn: for they will share in the day of comfort. Blessed are the meek: for "they will inherit the land." Blessed are they which do hunger and thirst: for "they will be filled." Blessed are the merciful: for they will obtain mercy. Blessed are they that are "pure in heart": for "they will see God." Blessed are the peacemakers: for they will be called children of God. Blessed are they who are persecuted: for theirs is the kingdom of God.[51]

Lay not up for yourselves "treasures upon earth," where worm and rust doth corrupt, and where thieves break through and steal. But lay up for yourselves "treasures in heaven," where neither worm nor rust doth corrupt, and where thieves do not break through nor steal. For where your treasure is, there will your heart be also.[52]

No man can serve two masters: for either he will hate the one and love the other; or else he will hold to the one, and despise the other. Ye cannot serve God and mammon.[53]

51. Matt. 5.3ff.; Luke 6.20ff. All these promises refer to the Messianic age. One name for it was "comfort," *nechama;* cf. Luke 2.25 and Paraclete which is *menachem.* The same is true of "inherit the land"; cf. Psalms 37.11. Also of "they will be filled"; cf. Isaiah 66.11 as well as Psalms 22.27 and 17.15. To "see God" was a common expression of that time for the world to come. For the phrase, "they will be called children of God," cf. Isaiah 61.6 and 62.12. Matthew toned down poverty by adding "in spirit," and hunger and persecution, by adding, in the manner of Paul, "after righteousness" and "for righteousness' sake." Luke says: "that hunger *now.*" In connection with "pure in heart," cf. Psalms 24.4; in connection with "see God," Psalms 17.15.
52. Matt. 6.19ff.; Luke 12.33ff. Parallels in the talmudic writings.
53. Matt. 6.24; Luke 16.13. Mammon is the Hebrew word of that time for money.

125

The Meaning of the Torah—Ye have heard that it was said to them of old time: "Thou shalt not murder"; "whosoever shall murder, shall be given up unto the court." And I say unto you: whosoever is angry with his brother, shall be given up unto the judgment. And whosoever shall say to his brother, *reka*—which is, interpreted, good-for-nothing—shall be given up unto the Sanhedrin. And whosoever shall say, *more*—which is, interpreted, renegade—shall be given up unto the Gehenna of the fire. Therefore if thou bring thy gift to the altar, and there rememberest that thy brother hath ought against thee, leave there thy gift before the altar and go thy way; first be reconciled to thy brother, and then come and offer thy gift.[54]

Ye have heard that it was said: "Thou shalt not commit adultery." And I say unto you: Whosoever looketh on a woman to covet her hath committed adultery with her already in his heart. It hath been said: "Whosoever shall put away his wife, let him give her a writing of divorcement." And I say unto you: Whosoever shall put away his wife, saving for the cause of fornication, causeth that adultery is committed with her: for whosoever marrieth her that hath been put away committeth adultery. From the beginning of the Creation it

54. Matt. 5.21ff. In these sentences, our translations say: *"But I say unto you."* In the Greek of the Gospel, the Greek word in question never implies any opposition, but always only a conjunction. All that is said here is meant not as a contradiction of the Torah but as a commentary: it is "oral Torah," and there are manifold parallels to these sayings in the talmudic writings. —The Hebrew word *more*, renegade, was occasionally translated in those days with the Greek word *moros*, fool, simply because of the almost identical sound; in fact, the vocative of the Greek word which is here used is *more*. Cf. also Tanchuma for Numbers 20.10.—Following Luke 12.57ff., Matthew adds another passage which is not at all in keeping either with the style of the preceding or the context.

hath been true: "male and female he created them"; "therefore shall a man leave his father and his mother, and shall cleave unto his wife, and the twain shall be one flesh"; wherefore they are no more twain, but one flesh. What therefore God hath joined together, let not man put asunder.[55]

Again, ye have heard that it hath been said to those of old: "Thou shalt not swear falsely"; "thou shalt perform unto the Lord thine oaths." And I say unto you: Swear not at all; not even by heaven—"it is God's throne"; not even by the earth—"it is his footstool"; not even by Jerusalem—"it is the city of the great King." Neither shalt thou swear by thy head—thou canst not make one hair white or black. "Your word shall be: Yea, yea; Nay, nay." Whatsoever is more than these cometh of evil.[56]

Ye have heard that it hath been said: "Love thy neighbour as thyself: I am the Lord." And I say unto you: Love your enemies, and pray for them which per-

55. Matt. 5.27f. and 5.31f. and 19.9; Mark 10.11; Luke 16.18 and Matt. 19.4ff; Mark 10.6ff. Cf. I Cor. 7.10 as well as Genesis 1.27 and 2.24. The translations here say: "causeth her to commit adultery"; but the exact and correct translation is that given above. The man who divorces his wife, saving for the cause of fornication, has led her that is now free to marry another man, into adultery.—Sentences expressing an ascetic outlook characteristic of a later age have been interpolated here, and such sentences also follow the last passage in Matthew.

56. Matt. 5.33ff.; cf. 23.16ff. As happens occasionally in the Haggadic literature, too, several biblical verses have been combined here: Leviticus 19.12; Psalms 50.14 or Numbers 30.3 and Deuteronomy 23.22. The other biblical verses which are cited here are Isaiah 66.1 and Psalms 48.3. The meaning of this saying is: an oath by heaven, by the earth, by Jerusalem, or by your head is, strictly speaking, no oath and not considered as such; but you should desist from this, too: for heaven, earth, and Jerusalem are God's, and even your head is not really yours.— That "your Yea should be Yea and your Nay, Nay," is a popular Jewish proverb which occurs again and again in the literature.

secute you; that "ye may be the children of your Father who is in heaven": for he maketh his sun to rise on the evil and on the good, and sendeth rain on the just and on the unjust. For if ye love them who love you, what reward have ye? Do not even the publicans the same? And if ye wish peace to your brethren only, what do ye more than others? Do not even the pagans the same? "Thou shalt be perfect as the Lord thy God is perfect."[57]

Judging—Judge not, that ye be not judged. For with what judgment ye judge, ye shall be judged: and "with what measure ye mete, it shall be measured to you again." And why "beholdest thou the mote that is in thy brother's eye" but "considerest not the beam that is in thine own eye"? Or how wilt thou say to thy brother: "Let me pull out the mote out of thine eye"; and, behold, "a beam is in thine own eye"? Thou hypocrite, first cast out "the beam out of thine own eye"; and then shalt thou see clearly to cast out "the mote out of thy brother's eye."[58]

How oft shall I, if my brother sin against me, forgive

57. Matt. 5.43ff.; Luke 6.27f. and 6.32ff.; and Leviticus 19.18. A later time added to the biblical "Love thy neighbour" the words which are alien and opposed to the Bible, "and hate thine enemy." These appended words, which moreover do not fit into this context at all, would deprive this saying of its evident tendency: its concern with the meaning of love of the neighbour. And our Gospel clearly omitted the last part of the biblical verse: "I am the Lord." But this conclusion alone furnishes the necessary transition to the sentence: "that ye may be the children of your Father who is in heaven."—The final sentence, "Thou shalt be perfect, etc.," is Deuteronomy 18.13, understood haggadically.
58. Matt. 7.1ff.; Luke 6.37f. and 6.41f. Luke interpolates a few sentences of commentary. The word of the measure with which ye mete and, no less, that of the mote and the beam are Jewish proverbs which are encountered in Jewish literature again and again.

128

him? Till seven times? Not until seven times, but until "seventy times seven."[59]

"If ye forgive men their trespasses, your Father in heaven will also forgive ye: but if ye forgive not men their trespasses, neither will your Father in heaven forgive your trespasses."[60]

. . *Good Deeds*—Take heed that ye do not your good deeds before men, to be seen of them: otherwise ye have no reward of your Father in heaven. When thou givest charity, do not sound a trumpet before thee, as the hypocrites do in the community houses and in the streets, that they may have glory of men. I say unto you: that is their reward. When thou givest charity, let not thy left hand know what thy right hand doeth: that thy charity may be "in secret"; and thy Father who seeth "in secret" himself shall reward thee.[61]

Give to him that asketh thee, and from him that would borrow of thee turn not thou away.[62]

59. Matt. 18.21f., placed in a particular situation in the Gospel. "Seventy times seven" is a quotation from Genesis 4.24, according to the ancient translation.
60. Matt. 6.14f.; Mark 11.25. This was a popular proverb: cf. Sirach 28.2ff. and Shabbath 151b.
61. Matt. 6.1ff. The two Greek words used here, *dikaiosyne* and *eleemosyne*, correspond to the Hebrew *zedaka* and *gemilut chessed*. When some of our translations translate the first word as "justice" or *Gerechtigkeit*, the inner connection of the first sentence with the second is destroyed. Moreover, the first sentence is then given a rather artificial sense. In the language of those days, *zedaka* and *gemilut chessed* belong together. We need only translate back into Hebrew or Aramaic to see the point. (The Authorized Version translates both words, "alms." *Tr.*)—"In secret" is an expression constantly used in the Hebrew of that time.
62. Matt. 5.42; Luke 6.30. Both the idea and the wording were quite common at that time. Cf., for example, Sifre for Deuteronomy 15.9.

The poor widow putteth two mites into the alms box, and she hath put in more than all the rich. For all they put in of their abundance, but she did put in of her want.[63]

Against the Zealots—Ye have heard that it hath been said: "An eye for an eye, and a tooth for a tooth." And I say unto you: Resist not evil; but whosoever shall smite thee on thy right cheek, turn to him the other also. And if any man will sue thee at the law, and take away thy coat, let him have thy cloke also. And whosoever shall compel thee to go a mile, go with him twain. And of him that taketh away thy goods, ask them not again.[64]

Is it lawful to give the tribute unto Caesar? On the penny here we see Caesar's image and superscription. Then give back unto Caesar what is Caesar's, but also "unto God what is God's."[65]

63. Mark 12.42ff.; Luke 21.1ff. This dictum has been embellished with an artificial situation: Jesus is made to observe the poor widow in the temple, under circumstances which are quite alien to the realities of that time. Moreover, the story speaks of "the treasury" of the temple instead of an alms box. And as a conclusion, the phrase has been added: "did cast in all that she had, all her living." For this, cf. the first words of Leviticus 2.1 in the ancient interpretations.

64. Matt. 5.38ff.; Luke 6.29f.; and Exodus 21.24; Leviticus 24.20; Deuteronomy 19.21. The first sentence of the reply is a variation of Isaiah 50.6. The last sentence has been preserved only in Luke where it is, however, combined with part of the sentence which follows in Matthew—a sentence which really does not belong to this saying. The meaning of this saying, and the next, can be understood only when it is recognized that both are directed against the Zealots.

65. Matt. 22.15ff.; Mark 12.14ff.; Luke 20.20ff. In all our Gospels this saying has been placed in a fictitious situation. Our translations say, "Render to Caesar etc." instead of "Give *back* unto Caesar etc.," as the text, *apodote*, requires. This word

The Gospel as a Document of History

Taking Thought and Praying—Take no thought for
your life, what ye shall eat; nor yet for your body, what
ye shall put on. Is not the life more than food, and the
body than raiment? Behold "the fowls of the air": for
they sow not, neither do they reap, nor gather into
barns; yet your Father in heaven feedeth them. Are ye
not better than they? Consider the roses of the field,
how they grow; they toil not, neither do they spin: and
I say unto you, that even Solomon in all his glory was
not arrayed like one of these. Wherefore, if God so
clothe the plant of the field, which today is, and tomorrow is cast into the oven, how much more you, O "ye of
little faith"? Therefore take no thought, saying: "What
shall we eat?" or "What shall we drink?" or "What
shall we put on?" After all these things do the pagans
seek. Your Father in heaven knoweth that ye have
need of all these things. "Take no thought for the morrow": for the morrow shall take thought for itself.
"Sufficient unto the day is the misery thereof."[66]

Ask, and it shall be given you. Seek, and ye shall find.
Knock, and it shall be opened unto you.[67]

When you pray, you shall not be as the hypocrites:
for they love to pray standing in the community houses
and in the corners of the streets, that they may be seen

"back" alone gives this saying its real point. The last part of
this saying is a quotation of a popular proverb—see Aboth 3.7.
And perhaps the old tradition also cited the conclusion of this
proverb: "For thou and whatever is thine are God's."
66. Matt. 6.25ff.; Luke 12.22ff.; and Psalms 8.9. Into this saying some sentences of commentary were interpolated. The first
half of the penultimate sentence and the whole of the last sentence were popular proverbs; and the phrase, "ye of little faith,"
was popular at that time, too. Cf. Sanhedrin 100b and Ber. 9b.
The word "life" at the beginning corresponds to the Hebrew
word *nefesh* which designates the soul as well as life.
67. Matt. 7.7; Luke 1.19. Several sentences of commentary were
added later.

of men. I say unto you: that is their reward. When thou
prayest, "enter into thy closet and shut thy door," and
pray to thy Father which is "in secret"; and thy Father
which seeth "in secret" shall reward thee.[68]

When ye pray, use not vain repetitions, as the pagans
do: for they think that they shall be heard for their
much speaking. Be not ye therefore like unto them: for
your Father knoweth what things ye have need of,
before ye ask him.[69]

The Kingdom of God—Enter ye in at the strait gate:
for wide is the gate, and broad is the way, that leadeth
to sin; and strait is the gate, and distressful is the way,
that leadeth to life.[70]

Seek ye first the kingdom of God; and all things shall
be added unto you.[71]

Whosoever hath, to him shall be given, and he shall

.

68. Matt. 6.5f. The words, "Enter into thy closet etc." are a
quotation from Isaiah 26.20.
69. Matt. 6.7f. There also follows a word concerning fasting.
But that this word is of late and foreign origin is apparent from
the fact that it involves a Greek play on words for which there
is no basis of any kind in Hebrew.
70. Matt. 7.13f.; Luke 13.23f. In the Gospel according to Matthew, some remarks have been interpolated into this sentence by
way of commentary. Our translations here speak of "the way
that leadeth to destruction." The Greek word in question, however, was used already in the Septuagint to translate sin. Sin
and life are ancient biblical opposites. Nor does this saying
refer to a "narrow" way, as most of the translations have it: the
Greek word, and the Hebrew word on which it is based, both
mean "distressful"—"afflicted with distress."
71. Matt. 6.33; Luke 12.31. This sentence was later interpolated into the saying about taking thought of one's needs and
thus given a false context. In Matthew, moreover, righteousness
has, in the manner of Paul, been placed beside the kingdom of
God.

have more abundance: but whosoever hath not, from
him shall be taken away even that he hath.[72]

How think ye? if a man have an hundred sheep, and
one of them be gone astray, doth he not leave the ninety
and nine in the mountains, and goeth and seeketh that
which is gone astray? And if so be that he find it, verily
he rejoiceth more of that sheep than of the ninety and
nine which went not astray. Likewise "joy shall be in
heaven over one sinner that repenteth more than over
ninety and nine just persons, which need no repentance."[73]

The Resurrection—The dead shall rise. God spake to
Moses at the bush, saying: "I am the God of thy father,
the God of Abraham, the God of Isaac, and the God of
Jacob." He is not the God of the dead, but the God of
the living.[74]

THE PARABLES

The Words of God—A scribe is like unto an householder, who gives away out of his possessions "things
new and old."[75]

72. Matt. 13.12 and 25.29; Mark 4.25; Luke 8.18. This saying
has the same meaning as the preceding one: Whoever has the
kingdom of God, has everything; but whosoever does not have it,
will find that all he has will come to nothing.
73. Matt. 18.12ff. and Luke 15.4ff. The last sentence is found
only in Luke. It is a Jewish proverb; cf. Sanhedrin 99a.
74. Matt. 22.31f.; Mark 12.26f.; Luke 20.37f.; Exodus 3.6. This
interpretation of the biblical verse has many parallels in ancient
Jewish literature. The meaning is this: the patriarchs have died,
but God still calls himself their God; for they will live again.
75. Matt. 13.52. The word "householder" is in Hebrew *ba'al
ha-bayith*, used to designate one who has possessions, particularly a house and a field. In accordance with the general
tendency against the scribes which characterized later times,
our Gospel has qualified the words "a scribe" with an expres-

133

Whosoever "heareth the words of God and doeth
them" is like a wise man which built his house upon a
rock. And the rain descendeth, and the floods come, and
the winds blow, and beat upon that house, and it falleth
not: for it was founded upon a rock. And whosoever
"heareth the words of God and doeth them not" is like
a foolish man which built his house upon the sand: and
the rain descendeth, and the floods come, and the winds
blow, and beat upon that house, and it falleth, and great
is the fall of it.[76]

A certain man had two children. And he came to the
first, and said: "Go today and work in my vineyard."
He answered and said: "I go, sir"—and went not. And
he came to the second and said likewise. He answered
and said: "I will not"—but afterwards he repented and
went. Whether of them twain did the will of his father?[77]

The Kingdom of God—The kingdom of God is like
to a grain of mustard seed, which a man taketh and
soweth in his field: which indeed is the least of all seeds;
but when it is grown, it is the greatest among herbs,
and becometh a tree, so "that the fowls of the heaven
come and lodge in the branches thereof."[78]

sion which is utterly alien to the thought and speech of that
time: "which is instructed for the kingdom of heaven." The
phrase "things new and old" is a quotation from the Song of
Songs 7.14: this verse was then applied to the interpretation
of the Holy Scriptures, the Haggada.

76. Matt. 7.24ff.; Luke 6.47. "Heareth and doeth" is a biblical
quotation—Deuteronomy 6.3; 27.10; and elsewhere—and always
refers to the word of God. In this place, a later age applied this
phrase to the words of Jesus.

77. Matt. 21.28ff. Later a parable about a vineyard was added
to prophesy Jesus' death and the Jewish people's rejection.

78. Matt. 13.31f.; Mark 4.30ff.; Luke 13.18f. The final sentence is a quotation from Daniel 4.18. In Matthew, these sentences are preceded by a parable about wheat and tares. It

The kingdom of God is like unto leaven, which a woman taketh and hideth in three *se-a's* of meal, and in the end the whole is leavened.[79]

So is the kingdom of God, as if a man should cast seed into the ground; and should sleep at night and wake in the day, and the seed should spring and grow up, and he seeth it not.[80]

᾿ Behold, a sower goeth forth to sow. And as he soweth, some seeds fall by the wayside, and the fowls come and devour them up. Some fall upon stony places, where they have not much earth, and forthwith they spring up, because they have no deepness of earth; and when the sun riseth, they are scorched; and because they have no root, they wither away. And some fall among thorns; and the thorns spring up, and choke them. But others fall into good ground, and bring forth fruit, some an hundredfold, some sixtyfold, some thirtyfold.[81]

The kingdom of God is like unto a treasure hid in a field; the which if a man hath found, he hideth again,

---

seems to belong to a later age and apparently reflects quarrels in the young Church; in its style and tendency it differs from the other parables. It is similar to the parable about catching fish which follows later in the same chapter.—The word "heaven" in the Greek text is, whenever it occurs in conjunction with the word "kingdom," a designation of God.

79. Matt. 13.33; Luke 13.21. A *se-a'* was a large measure, and three *se-a's* amounted to about ten gallons. The point of this parable, as of the preceding one, is this: the great effect of an apparently small force. Leaven was a frequently used metaphor in this connection.

80. Mark 4.26f. The sentence construction here is completely Hebrew. Later a sentence of commentary was added; also a concluding sentence, echoing Joel 4.13.

81. Matt. 13.3ff.; Mark 4.3ff.; Luke 8.5ff. This parable is followed by a lengthy exposition, intended as a commentary.— Our translations always use the past tense in these parables, which does not correspond to the meaning of either the Greek tense or the original Hebrew.

and for joy thereof goeth straightway and selleth all that he hath, and buyeth that field.[82]

The kingdom of heaven is like unto a merchant man, seeking goodly pearls: who, when he hath found one pearl of great price, goeth and selleth all that he hath, and buyeth it.[83]

The kingdom of heaven is like unto a certain man, which prepareth the marriage of his son, and sendeth forth his servants to call them that were bidden to the wedding: and they will not come. Again he sendeth forth other servants, saying: "Tell them which are bidden: Behold, I have prepared my dinner: my oxen and my fatlings are killed, and all things are ready: come unto the wedding." But they despise it and go their ways, one to his farm, another to his merchandise. Then the man becometh wroth and saith to his servants: "Go ye into the highways, and as many as ye shall find, bid to the wedding."[84]

The kingdom of God is like unto a fig tree: when it putteth forth young branches, and the leaves come forth, ye know that the harvest is nigh.[85]

82. Matt. 13.44. The image of the treasure is a common metaphor of that time.
83. Matt. 13.45f. With this and the preceding parable, cf. the sayings about the kingdom of God which speak of those to whom "all things" are given, page 00 above.
84. Matt. 22.1ff.; Luke 14.16ff. In Matthew, the word "king" is in the beginning added to the word "man"; and then "king" remains the subject. In both Gospels the parable was amplified, particularly to suggest more of the Last Judgment.
85. Matt. 24.32. This parable is based on the biblical verse, Song of Songs 2.13, which was at that time interpreted messianically. It is also based on a play on words: *kez* means end, Messianic Age; and *kayyitz* means harvest, summer. Cf. Amos 8.2 and Hosea 6.11. Cf. also the story in Matt. 21.18ff. and Mark 11.12f., as well as page 115, note 31, above.

3

THE FAITH OF PAUL

There are few great historical personalities who give us an insight into their characters in the same degree as Paul. It is the salient feature, indeed, a distinctive mark of Paul's letters—those which are beyond doubt genuine—that they are substantially confessions. In them Paul discloses himself, and he does so with great frankness and a remarkable capacity for self-diagnosis. He could not preach his faith without searching and revealing his heart. He could not be detached; his "I" was always fully engaged; his speech was often excited, even passionate. What he sends out to a community is not an "epistle," but a "letter."[1] In Deissmann's phrase: "an 'I' is writing to a 'thou.' "

It is of some significance that his appearance is described to us. To see a man sometimes facilitates our opinion of him. In the "Acts of Paul and Thecla" Paul is described as: "a short man, bandy-legged, with a bald head, a prominent nose, and the eyebrows grown

1. Morton Scott Enslin, *Christian Beginnings*, p. 213.

together—of dignified bearing and full of kindliness."[2]
The "Acts of Paul and Thecla" were composed more
than a hundred years after Paul's death, but it appears
that his picture was handed down by faithful tradition.
The more so since it is scarcely intended to flatter. The
motif in this portrait of Paul is clearly the *atopia*
(oddness), that *atopia* which was once emphasized in
regard to Socrates. Some features in Paul's portrait are
due perhaps to this motif.[3]

But the main source of our knowledge of Paul is his
genuine letters. Four letters must at any rate be recognized as authentic: the letter to the Romans, the two
letters to the Corinthians (with the exception of the
passage in the second letter, 6.14-7.1, which is most
probably an interpolation), and the letter to the Galatians. They show the same style and rhythm, a distinctive style and rhythm, the first traces of which we can
perceive in the Books of Ezra and Nehemiah and then
more clearly in the Book of Daniel. These three biblical
books seem to have exerted some influence on Jewish
style, vocabulary, manner of arguing, and doctrine.
Attention should also be paid to the fact that the word
ekklēsia, refers in Paul's genuine letters to individual
congregations, and not, as in other letters attributed
to Paul, to the mystical body of the faithful.[4] All these

2. *Neutestamentl. Apokryphen,* ed. Ed. Hennecke, 2nd ed.,
p. 198.
3. There are references to Socrates in Christian apologetical
literature. Justin Martyr, for example, draws a parallel between
the Gospel and Xenophon's *Memorabilia.* The fact that the
Gentile philosopher Celsus drew a parallel between Socrates and
Christ is equally significant. Cf. A. v. Harnack, *Reden und
Aufsätze,* i, 27ff.
4. This latter meaning of the term is met in the letter to the
Ephesians (1.22; 3.10; 3.21; 5.23-32) ; and it is noteworthy that
there is full correspondence between the Revelation and Paul's
genuine letters, as far as the former meaning of the term is
concerned.

140

four letters together give us a clear picture of the nature of Paul's faith.

A source that is in every regard secondary is the Acts of the Apostles (*the* Apostles being here Peter and Paul), composed in the second generation after Paul, obviously by the same author as the third Gospel. Apart from other evidence that might be produced for this assertion, the identity of the character of the writer of the two works is strikingly manifest. The author takes pains to show that he is an educated man; he aims at displaying a good acquaintance with historical, local, and personal detail. He commands a certain literary skill and adroitness, and is well versed both in the language of the Septuagint and in the common religious tongue of the Greek. He has also an artistic, even a poetic talent, and he delights in this and is seduced by it. He is prompt to color and embellish, and enjoys arranging situations; and takes pleasure in speeches and prayers. Moreover, he is in love with the miraculous, the extraordinary, and the superlative, as he sees them in events and as he describes them in his narrative. The stories he tells abound in wonders and portents and in coincidences too, and his tale, therefore, is rather a series of single stories than a continuous and interconnected narration. There is no doubt that he invents particulars. Eduard Norden produced the evidence for it in his classic treatise *Agnostos Theos*.[5] On the whole, it must be said that the third Gospel and the Acts present us with historical fiction

5. Norden's book (first edition, 1913; second edition, 1926) provoked a vast literature. In spite of many critical attempts, his principal points have never been refuted. From recent books on the N.T., as for instance, A. M. Hunter's suggestive *Interpreting the New Testament, 1900-1950* (1951), one would think that Norden's most significant work has now fallen into oblivion. Cf. also Ad. Deissmann, *Paulus*, 2nd ed., pp. 226ff.

rather than history. Behind them lies a charming personality, an attractive writer, but not an authority to rely upon. The Acts are of some help, but only when their information is confirmed by the letters.

These are our sources. What do they offer that may allow us an insight into the nature of Paul's faith? The first thing we see is that there is a center round which everything turns. The point on which everything depends, round which everything revolved in Paul's life, and the point at which his faith became his life was the vision which overpowered him when one day he saw the messiah and heard his voice. This vision immediately became, and remained, the central fact of Paul's life. Such an experience cannot be argued about.[6] One must start from it in order to understand Paul, his personality, and his confession.

It was a vision that had seized him, and to the Jew as he was and as he never ceased to be, to the Jew whose spiritual, intellectual, and moral world was the Bible, his vision must have meant the call: the call to the new way; no longer was he allowed to follow the old course. A Greek who had experienced such a vision would have reflected, talked, and mused, or spoken and written about it; he would not have heard the Jewish command: "Go"—"Thou shalt go." The Greek had no God who laid a claim on him and sent him out to be His messenger. Only the Jew would be always aware that the revelation entailed the mission, that a prompt readiness to follow the way was the first sign and testimony to the faith. Paul knew now that to him had fallen the apostolate in the name of the messiah. The last Jew in

6. Some fine remarks on the general character of the vision can be found in C. G. Jung's *Psychologische Typen*, 4th ed., pp. 82ff.

the young Church was its last apostle. With the Greek succession a new chapter in the history of the Church opened.

It is customary to speak of Paul's conversion. But such a term is inadequate. What happened in Paul's life was not just a conversion in the usual meaning of the word but rather a revolution, a transformation. What Paul tells us of his inward change indicates clearly the suddenness of it. It was an instantaneous crisis. Nobody had approached or taught him, nobody was a helper or agent. The vision and Paul himself were the sole constituents of the event. Therefore he alone could and must act on it here on earth. Thus, his first step was in the direction not of man but of the desert, unto that place of lonely decision to which men of the Jewish people had often withdrawn so that they might meditate upon the way that lay before them. "Immediately I conferred not with flesh and blood, neither went I up to Jerusalem to them which were apostles before me, but I went into the desert (Arabia)"[7] (Gal. 1.16f.).

Paul's transformation was not that *subita conversio ad docilitatem* which Calvin experienced and of which he spoke in the Preface to his *Commentary to the Psalms*—that "sudden conversion to a readiness for learning." Paul had nothing further to learn: the vision had made him aware of everything. He had rather to forget many things. A new principle had been established, a new point of view was taken. The world from

7. The word *Arabia* (a mistake for *Araba*) is not a geographical name signifying the Arabian country, but an appellative meaning the desert. The Hebrew word ערבה = *desert* had entered into the Greek language of the Septuagint; cf. Deut. 2.8; 3.19; 4.49; Jos. 3.16 *et passim*, and on the other hand Deut. 1.1 *et passim*. In Gal. 4.25, it is the *nomen proprium*.

which it came was not a sphere into which one could be initiated by a preparedness for learning. It could only be accepted by him, or refused, at once and for ever. Perhaps a word of Kierkegaard's, although bizarre in its expression, might serve here as an illustration: "The apostolate is a paradoxical fact which in the first and last moments of his (the apostle's) existence is outside his personal identity with himself."[8] A parallel that may help us to understand such a "paradoxical fact" is the "crisis" in Mohammed's life.

When Paul speaks of his new life he emphasizes both things together: the "revelation" and the "mission"; at bottom they meant to him the same thing. He was not authorized or invested by man. But he is conscious of having received the mark from above. Not an ordination, but a "manifestation" made him an apostle. All four letters begin in a similar manner: "Paul, a servant of Jesus Christ, called to be an apostle, separated unto the gospel of God" (Rom. 1.1); "Paul, called to be an apostle of Jesus Christ through the will of God" (I Cor. 1.1); "Paul, an apostle of Jesus Christ by the will of God" (II Cor. 1.1); "Paul, an apostle, not of men, neither by man, but by Jesus Christ, and God the Father, who raised him from the dead" (Gal. 1.1). He stresses this point over and over again: "The gospel which was preached of me is not after man, for I neither received it of man, neither was I taught, but by the revelation of Jesus Christ" (Gal. 1.11 and 12). These words are not mere introductory phrases, they lie at the root of his faith.

It is remarkable with what chastity, if one may say

8. Quoted by Karl Barth in his *Commentary to the Letter to the Romans*, 1.1. As for the spiritual background of that sentence cf. E. L. Allen's penetrating book, *Kierkegaard, His Life and Thought*, 1935, pp. 148ff.

so, Paul relates the event of the manifestation. He writes to the Galatians: "When it pleased God, who separated me from my mother's womb and called me by his grace, to reveal his son in me, that I might preach him among the heathen . . ." (Gal. 1.15f.). And with still more reserve he writes to the Corinthians: "Have I not seen Jesus Christ my Lord?" (I Cor. 9.1 and 15.8).[9] He says no more and no less. It is left to the author of the Acts to tell us more in a story full of circumstance and a poetry which is rightly among mankind's greatest possessions (22.6ff.). Paul himself mentions no such occurrences when speaking of the vision. If anything like this had happened he would have spoken it.[10] It seems that his very simplicity of expression represents the truth here, and shows that it is the whole truth.

This vision, as we have said, became the permanent center of Paul's faith and life. There was, of course, also a background: Jewish messianic thought and sentiment, which had a firm hold on the bulk of the Jewish people, particularly in Palestine. There is no doubt that Paul at first very actively opposed those who believed that the messiah had come in their own day, that Jesus of Nazareth was the Christ. They had seen and heard him healing and preaching and comforting, until the Romans crucified him for having been hailed King of the Jews. They were convinced that, soon afterwards, on the third day, he was raised, in accordance with the word of the prophet, and that on the appointed day which they were expecting he would reappear in the

9. One should hardly consider II Cor. 4.6, as is sometimes done, a reference to the "vision."
10. See R. Bultmann in *Religion in Geschichte und Gegenwart*, ii, IV (1930), p. 1022, and also E. Buonaiuti, "Christus und Paulus," in *Eranos-Jahrbuch*, 1940-41, p. 259f.

145

fullness of his glory. Paul relates how strongly he contended against the congregation of the faithful: "Beyond measure I persecuted the Church of God, and wasted it" (Gal. 1.15 and 23), or, to translate the Greek text more accurately: "Beyond measure I harried the Church of God and pressed hard upon it."[11]

But all this was only a preliminary stage in the process of Paul's inner life, which had its beginning in the "vision." Here we meet the most essential factor, from which everything else derives. In his vision Paul saw the Christ; his faith henceforth was Christ-centered. It was not God who had awakened him and spoken to him and called him, but the Christ. When Paul remembers the great hour he says: "Have I not seen Jesus Christ our Lord" (I Cor. 9.1). One sees at once the distinctive character and the implication of the vision when one compares it with Isaiah's: "Mine eyes have seen the King, the Lord of hosts" (6.5), or when one realizes that the old prophets were all called to be messengers of God, while Paul was "called to be a messenger of Jesus Christ" (I Cor. 1.1).

The prophets' task was theocentric, Paul's task was Christ-centered. This is the emphasis in the letter to the Romans: ". . . Jesus Christ our Lord by whom we have received grace and apostleship" (1.4f.).

A turning point in the history of religion, of monotheism, is seen here. The old theocentric faith of Judaism is superseded by the new Christ-centered faith. The belief in God, the One, has receded before the belief in

.

11. The Greek word *diokein* seems to be here the equivalent of the Aramaic 'ר = to harry, to taunt, which was the usual term for arguing maliciously and spitefully, and *porthein* seems to mean: pressing hard (cf. *Herodotus*, i, 162), like the Latin *oppugnare*. Again, it is instructive to compare the short sentence used by Paul with the superlatives in the Acts (9.1ff.; 22.1f.; 26.9ff.), not to mention the historical lapses in the latter.

the Christ. Here is a parting of the ways in religion. It is true, the faithful would not think of the Messiah without being conscious of God; they would not lift up their minds toward the Son without at the same time being aware of the Father. But the human mind is such that an older belief is impaired by a new one, and the new belief commands the way of the future. What happened or evolved afterward was involved already in the beginning. God, as it were, was removed into the background. He became the *Deus absconditus* surrounded by the dark and tremendous mystery. The bright light, the broad glory shines now round the Christ. His is the eternal drama, where God has only eternal existence. His are the great attributes of savior, redeemer; he is known now as the Lord, the *Kyrios*,[12] the very same word by which the Septuagint had rendered the Tetragrammaton, the "I am[13] that I am," or as the Septuagint has it, "I am he who is."

Moreover, the very idea of the messiah had for long shown a modification which deserves closer attention than it usually receives. There was, on the one hand, the picture drawn by the prophets. The messiah is the "son of David," the "child born unto us, the son given unto us," upon whom "the spirit of the Lord shall rest." One day he will be born to be the true king, to deliver the tribes of Israel and to show mankind the way of

12. One should notice the distinctive difference between the Pauline letters and Revelation in regard to the content of the term "the Lord." There is a similar disparity between the Pauline term "the Lord" and "the Son of man sitting on the right hand of power" (Matt. 26.64). See on this W. Bousset, *Kyrios Christos*, 2nd ed., 1921.
13. One should contrast the Pauline term *Kyrios* with the manner in which the author of "Revelation" treats *ho on* (derived from Exodus 3.14), as an indeclinable noun.

religion. Before his coming God will "send Elijah the prophet" to pave his way. The line of hope and thought is here the line of history, of universal as well as Jewish history: it is so to speak a horizontal line. It proceeds from the first day and from the first word in the Bible, the sublime *bereshit*, "in the beginning," and passes on to the last day of fulfillment, to the sublime biblical *be'harit*, "and it shall come to pass in the *'aharit, in the last days . . .*" the line goes from the *archē* to the *eschaton*. One day the world was created, and one day the world will be achieved, and history between the two "days" is like the arc of tension which the course of humanity must take on earth.

On the other hand, there was a different conception of the messiah. It originated with the Book of Daniel, one of the most effective books of the Bible.[14] Here the messiah is not born nor is he "a rod out of the stem of Jesse." His root is in another sphere altogether, that of pre-existence. From that sphere he will come down, "in the clouds of heaven with power and great glory."[15] Here the relation is no longer between the first and the last day, but between the "world below" and the "world above," the *'olam hazzeh* and the *'olam habba*, this present world and the world that is to come. All trust, desire, and belief are centered not on the "days to come," the *yamim ba'im*, of the prophets, but on that *'olam habba*, that "world to come," which the "vision"

14. It may be noticed here that the first to point out this turning point marked by the Book of Daniel, was Wilhelm Baldensperger in *Das spaetere Judentum als Vorstufe des Christentums* (1909). Baldensperger was a man from Alsatia like Albert Schweizer, who resembles him in style and method. He is now forgotten—to the detriment of New Testament studies.
15. Matt. 24.30 and 26.64, and their parallels, are fragments of an old apocalypse inserted in the Gospel.

148

had offered. The line is here no longer horizontal but vertical, from the "above" to the "below" and from the "below" to the "above," and between the two worlds there is now the tension of contrast.[16] No room is left here for the forerunner, the Elijah; his place is only in the former, the old prophetic view.

Attention must be paid to the fact that the manner of contrasting the "below" with the "above" is characteristic also of the Alexandrian Greek philosophy. The Book of Daniel was composed when Palestine had for a century been part of the Ptolemaic Egyptian kingdom and under its intellectual influence. Even later, when a frontier separated Jewish Palestine from Egypt, it was more a political than a cultural frontier. There was a mutual and continual "give" and "take" in the spiritual field.[17] We cannot tell whether the new messianic conception which appears in the Book of Daniel had its origin in Palestine or Egypt. In any case this new form of messianic idea is strikingly congruent with the basic idea of Alexandrian philosophy. A powerful ally and at the same time a bold seducer could, and must have, come into contact with the vertical messianism.

Within the world of Jewish faith the two messianic conceptions existed side by side. Once the religious principles were safeguarded, there was a characteristic large-mindedness in the Jewish people. The pronouncement concerning the controversy of the schools of Hillel and Shammai that "both are words of the living God" reflected a common feeling. The "horizontal" messian-

16. Cf. Leo Baeck, *Aus drei Jahrtausenden* (1936), pp. 326ff., and *The Pharisees and other Essays* (1948), pp. 114f. [See also the first essay in this volume. *W.K.*]
17. *Ibid.*

ism appealed to all those whose hearts were alive to
the task of establishing the kingdom of God; their ears
were open to the words of the prophets. Those who
impatiently desired to receive the kingdom of God here
and now were attracted by the other way, the "vertical" messianism; they desired ardently to see and to be
absorbed in the vision. Two forms of the idea of the
kingdom of God are revealed here; but there was no
rigid boundary between them.

In the Gospel we see both forms, the prophetic and
the apocalyptic. The messiah is the son of David; his
descent is from Jesse. "Two blind men follow him cry-
ing: Thou, son of David, have mercy on us." "The
people say: Is not this the son of David?" In Jerusalem
the multitudes shout: "Hosannah to the son of David"
(Matt. 9.9, 22; 12.23; 21.9; and the parallels). But at
the same time we come across sentences from an
apocalypse intercalated in the Gospel speaking of him
as "coming in the clouds of heaven."[18] Moreover, we
can observe here a decided attitude of opposition to the
"son of David." All three synoptic gospels contain a
discourse which bears distinct witness to such a rejection: "And Jesus answered and said, while he taught
in the temple. 'How say the scribes that Christ is the
son of David? For David himself said by the Holy
Ghost, The Lord said to my Lord, Sit thou on my right
hand, till I make thine enemies thy footstool. David
therefore himself calleth him Lord; and whence is he
then his son?"[19] This was, indeed, the issue: "the son

18. See above, p. 29.
19. Mark 12.35ff.; Matt. 12.42ff.; Luke 20.41ff. Vincent Taylor
in his excellent *Commentary on Mark* (1952), pp. 490ff., records
all the different interpretations of these verses, but it seems that
the essential point has been missed. Here, in this discourse, we
may see the first step toward the *Kyrios Christos.*

of David" or "the son of man sitting on the right hand of power."[20]

There can be no doubt as to which of the two ideas Paul embraced. To him had been allotted the vision, and the "vision" disclosed the "above," the celestial. It is true that the introduction to the letter to the Romans (1.3) says: ". . . his son Jesus Christ our Lord which was made of the seed of David according to the flesh." But the prefaces to the other letters, although their diction is similar, do not have these words, nor are they contained in the letters themselves. It sounds rather like the quotation of a coined phrase that was usual in the congregations.[21] The messiah is, for Paul, only the "son of God." This is the whole fullness of the messianic thought. What Jesus had said or done, his preaching or his working wonders are, at least comparatively, insignificant. He came on this earth only in order to die and to be resurrected. The resurrection is the gospel and nothing else. "If Christ be not raised, our faith is vain," "If Christ be not risen, then is our preaching void, and your faith is also void" (I Cor. 15.14 and 17). This is the only tradition Paul refers to. Twice he says: "I have received of the Lord that which also I delivered unto you,"[22] and of the two sentences that follow this announcement the former refers to the very commencement of the resurrection—to the last supper—and the latter to the resurrection itself. This is the sole theme. Here is contained already the distinction between Paul and the disciples which has continued in the Church: the distinction between those who

20. Matt. 26.64. Concerning the term "son of man," see L. Baeck, *Aus drei Jahrtausenden*, pp. 313-325 [or the first essay in this volume. *W.K.*].
21. Cf. II. Tim. 2.8.
22. I Cor. 11.23 and 15.3; cf. II Thess. 2.15.

demanded the *imitatio Christi* and those who first taught "belief."[23]

Paul's mind, however, could encompass many things. Provided that the essential point was faithfully adhered to, he was prepared to concede some latitude to the expression.[24] He was conscious of the completeness of the vision he had had, but at the same time of the incompleteness of the utterance he could give it. "By part we judge, and by part we prophesy" (I Cor. 13.9).[25] Thus he did not object to *extasis,* nor to "speaking in odd tongue," nor to "prophesying." Paul's mind was able to embrace many a thing;[26] his genius turned rather toward analogy than toward analysis.

Yet another point should be mentioned here. The nature of the messianic idea as apprehended by Paul invited "analogies" and "relations." Paul was brought up in Tarsus,[27] a place of Hellenism, with all its philos-

23. The term itself *imitatio Christi* is based upon a Pauline word, I Cor. 11.1: *Imitatores mei estote, sicut et ego Christi.* But this word does not refer to the human personality of Jesus, to the Sermon on the Mount, to the lovingkindness, to a moral heroism, but to the Christ of the Pauline doctrine. It means about the same thing as I Cor. 15.11.

24. I Cor. 14.37f. That whole chapter has as its object to show the insignificance of the "expression."

25. The word *ginoskein* here apparently does not mean, as the Authorized Version gives it: to know, but rather: to judge, *judicare.*

26. It may be doubted whether he allowed eschatology. It seems that I Cor. 15.23-28, is an interpolation. The context is obviously interrupted. Verse 29 is the continuation of verse 22, the word *epei* that begins verse 29 would be without any meaning should it be consecutive to verse 28; but it has its clear significance as continuing verse 22. Moreover, Paul's structure of faith is contrary to eschatology.

27. Jerome's statement that Paul's parents came to Tarsus from Giskala in Palestine and that Paul himself was born there may be an old tradition. The word *gegennemenos* in Acts 22.3 can signify both "born" and "grown up."

ophies, beliefs, annunciations, and cults. However wrong some of them must have appeared to the Jew, there was in them something which seemed not so alien to him. There had existed a simple and easy answer to the forms of ancient heathendom: they were all vain and void. But, faced with the Hellenistic thoughts the feeling of a Jew was somehow more complex. Something reminded him here of Jewish speculation, especially that fostered by the schools of Jewish "wisdom." No Jew could reject such aspects of "Hellenism" without renouncing a part of his own self. One was, indeed, prepared to ascribe to Hellenistic teachers the "wisdom" of which the Bible spoke. A Jew, on meeting such a teacher, had to praise God for "having given of His wisdom to a human being."[28] The heathen teachers, although not possessing the fullness of the Torah, had, nevertheless, this "wisdom," this ḥokhmah. Nor should it be forgotten that for the Jew "wisdom" was the intellectual, the moral, and the cosmical power;[29] it meant very much to him. He could also hope to win over the best of the Gentiles and convince them that, being engaged already in the right way, they should reach out for the final goal: the Jewish creed. Many conversions were accomplished in this manner.

To Paul, Hellenistic thought would have meant both

28. B. Berakhoth, 58a.
29. Cf. L. Baeck, *The Pharisees and other Essays*, p. 27, and his *Aus drei Jahrtausenden*, pp. 162ff. We can distinguish in the Jewish literature of the Hellenistic period two courses. In the older, "wisdom" and *Torah* are identified, cf. *Sirach* 24.8-11 and 23; *Henoch* 62; *I Bar.* 3.38ff. ("wisdom" is equivalent also to the Stoic *Logos*, cf. *Sap. Sal.* 7.24). In the other, the two are kept distinct; *Torah* is given a special high place (cf. Josephus, *Ant.* xx, 11, 2) and declared to be pre-existent (cf. *Sifre* on Deut. 2.10; Ber. R., 1, 5). The whole material is now well expounded by W. D. Davies in his fine book, *Paul and Rabbinic Judaism*, pp. 150ff.

an appeal and a hope. Although he was not, as has often been said, a "Hellenist," his approach to the Hellenistic world was the same as that of some Palestinian teachers. Paul's relation to Hellenistic thought can be easily traced. He speaks, in the manner of Greek, especially Stoic philosophic terminology of a natural knowledge of God (Rom. 1.18ff.), of the Christ being "the wisdom of God" (I Cor. 1.24) and he says of God, that "of him and through him and to him are all things" (Rom. 11.26 and I Cor. 8.6); he avails himself of the terms "conscience" (Rom. 2.15, etc.), "the proper" (Rom. 1.28), "nature" (I Cor. 11.14), etc.; "the elements of the world" (Gal. 1.4, 3, and 9). By doing so Paul was within the Jewish compass.[30]

But from the same Hellenistic thought, although from a different level, other images and other voices would come to Paul—images and voices that would still appear as something akin to Jewish Christology, but, in fact, were different. Paul was carried away by them far outside the Jewish boundaries. The different level of Hellenistic thought was formed by the colorful mystery-cults and the ambiguous mystery-doctrines which became a victorious creed appealing both to the refined and the simple. It flourished in Tarsus. Each of those multifarious cults and doctrines had its own particular feature, but essentially they were all the same thing and they offered the same message; the distinctions were without a difference. They all spoke of a savior, a redeemer, of a Lord, a godhead that had

30. The extent of harmonizing Jewish and Hellenistic thought is shown by the fact that one of the old Aramaic versions, the so-called *Targum Yerushalmi*, renders the first words of Genesis: בחוכמא ברא which Jerome (*Quaest. hebr. in Gen.*) translated: *in filio creavit*. A term corresponding to *ḥokhmah* is *derekh 'eretz*, "way of mankind," cf. G. Klein, *Der aelteste christliche Katechismus*, pp. 61ff.

died young and was raised from death, and who by
his death and resurrection had subdued death itself,
and now bestowed the real life, the lasting days on
those who believed in him and became united with him
by means of sacraments: the baptism, the unctions, the
consecrated substances. There were only two articles
of faith common to all these doctrines: sacrament and
resurrection, the former, the indispensable "way"; the
latter the fulfillment.

The sacrament was, thus, something absolutely essential. Nothing else but the sacrament could open for
man the supernatural realm—to make him die, be
raised again, and live in the godhead which had vanquished death. Furthermore an experience of "imme-
diateness" was given to man. After the initiation, there
was no proceeding step by step, no waiting or watching; the savior did not come again, did not reappear
in order to bring salvation. Here and now, and all at
once redemption was achieved. The fullness, the perfection was not only a "promise," an "expectancy";
it was intimate and enduring "presence."

This creed as well as its expression bear a likeness
to what is proclaimed in Paul's letters. This likeness
should not be overlooked. But, when in the beginnings
of this century[31] attention was first drawn to these
congruities, by eminent scholars, a conclusion was
reached in the form of an overstatement. Paul was
described almost as the founder of a new type of
mystery-religion, who opened the last and all-
embracing chapter in the history of these mysterious
creeds and cults. Afterward, and as a natural reaction,
the opposite course was followed; an understatement,

31. It should be noticed that the great philologist Isaac Casau-
bonus pointed out the similarities between Paul and the mystery-
cults in his *Exercitationes de rebus sacris*, Geneva, 1655.

even a belittling of Paul's contacts with the mystery-cults. The right things were cast away together with the wrong ones. Careful examination of all the issues involved leads to the conclusion that conformities between Paul and the mystery-cults should not be denied —conformities pointing to influence.

Paul was a Jew of Tarsus, not a Syrian or Persian or Egyptian of Tarsus. His belief was Jewish messianism such as was determined by the Book of Daniel and the books which sprang from the latter. His starting point was the vision allotted to him which gave him the assuredness that Jesus was the Christ. His background was that of his Jewish people. But his vision, and the certainty it gave him, received a new significance and, to his mind, a new amplitude as well as a new confirmation through the mystery cults and creeds. What had been achieved in the sphere of "wisdom," the first gathering in of the Gentiles, appeared to Paul as a task to be performed in the large realm of the mystery cults. In the sphere of "wisdom," the One God as revealed to the Jewish people, was preached—the One from whom all "wisdom" comes forth and beside whom there is none else. The proclamation in the new sphere was "wisdom," but more than "wisdom,"[32] it was even "the power of God" (I Cor. 1.24), the messiah, Jesus Christ, who was first manifested to the Jews. He was, in truth, the only savior, from whom all redemption comes and besides whom there is none else, no Attis, no Osiris, no Mithras. "To us then is but one

32. The purpose of I Cor. 1.18-28 is to show that "wisdom" as such is nothing final, but attains the truth only by acknowledging the Christ and the resurrection. Paul does not discard or disregard "wisdom," but he seeks to point out its real correlate, "the power of God." Cf. Marc. 6.2 where *sofia* and *dunamis* are joined together.

156

God . . . and one Lord Jesus Christ . . ." (I Cor. 8.6).[33] The one God and the one savior must be proclaimed unto the self-assured Greek for whom it could only mean "foolishness," "stupidity," and unto the self-conscious Jew for whom it must be "seduction," "the snare."[34]

This was for Paul the final answer, the conclusive manifestation that comprehended everything, philosophy and mystery, and, thus, gave to the whole mankind the whole truth—"wisdom" and "power" united, or, as Paul puts it in Daniel's words: "Christ the power of God and the wisdom of God" (Dan. 2.20; I Cor. 1.24). It would be useless to speculate how in Paul's mind the single threads became interwoven, what came first and what followed, where and when they joined each other. But the texture itself is manifest; it can be clearly seen: only by perceiving it can the two distinctive characteristics of Paul's preaching and teachings be discerned; the significance given by him to baptism and to the "days of the messiah."

Baptism, as preached by Paul, is something quite different from the baptism which from ancient times was the sacred rite in Judaism, and in Paul's days, especially, the practice in the circles of the Essenes, the *tobhle shaḥarin*, the "Hemerobaptists,"[35] as well as the baptism of John the Baptist. It purified those

---

33. As to "Lords many" (I Cor. 8.5), cf. K. and S. Lake, *Introduction to the N.T.*, pp. 237ff.

34. The meaning of *skandalon* in the New Testament language is: *seduction, seducer*; Satan is *skandalon* as well as Balaam (Rev. 2.14).

35. We do not know whether the *tobhle shaḥarin* (Berakhoth 22a), or, as the Talmud Yerushalmi calls them, the *tobhle shaḥarith* (Berakhoth 6c), were a section of the Essenes, or a special sect, or a distinctive name of the Essenes. Nor can we positively know if John the Baptist means John the Essene.

who had been polluted by means of submersion in clear water. The water itself was of no significance, it was nothing else but water. It was like the water in which vessels were cleaned that had become ritually unclean. And it was the man himself who had polluted and cleansed himself through this baptism, it was his own action. It was not administered to him by someone else; he was not baptized by another man. The Hebrew and the Aramaic words for baptizing, *ṭabhol, ṭebhal,* are used, in relation to human agents, exclusively as intransitive verbs.[36] The people who came to John the Baptist were not baptized by him, they baptized themselves,[37] they became, so to speak, baptists like him. Baptism was something quite different in the mystery cults. It was not a ceremonial rite, but a magic sacrament, indeed, a magic event. Man had to be baptized, he became the object of something that was to be done to him,[38] and baptism worked upon him *ex opere operato*. Moreover, he was not cleansed, but transformed. By virtue of baptism he was lifted from this life and elevated to another one, to the true and lasting life that is stronger than death. He became united with deity, to share the same existence. *Charizomenē sōteria,* "redemption by grace," became his share.

36. Only in relation to things are they used transitively.
37. It stands to reason that the victorious Paulinism has exerted its influence on the final form of the synoptic Gospels. Thus the word *baptizein* was given a new meaning. One of the readings of Luke 3.7 which has *enopion autou* still shows the original situation. In Greek writers the word *baptizein* means "to be submerged, to be immersed," *i.e.*, about the same meaning as the Hebrew and Aramaic טבל.
38. It is noteworthy that Aristotle when explaining the character of the mystery cults indicates as a particular mark that they mean a *paschein*, that is, that the initiated are mere objects (*Aristotelean fragment*, quoted by Synesios [Migne, *Series Graeca*, lxvi, 1136A]).

When we read what Paul says of baptism, how he refers to it as being "baptized into Jesus Christ," "baptized into his death," being "buried with him," in order to be "in the likeness of his resurrection" (Rom. 6.3ff.), as "putting on Christ" (Gal. 3.27), as being "all baptized into one body" (I Cor. 12.13), how he even speaks of "being baptized into one body" (I Cor. 15.29)—when we grasp all this we can find nothing, except the words themselves, that is common with what Jewish teachers, or John the Baptist, or the disciples of Jesus would understand by baptism. On the other hand, we can scarcely fail to recognize the distinctive features of "baptism" in the mystery-religions. The term used by Paul is the Jewish term, but the content given to it points to those other spheres,[39] with which Paul was very well acquainted. It is difficult not to suppose that Paul was captivated by the analogies that they offered. They showed him the province where the Gentiles came near to his own gospel of the savior, of the Lord who had died on the cross, and was resurrected in order to grant resurrection to the believer. He saw the Gentiles as marching on the same road. His task became now to show them their true goal, exactly like what had formerly been done in the field of "wisdom": the Christ who was both "the power and the wisdom of God."

The striking parallel between the Christian baptism and the initiatory rite of the mystery-cult was recognized by Tertullian in later days when Christianity advanced and paganism retreated. In his treatise on baptism Tertullian asserts that the devil counterfeited

39. What Paul writes to the Corinthians: "Christ sent me not to baptize, but to preach the gospel," shows, perhaps, some first sign of reluctance in him (I Cor. 1.17). But one could interpret these words in some other manner, namely, that Paul considered his real task to preach his vision.

Christian baptism in his desire "to rival the things of God," by "practicing baptism in his own subjects," by arrogating to himself the "cleansing," the "absolving," the "washing away of sins."[40] The parallel is so strong, that no other expedient seemed to be available than the recourse to Satan's malignity. The fact was indeed a hard one, and could not be denied.

Another point of great consequence was involved in Paul's baptism, namely, the problem of the kingdom of God. The "kingdom of God" is neither a frequent nor a significant term[41] in Paul's creed and doctrine.[42] In any case the idea itself is different from what it meant in Judaism, where it referred to the "days to come," which the faithful expected and for which he prepared himself. Paul did not preach expectancy of a future age. By proclaiming the resurrected Christ he proclaimed the presence of God's kingdom. Man was to be resurrected by virtue of the sacrament and to live in the Christ. "The testimony of Christ was confirmed in you: so that ye come behind in no gift; waiting for the coming of our Lord Jesus Christ" (I Cor. 1.6ff.). The kingdom has become an actuality for Paul, a full consummation. The final day of judgment would only seal what was already accomplished.[43] The faithful was in the midst of the days of promise, in the midst of the days of the messiah. Here was the core and the strength of Paul's faith. The word "now" is Paul's: "Now the righteousness of God without the law is manifested";

40. *De baptismo*, ch. v. Cpr. also Luke 22.31.
41. See R. H. Charles, *Eschatology*, p. 390ff.
42. See Rom. 14.17; I Cor. 4.20; 6.9 and 10; 15.50; Gal. 5.21. All these sentences apparently quote old sayings handed down by tradition and familiar to the people like household words. I Cor. 15.24 is, as mentioned before, part of an apocalypse interpolated in the text of the letter.
43. Cf. I. Cor. 1.8 and II Cor. 1.13f.

160

"being now justified by his blood." "Our Lord Jesus
Christ by whom we have now received the atonement"
(Rom. 3.21; 5.9, 11). "Whether things present or
things to come, all are yours" (I Cor. 3.22). Here, too,
his way and that of Jesus' disciples parted asunder,
and although Paul retained the old word he gave to it
another significance.

Another momentous problem had to be solved by
Paul. Jewish teaching in his days was that the course
of history was divided into three different epochs succeeding each other. An old tradition, as shown by its
introductory solemn formula: "It was taught in the
school of Elijah"[44] states: "There are three epochs: two
thousand years of chaos, *tohu wabhohu*; two thousand
years of Law (*Torah*), beginning with the revelation
on Mount Sinai; two thousand years of the Messianic
age"[45] which will be finally followed by "that world
which is wholly *Shabbath*, the rest in the life of eternity."[46] There is, thus, not a perpetuity, but a "period,"
of the Torah. If the "Days of the Messiah" have commenced, those of the Torah came to their close.[47] On
the other hand, if the Law, the Torah, still retained its
validity, it was proclaimed thereby that the messiah
has not yet appeared. Such was the alternative, and
such was the problem that had to be determined.

It was not a Hellenistic but a Jewish problem, since

44. It would seem that in the field of Haggadah, the term
תנא דבי אליהו has the same meaning as the term הלכה למשה מסני
in the field of the Halakha. Cf. W. Bacher, *Tradition und Tra-
denten*, pp. 25ff. and 233f.
45. B. Sanhedrin 97a and *Pesiqta Rabbati* 4a—cf. Yer. Megillah
70d.
46. Tamid vii, 4. The whole question of "Messianic Age" is discussed by G. F. Moore, *Judaism*, II, 323ff.
47. The term תורה חדשה "the new Torah" (Lev. Rabba xiii) may
also be mentioned here. Cf. Yalqut to Isaiah 26.2; Niddah 61b,
Pesaḥim 50a. The new Torah supersedes this Torah.

it followed necessarily from the doctrine of the
"epochs." Time and again, throughout the centuries,
this problem has engaged the Jewish mind. Different
schemes of determining the "periods," were in existence, but the basic idea remained always that one
"period" would replace the other, and that the "epoch"
of the Torah would come to an end, and that the
"period" beyond the Torah would be ushered in. This
conception prevailed both before Paul and after.
Simeon ben Eleazar,[48] the disciple of Meir (second half
of the second century), significantly, interpreted the
words of the Ecclesiastes 12.1 ("the years draw nigh,
when thou shalt say 'I have no pleasure in them' ") in
the following manner: "the years draw nigh, in which
thou shalt say, I need no will,[49] no choice"; and explained that "this relates to the 'Days of the Messiah,'
for in them there will be no merit or guilt." The parallel
to Paul's sentence: "All things are lawful unto me"
(I Cor. 6.14) is obvious. Paul would speak so, only
because he was convinced that the "messianic days"
have dawned upon earth.

The primary question, which Paul's faith had to face
was: which "period" was it, that of the Torah or that
of the messiah? Was the appearance of Jesus Christ
only the beginning, however momentous, or was it
"finality" already? Or, to put it in the words of
Matthew: Is "all fulfilled" already and the "law" is
superseded, or it is not yet fulfilled and "one jot or one
tittle shall in no wise pass from the law"?[50] Now it is

---

48. B. Shabbath 151b, and *Yalqut* to *Ecclesiastes* 12.1; in both
passages Simeon ben Eleazar is mentioned as the author. In
Midrash to *Eccles.* 12.1, the author is Hiyya ben Nehemiah.
49. Simeon b. Eleazar takes the word חפץ not in the connotation
of "pleasure," but in its primary meaning: "the will, the decision."
50. In this sentence (Matt. 5.18) the stress is placed on the
last words, "till all be fulfilled."

clear why Paul fought, not against "law," but against the "present" validity of the law; and fought this fight with all the determination of his faith and his will. Not the "law" as such but the messiah, his presence, his actuality, were at stake. Paul's whole religion was involved in this fight. If by God's decree full redemption was, in fact, allotted to Paul and the community of the faithful, it followed that the law had ceased rightly to subsist. Were it still to be in force, then the gospel of the fulfillment, of the consummation, was denied. The line of division was clearly drawn: whoever maintained that the law was still binding was an unbeliever, he did not believe in the presence of the Christ. Either "law" or "redemption," this was the choice. We are, therefore, not entitled to say that Paul rejected or condemned the law—if he had done so he would have broken asunder the structure of his belief. To the contrary, to him "the law is holy, and the commandments holy and just and good" (Rom. 7.12), he could say, indeed: "we establish the law" (Rom. 3.31). This is not, as some scholars have assumed, an inconsistency. Quite to the contrary, it shows the congruity of Paul's thinking. He had to speak of both: of the law, and of the Christ. He could not tell the one without telling the other. There is an interconnection between them, the same as there is between the route and its goal, or that between what is "written" and what is "fulfilled." The two together prove the truth, and display the nature of the divine ordinance and dispensation.

By preaching the new "epoch," the "days beyond the law," Paul, and this point must be stressed again, did not step out of the Jewish compass and the Jewish purview. He was strongly convinced that he was, and remained, within the Jewish sphere. What severed him from the others, was, so to speak, not the *quaestio juris*, but the *quaestio facti*. That a new epoch was to begin one day was not contended by anybody; it was the common belief of the Jewish people. Moreover, it was a belief the Jewish people could never dispense with, nor do without. What separated Paul from the Jewish people was the question of fact—the problem whether the messiah had, finally, been manifested, whether his kingdom had come in in truth. Paul never thought of rejecting or disregarding his Jewish people. It was his people, which he could not forsake without forsaking his own faith, which he could not dismiss without dismissing his hope and his love. Or, to quote his own words: "I say then, hath God cast away his people? God forbid" (Rom. 11.1)—or, to render this last phrase, the Greek *mē genoito*, corresponding to the Hebrew חלילה according to its full meaning, as in the Septuagint: *mēdamōs* "on no account," or as the Aramaic version, the so-called Targum Jonathan, often has it: חולין הוא לך "it would be a profanation."[51] Paul could not even imagine that God "has cast away his people."[52] The eleventh chapter in the Letter to the Romans is the most moving thing Paul has ever written. The sincerity of this man, the depth of his feeling rooted in his Jewish people, are all revealed here.

But at the same time it can be seen here, how Paul's thoughts are interlocked. God can never be entirely known, He is the *Deus absconditus*. Yet He has manifested Himself to mankind through His revelation to the Jewish people—a revelation which is at the same time also redemption; the two concepts are, therefore,

51. See Septuagint and *Targ. Jon.* to Gen. 18.25 and I Sam. 2.30.
52. Is it mere contingency that this phrase *me genoito* appears only in the letter to the Romans, the first to the Corinthians, and the letter to the Galatians, which are mostly concerned with the Jewish people?

interconnected. "Unto the Jews were committed the sayings *(ta logia)* of God" (Rom. 3.2). "For I would not, brethren, that ye should be ignorant of this mystery" (Rom. 11.25).

The word mystery *(mustērion)* which had passed into the Hebrew language in the Hellenistic period and become a Hebrew word, signifies here something more than the word "mystery" means today. It means here that whereby and wherein the "unknown God" becomes the "knowable," whereby the divine secret becomes visible somehow and somewhere. Both must be stressed here: the "unknown" and the "knowable."[53] Thus in talmudic literature the prophet is said to stand in God's "mystery,"[54] thus the "Oral Law" is called "the mystery,"[55] and circumcision likewise.[56] As a part of God's manifestation, as belonging to the sphere of the "mystery" the Jewish people is an essential part of Paul's faith. Nor did Paul, by stressing his apostolate to the Gentiles, deviate from the genuine Jewish creed. It is not only history that tells us of the Jewish mission and its extension; of the large-mindedness it showed to the "godfearing." There is something more: Jewish philosophy, or theology, or history, includes always the Gentiles. The terms, "Jewish people" and "Gentiles" are interrelated in their meaning. There could be no fulfillment without the one and the other. The Magna Charta of the messianic rights, in the second chapter

53.   Hence what Karl Barth says in explaining Rom. 11.25 that *mustērion* corresponds to our term "paradox," seems to be not quite correct, although the problem of the "paradox" is of greatest importance here, too.
54.   *Exod. Rabba* xviii.
55.   *Pesiqta Rabbati* v, and *Cant. Rabba* to 2.7.
56.   *Tanhuma* to Gen. 17.2, ed. S. Buber, p. 40a.

of the book of Isaiah, places Jews and Gentiles side by side together. The "coming" of the messiah and the "coming" of the Gentiles are interconnected.

This is Jewish faith, and such was Paul's faith. Paul longed for the first response to his gospel from his Jewish people. When the response failed—Jews were still prepared to hope and to wait (patient expectation was not one of Paul's qualities)—Paul went to the Gentiles, recognizing both their "wisdom," as the Jews had done, and their "dynamics," which the Jews had rejected. The Jewish people remained, however, interwoven with Paul's messianic, "Christian" faith. The eleventh chapter of the Letter to the Romans shows it very clearly.

Such is Paul's faith and its characteristic traits. But Paul was a theologian too. He was a theologian, not "incidentally" as has been said,[57] and often repeated; he was so by his whole nature and life, one could almost also say: by his nationality. As a Jew, his life was contained in the Bible, and as a Jewish scholar he had to justify before the Bible whatever he would say and do. He must expound the Bible, he must lay open the meaning of its words. This explanation of the Bible only could legitimize his preaching, that is to say: he had to be a theologian too.

It is a principle in Judaism that truth has to be discovered in, and through, the Bible. The book of "revelation," must again and again be revealed by the teacher. For every sentence and story in this book not only tells something, it also means something. It does not merely describe what has been and now ceased to be. It manifests something permanent that attains actuality again

—

57. By Dean Inge in his classical essay on St. Paul (*Outspoken Essays*, First series).

and again. A particular kind of logic had been evolved.
Association of words and meanings became method.
The Holy Scripture became the cosmos in which every
detail had its allotted place, and its particular significance within the whole. Each detail must be compared
with other details, it is a link in the great system of
God's manifestation. Everything points to something
else and it means something that is present now. An act
of recognition takes place. "This is he that is spoken
of" (Matt. 3.3). One may call this reasoning by analogy. Aristotle explained and justified the rule of analogy: *Ho theos kai hē fusis ouden matēn poiousi,* "God
and nature do nothing aimlessly"—similarly, one might
say here: this is the word of God, and God speaks nothing that is aimless.[58]

Such was Paul's method; the way of his theology.
Analogy prevails in Paul's manner of thinking and proceeding. Perhaps, when Paul became acquainted with
the mystery-religions an act of recognition implied in
this method decided, or at least influenced the issue.
Paul's theology was constructed by this method, and it
reveals both his mind and the breadth and complication
of the Jewish background which nurtured him.

Paul's achievement influenced Judaism itself, although his name is not mentioned in talmudic literature. His "antinomism," and more so that of his successors, provoked a strengthening of "nomism" within
the Jewish sphere. The only sentence in talmudic literature, which, without mentioning Paul by name,
points apparently at him, refers to him as the "man,"
whose "way is forward and strange" (Prov. 21.8), and
explains that this "man . . . made himself strange to the

58. Cf. Leo Baeck, *The Pharisees and other Essays,* pp. 53ff.

circumcision and the commandments."[59] The sentence
is contained in a sermon preached on Jewish Pentecost
"the season of the giving of our Torah," and it was
inserted in the Midrash on the Book of Ruth that is
read on that feast day. In the Midrash another sermon
follows immediately which has the very same subject as
chapter 11 in the Letter to the Romans: God "cannot
cast away his people." The Jewish preacher says:
"God, as it were, speaks: 'To cast them away for another people—I cannot do it. I can but visit them with
afflictions.' "[60] This "mystery" remained the core of
the Jewish faith. The idea of the suffering messiah
and the idea of the suffering people become very nearly
one and the same idea.

59. *Ruth Rabba., Petiḥa,* iii; שעשה עצמו זר למצוה וזר למילה. The
sentence *'Aboth* iii, 15, by Elazar of Modiim, reflects a different
period. Cf. W. Bacher, *Agada der Tannaiten* i, p. 190.
60. *Ruth Rabba., Petiḥa,* iv; להחליפן באומה אחרת איני יכול הריני מייסרן
ביסורין.

4

MYSTERY AND
COMMANDMENT

There are two experiences of the human soul in which the meaning of his life takes on for a man a vital significance: the experience of mystery and the experience of commandment; or, as we may also put it, the knowledge of what is real and the knowledge of what is to be realized.

When man wants to be certain of his existence, when he therefore listens intently for the meaning of his life and life in general, and when he thus feels the presence of something lasting, of some reality beneath the surface, then he experiences the mystery: he becomes conscious that he was created, brought into being—conscious of an undetectable and, at the same time, protective power. He experiences that which embraces him and all else. He experiences, in the words of the ancient metaphor in the Blessing of Moses, "the arms of eternity."

And when man looks beyond the present day, when he wishes to give his life direction and lead it toward a goal, when he thus grasps that which defines his life

171

and is clear about it, then he is always confronted with
the commandment, the task, that which he is to realize.
The foundation of life is the mystery; the way of life
is the revealed. The one is from God; the other to be
achieved by man. To cite another thought from the
Bible: "That which is concealed belongs unto the Lord
our God, but that which is revealed belongs unto us and
unto our children forever, that we may do all the words
of this Torah." And both, mystery as well as commandment, represent certainty—the certainty of life, the
certainty of the self.

This twofold experience could also be called humility
and reverence. The humility of man is his recognition
that his life is framed by infinity and eternity, by that
which transcends all human knowledge and apprehension, and surpasses all that is natural and existent; that
his life is absolutely dependent; that the unknowable
and unnamable, the unfathomable and unthinkable
enters into his life. Humility is the feeling for that deep
and mysterious sphere in which man is rooted; the
feeling, in other words, for that which remains in being
and is real—the great quiet, the great devotion in all
philosophy and all wisdom. And reverence is man's
feeling that something higher confronts him; and
whatever is higher is ethically superior and therefore
makes demands and directs, speaks to man and requires
his reply, his decision. It can reveal itself in the small
and weak no less than in the sublime; it can manifest
itself in the other as well as in oneself. Reverence is
thus the recognition of the holy, that which is infinitely
and eternally commanding, that which man is to accept
into his life and realize through his life—the great im-
pelling force, the active aspect of wisdom.

This twofold experience can also be intimated in this
way: the consciousness that we have been created

172

versus the consciousness that we are expected to create. The former is our certainty of that through which all that lives has life; our certainty that, at heart and in truth, we are related to the oneness of all life; our certainty of that which is omnipresent and enduring. It is the capacity of the soul for grasping the invisible in the visible, the lasting in the momentary, the eternal in the transitory, and the infinite in the earthly and limited. It is this faith which ever and again grasps that which has reality and which is the principle and source of life. The latter, on the other hand, is the capacity to be aware of the demand and determination of the hour; it is the certainty of the task, of that which admonishes, points ahead, and directs our life; the certainty that every man's life can do its share and accomplish its function; that man has some quality that lifts him out of the universe which has been created even as he himself has been created—a quality which gives man a quite personal aspect, a quite individual place and a unique direction and freedom, a capacity for decision by virtue of which man comprehends again and again what he is supposed to fulfill.

These are the two experiences of the meaning of life. And what is peculiar to Judaism is that these two experiences have here become one, and are experienced as one, in a perfect unity. And it is thus that the soul becomes conscious of its own unity and totality; it is thus that piety springs up in the soul. From the one God come both mystery and commandment, as one from the One, and the soul experiences both as one. Every mystery means and suggests also a commandment; and every commandment means and suggests also a mystery. All humility also means and suggests reverence, and all reverence, humility; all faith, the law, and all law, faith. All consciousness that we have been created means and suggests the demand to create, and every demand to create means and suggests the consciousness that we have been created. What is evident is here rooted in that which is concealed, and what is concealed always has its evident aspect for man. The profundity of life cannot be grasped without its also speaking to us of duty in life; and not a single duty of life is perceived truly without at the same time proclaiming the profundity of life. We cannot have knowledge of the foundation of our life without at the same time beholding our way, and we cannot understand this way without penetrating to the foundation of our life. We cannot fully take to heart that we are the creatures of God without apprehending also that we ought to be the creators of our own lives; and we cannot be in full possession of this commandment to create unless we remain aware that we ourselves have been created—created by God that we ourselves may create, and creating because we have been created by God. This unity of both experiences in the human soul constitutes Jewish piety and Jewish wisdom; the meaning of life reveals itself here in this form.

Therefore Judaism is not marred by the split which is introduced by other conceptions of God. Judaism lacks any foundation for the conflict between transcendence and immanence. Jewish piety lives in the paradox, in the polarity with all its tension and compactness. That which is a contradiction in the abstract world of mere theory is made a unity and a whole in the religious consciousness. For this consciousness there is no such thing as this world without any beyond, nor a beyond without this world; no world to come without the present world, and no human world without that which transcends it. Whatever is on this side is rooted in the beyond, and whatever is beyond demands completion on this side by man. The infinite appears in the finite, and whatever is finite bears witness to the infinite. The life of man leads from God to man and from man to God. God is He in whom is all being, and God is also He that is positively different. God gives man life, and God demands man's life from him. Our soul is what is divine in us, it is our mystery and shares the mystery of all souls; and yet it shows also our individual stamp, that which is unique within us, our very self, that which belongs to it alone. The human dwells in the divine, and the divine demands of every man his humanity. This unity of both, the meaning which emerges from this opposition, alone is truth and pregnant with thoroughgoing certainty.

Hence any opposition between mysticism and ethics has no place here either. The religious consciousness here is never without its immediacy, its experience—nor without that which has been commanded and still is to be realized in life. No experience without tasks and no tasks without experience; life dwells only where both are present. In Judaism, all ethics has its mysticism and all mysticism its ethics. This applies to the whole far-flung history of its ideas. For Jewish mysticism the energies welling up out of God are energies of the will. Floods of mystery full of commandments and floods of commandment full of mystery issue from God. And the deed which fulfills God's commandment opens up a gate through which these floods surge into man's day. All absorption in the profundity of God is always also an absorption in the will of God and His commandment. And all Jewish ethics is distinguished by being an ethic of revelation or, one might almost say, an ethic of experience of the divine: it is the tidings of the divine. Every "thou shalt" is confronted with another word which introduces it and simultaneously replies to it—another word which is at the same time the word of mystery: "Thus saith the Lord." And it is followed by this same word both as a conclusion and a new beginning: "I am the Lord thy God." Ethics is here rooted in the profundity of living experience, and it is significant that in the Hebrew language of the Middle Ages the same word is used to designate an ethical disposition and a mystical absorption. The history of Judaism from ancient times to the present could be written as a history of mysticism; and the history of Judaism from its origins until now could also be written as a history of "the Law"— and it would be the same history. And for the most part it would be the history of the very same men. Many of the most influential and decisive teachers of the law have been mystics; for example, the author of the oft-cited *Shulhan Arukh*.

Of course, mystery and commandment were not always emphasized equally in Judaism. Now the one was stressed more, now the other; and this distinguishes different spheres and epochs. Only where one or the other was supposed to constitute the whole of religion, only where the whole of piety was exclusively identified with one or the other, did the religion cease to be Judaism. Judaism ceases where the mood of devotion, that which is at rest and restful, would mean everything; where faith is content with itself, content with mystery; where this mere faith finally extends its darkling glimmer to the point where it drowns the world and dreams become the stuff of life. The religion of mere passivity, devoid of commandments, is no longer Judaism. Nor is Judaism to be found where the commandment is content with itself and is nothing but commandment; where the whole sphere of life is supposed to be embraced by commandments and only that which lies under the rays of their cold light is presumed to be the meaning of life;

where man thinks that he has seen everything when he sees the way on which he is to proceed. The religion of mere activity without devotion—this religion which becomes an ethic of the surface, or no more than the custom of the day—is not Judaism. The world of Judaism is to be found only where faith has its commandment, and the commandment its faith.

This is why Paul left Judaism when he preached *sola fide* (by faith alone) and thereby wound up with sacrament and dogma. Mystery became everything for him, not only that which is concealed but also that which is manifest. Hence mystery finally had to become for him something tangible, namely, sacraments, and something that can be molded, namely, dogma. For it is always thus: sacraments are a mystery into which man enters, a mystery of which man can take hold; and dogma, like myth, is a mystery which man can build up and shape. The gospel—that old gospel which had not yet been adapted for the use of the Church and made to oppose Judaism—was still wholly a part of Judaism and conformed to the Old Testament. It is relatively less important that it was written in the language of the Jewish land and thus was a piece of Jewish literature. A full understanding of Jesus and his gospel is possible only in the perspective of Jewish thought and feeling and therefore perhaps only for a Jew. And his words can be heard with their full content and import only when they are led back into the language he spoke. The boundary of Judaism was crossed only by Paul at the point where mystery wanted to prevail without commandment, and faith without the law.

Judaism, however, can be abandoned no less on the other side. The very ground on which it rests is abandoned when these other developments take place: when it is assumed to be merely an ethic or the support for

177

an ethic; when it becomes a mere edifice of ideas, a doctrine; or when that which the mystery intimates is no
longer supposed to be the foundation of man's life but
merely some postulate of his thought—when Judaism
is taken to be a Judaism without paradox. There is no
such thing as a Judaism which is nothing but Kantian
philosophy or ethical culture, nor a Judaism in which
the idea of God is merely a decorative embellishment or
a crowning pinnacle. And the distinctive essence of
Judaism is lost, too, where the abundance of its laws
may still prevail, but merely as something that is performed, severed from its roots in mystery, void of
devotion.

Jewish piety and Jewish wisdom are found only
where the soul is in possession of the unity of that
which is concealed and that which is evident, of the profound and the task—the unity of devotion and deed.
What matters is the unity experienced in the soul, a
unity which is born of a reality and points toward a
truth—not a mere synthesis, and least of all syncretism.
A synthesis merely puts two things alongside each other
or at best into each other; but however closely it connects them, it merely connects one thing with another.
A unity, on the other hand, involves no mere connection
but a revelation: one thing is grasped and experienced
through the other and each receives its meaning only
from the other. Mystery and commandment are not
merely connected and interwoven but proclaim each
other and give each other their distinctive essences. The
commandment is a true commandment only because it
is rooted in mystery, and the mystery is a true mystery
because the commandment always speaks out of it. Because it is rooted in mystery, the commandment is unconditional and absolute, independent of the ephemeral
and useful, urgent and triumphant. It has the force of

unconditional unity, of the unity of morality, or—and
this is merely another way of putting it—it has the
capacity for taking itself absolutely seriously, to think
itself through; and this gives it its entire meaning. And
because mystery here cannot be without commandment,
it has its own blessing and creative power, and remains
fertile; it has the power to demand real life and to give
real life; it can let the well of profundity rise into the
light of day and introduce the eternal into the present
hour; it has the gift of being in everything and giving
unity to everything or—and this is just another way of
putting it—the gift of being real instead of merely
existent. And it is this alone that gives mystery its full
meaning. This totality and unity—this peculiar way in
which each is grasped by way of the other—this is
Judaism.

Not only the individual's life but history, too, receives
its meaning from this. There is history because there is
a unity of creation and future. Creation is unthinkable
apart from a future, and the idea of the future is in-
separable from the certainty of the divine creation.
Every commandment that issues from God, every commandment through which God speaks to man whom He
has created, has its own infinity, its everlasting future.
It creates and begets, it commands on and on, it transcends itself; every duty begets another duty. This end-
lessness of the law impressed Paul particularly; and it
was his opposition to this, his rebellion against that
which could not be fulfilled once and for all, that trou-
bled his soul and eventually gave birth to his faith in a
redemption that was fulfilled, in a salvation that had
been accomplished. For Judaism, however, this endless-
ness is something positive, it gives man something. A
commandment that can be fulfilled completely is merely
a human law. The commandment of God is a command-

ment which leads into the future and involves a mission which, in the words of the Bible, continues "from generation unto generation." It contains a promise, it has a life that continually comes to life, it has a messianic aspect. All creation has its future; in the words of an ancient Jewish parable: "The creation of the world contained the idea of the Messiah." Thus the future is not merely something historical or a mere result, not merely a synthesis of theses and antitheses of the past, but it signifies the certainty that God has created. All future issues from creation; it is the reply to the question of man's nature; it is that which man must expect —not miracle, nor myth, nor fate, but the future of the way, life begotten by Life. Creation and future, mission and confidence depend on each other and reveal each other. And all ages, too, have their unity. God has made a lasting covenant with man.

Therefore religion is not, in our case, a faith in redemption from the world and its demands, but rather— and this has often been called the realism of Judaism —trust in the world or, to be more precise, the assurance of reconciliation. All reconciliation is the reconciliation of the day with eternity, of the limited with infinity, of that which is near with that which is distant, of existence with being, with that which is real and therefore shall be realized. Reconciliation is the liberating assurance that even now, during our life on earth, while we are coping with what is given and assigned, we are related to God. When we speak of the meaning of life, we have in mind such reconciliation. Wherever we find both mystery and commandment, we also encounter the possibility of such reconciliation; for there it is possible for man to become certain of his origin as well as of his way, and so turn back to devotion and to the task of his life—he can always return to himself. Reconciliation

and redemption are correlative here. Redemption here
is not redemption from the world, but in the world, consecration of the world, realization of the kingdom of
God. Mere redemption means that the spheres of mystery and commandment, of this world and the beyond,
are separated as two realms which are in a sense opposed to each other. Reconciliation, however, means that
they belong together and that everything is unified in
the one God. Whatever is beyond enters into this world,
and this world bears witness to the beyond. A sentence
in the Talmud exhibits the paradox which characterizes
Judaism: "One hour of returning to God and good deeds
in this world is more than all the life of the world to
come; one hour of peace in the world to come is more
than all the life of this world." The kingdom of God
comprehends everything: mystery and commandment,
the beyond and this world; it is the kingdom of reconciliation. "The whole world is full of His glory."

Thus religion is everything here. It permeates the
whole of life, carries the meaning of all days, and comprehends the meaning of all ways. There is nothing left
that could be called mere "world," and nothing set aside
as basically merely "everyday"; there is no mere prose
of existence. That which is seemingly commonplace
speaks, too, with a voice that comes from the depths;
and all prose is also a parable and speaks of that which
is concealed. Religion here is nothing isolated, nothing
that is shut off; it does not exist only alongside our life
or only under or above our life. There is no mystery
outside of life and no life outside the commandment.
Even all solitude is the solitude of life and has its place
in the social sphere. Again there is a unity even in opposition. The depth of life always leads to solitude because
it leads us away from the merely human to God; and
the task of life leads us into the social realm because it

181

is to be fulfilled by man among men. Yet every commandment should issue from the depths of the self, from that solitude in which the human is surrounded by the divine and in which man perceives the voice of God; and all depth, all solitude is here meant to be the beginning of that way on which the commandment guides us and where we hear the voice of our fellow men. And all thinking of God and searching for God, too, places us in the midst of life. Knowledge of God is not the conclusion of some speculation or the end of some ecstasy, but the ethical, the commandment, something demanded and demanding, a challenge to man's personality. The prophetic dictum places it alongside faithfulness and love. It is owned by piety, by humble reverence for the Lord, by the fair of God. "Behold, the fear of God is wisdom."

As soon as we understand these traits and trends of Jewish religion, we can also comprehend that which many would consider its only aspect: the profusion of rules and customs with which the community surrounds itself, its so-called Law. In Judaism the attempt has been made to give life its style by causing religion to invade every day and penetrate the whole of everyday. Everything is in a sense divine service and has its mood and its dignity. In the view of the earthly, the spirit is to be safeguarded; and in the view of the desire, the freedom is to be kept. Judaism cannot do without this ascetic trait unless it wants to forego all that is inward and religious. It does not lead man out of his everyday world, but relates him to God within it. Every partition of life into the profane and the sacred is to be avoided, and the sanctuary dare not possess merely one day beside all the other days. The word "remember" is inscribed above this law: "That you may remember and do all my commandments and be holy unto your God."

Thoughtlessness is the true Godlessness; it is the home-lessness of the soul. And the Law would guard man against this state in which he is without mystery and commandment; it would give every surface its symbolic function and every bit of prose its parable. Every man is to be made the priest of his own life. Therefore are we confronted with such an abundance of customs, ar-rangements, and orders which surround everything, "when thou sittest in thy house, and when thou walkest by the way, and when thou liest down, and when thou risest up"—all the way to the ample prose of eating and drinking. All this has helped to consecrate the day and especially also the evening; and it is in his evenings perhaps even more than in his days that man really lives, and it is in his evenings that he dies. A form of life has been fashioned here, though it is, of course, not entirely free from the danger which confronts every style of life: it may cease to be something personal and alive and degenerate into something purely external, into mere tradition. The "Law," too, has sometimes been degraded in this way: that which was meant to be consecration has at times become a mere routine, the fulfillment of something handed down. But even then it was preferable to pure lack of style. And it contains the power of always coming to life again and retrieving its soul.

The whole love of the "Law" has been lavished on and has cherished the Sabbath. As the day of rest, it gives life its balance and rhythm; it sustains the week. Rest is something entirely different from a mere recess, from a mere interruption of work, from not working. A recess is something essentially physical, part of the earthly everyday sphere. Rest, on the other hand, is essentially religious, part of the atmosphere of the divine; it leads us to the mystery, to the depth from which all commandments come, too. It is that which re-creates and reconciles, the recreation in which the soul, as it were, creates itself again and catches its breath of life—that in life which is sabbatical. The Sabbath is the image of the messianic; it proclaims the creation and the future; it is the great symbol. In the words of the Bible, it is "a sign between God and Israel"; or, in the words of the Talmud, it is "the parable of eternity." In the Sabbath, life possesses the great contradiction of any end, a perpetual renaissance. A life without Sabbath would lack the spring of renewal, that which opens the well of the depth again and again. An essential and fruitful aspect of Judaism would dry up in such a life; it could still be an ethical life, but it would lack that which defines the Jewish life. Therefore the Jewish community clings to the Sabbath as its possession in spite of all civic difficulties and troubles. The care for the Sabbath is one of the fundamental cares of Judaism.

The Law, and quite especially the sabbatical element in it, has educated that capacity in man which is born only of the depth of life—the capacity to be different. Without this, life cannot be unique. Whoever experiences mystery and commandment becomes unique among men, different, an individual within the world. Whoever knows only mystery becomes merely unique and knows only the day of silence. Whoever knows only the tasks is only among men and knows only the days of work and times of recess. But whoever experiences both, both in unity, lives in the world and yet is different, is different and yet is in the world, lives for other men and with other men and yet within himself, within himself and yet also for other men and hence also with them. This is the gift and possession of Judaism. And

184

it may well be its historic task to offer this image of the dissenter, who dissents for humanity's sake.

It is one of the capacities of religion to sustain, to conserve; and the old spirit of China created a religion in this sense—but only in this sense. Elsewhere we find that it is also one of the capacities of religion to assuage and to still, to teach denying and diverting; and the soul of India was able to do this—and this alone. The distinctive feature of Judaism—and its history also lives on in those religions which issued from it either immediately or mediately—is the power to liberate and renew, this messianic energy. Wherever Jewish piety is found, we encounter this strong drive to create, to fashion for the sake of God, to build the kingdom of God. We encounter this urge to exhibit the strength which is derived from the source of all things, from that which is beyond all strength; we encounter this decision which grows only in the man who knows mystery, not to bow and not to yield, to speak out and contradict. This demanding faith, this demand prompted by faith, is encountered where the soul experiences its depth and its task, that which is concealed and that which is evident, each in the other and each through the other. It is found in the religion of paradox and reconciliation, that religion which lives on the strength of the unity of mystery and commandment in the soul of man.

5

ROMANTIC RELIGION

If we classify types of piety in accordance with the
manner in which they have historically become types
of religion, then we encounter two forms above all:
classical and romantic religiousness, classical and romantic religion. The distinction and opposition between
these two types is exemplified especially by two phenomena of world history. One of these, to be sure, is
connected with the other by its origin and hence remains determined by it within certain limits; and yet
the significant dividing line separates them clearly.
These two religions are Judaism and Christianity. In
essential respects they confront each other as the classical religion and the romantic religion.

What is the meaning of romantic? Friedrich Schlegel
has characterized the romantic book in these words:
"It is one which treats sentimental material in a phantastic form." In almost exactly the same words one
might also characterize romantic religion. Tense feelings supply its content, and it seeks its goals in the now

189

mythical, now mystical visions of the imagination. Its world is the realm in which all rules are suspended; it is the world of the irregular, the extraordinary and the miraculous, that world which lies beyond all reality, the remote which transcends all things.

We can observe this disposition of the soul in relative historical proximity when we consider the German romantic of the last century. For him, everything dissolves into feeling; everything becomes mere mood; everything becomes subjective; "thinking is only a dream of feeling." Feeling is considered valid as such; it represents the value of life which the enthusiastic disposition wants to affirm. The romantic becomes enraptured and ecstatic for the sake of ecstasy and rapture; this state becomes for him an end in itself and has its meaning within itself. His whole existence is transformed into longing—not into the longing for God, in which man, raising himself above the earth, overcomes his earthly solitude; nor into the powerful longing of the will which thirsts for deeds; but into that sweet wavelike longing which pours itself out into feelings and becomes intoxicated with itself. Suffering and grief, too, become a good to him, if only the soul is submerged in them. He revels in his agonies as much as in his raptures.

Thus something agitated and excited, something overheated or intoxicated easily enters the feelings— and not only the feelings, but the language, too. Every expression seeks to excel in this direction; voluptuousness becomes a much sought-after word. The feelings talk in terms of superlatives; everything has to be made ecstatic. Fervently, the romantic enjoys the highest delight and the deepest pain almost day after day; he enjoys the most enchanting and the most sublime; he enjoys his wounds and the streaming blood of his heart.

Everything becomes for him an occasion of enraptured shuddering, even his faith, even his devotion. Thus Novalis praises his Christianity for being "truly the religion of voluptuousness."

These souls can always be so full of feeling because their abundant suffering is, for the most part, only reverie and dream; almost all of it is merely sentimental suffering. They like so much to dream; the dim distances, twilight and moonlit night, the quiet, flickering hours in which the magic flower lowers its blossoming head, represent the time for which they are wearily waiting. They love the soft, the sweet illusion, the beautiful semblance; and whereas Lessing had said to God, "Give me the wrestling for the truth," the romantics implore, "Accord me lovely illusions." They want to dream, not see; they shun the distinctness of what is clearly beheld in the light, to the very point of antipathy against fact. Disgruntled they confront reality; and in its stead they seek the less clear attraction of fluctuating feelings to the point of outright delight in confusion. What is within and without becomes for them a semblance and a glimmer, resounding and ringing, a mere mythical game; and the world becomes a sadly beautiful novel, an experience to be felt. As Hegel once put it: "The sense for content and substance contracts into a formless weaving of the spirit within itself."

The desire to yield to illusion, justifiable in art, here characterizes the entire relation to the world. In the deliberately sought-out twilight of longing and dream, the border lines of poetry and life are effaced. Reality becomes mere mood; and moods, eventually, the only reality. Everything, thinking and poetry, knowledge and illusion, all here and all above, flows together into a foaming poem, into a sacred music, into a great transfiguration, an apotheosis. In the end, the floods should close over the soul, while all and nothing become one, as the grandson of the romantics celebrates it:

> "In the sea-like rapture's billowy swell,
> In the roaring waves of a drowsy smell,
> In the world-breath's flowing all—
> To drown—
> To sink down—
> Unconsciousness—
> Highest bliss."

In this ecstatic abandonment, which wants so much to be seized and embraced and would like to pass away in the roaring ocean of the world, the distinctive character of romantic religion stands revealed—the feminine trait that marks it. There is something passive about its piety; it feels so touchingly helpless and weary; it wants to be seized and inspired from above, embraced by a flood of grace which should descend upon it to consecrate it and possess it—a will-less instrument of the wondrous ways of God. When Schleiermacher, defined religion as "the feeling of absolute dependence," he condensed this attitude into a formula.

Romanticism therefore lacks any strong ethical impulse, any will to conquer life ethically. It has an antipathy against any practical idea which might dominate life, demanding free, creative obedience for its commandments and showing a clearly determined way to the goals of action. Romanticism would like to "recover from purpose." All law, all that legislates, all morality with its commandments is repugnant to it; it would rather stay outside the sphere of good and evil; the highest ideal may be anything at all, except the distinct demands of ethical action. From all that urges and admonishes, the romantic turns away. He wants to dream, enjoy, immerse himself, instead of clearing his

192

way by striving and wrestling. That which has been and rises out of what is past occupies him far more than what is to become and also more than what wants to become; for the word of the future would always command. Experiences with their many echoes and their billows stand higher in his estimation than life with its tasks; for tasks always establish a bond with harsh reality. And from this he is in flight. He does not want to struggle against fate, but rather to receive it with an ardent and devout soul; he does not want to wrestle for his blessing, but to experience it, abandoning himself, devoid of will, to what spells salvation and bliss. He wants no way of his own choosing. For the romantic the living deed is supplanted by the grace whose vessel he would be; the law of existence, by mere faith; reality, by the miracle of salvation. He wants to exist, without having an existence of his own; he wants less to live than to experience—or, to use the German, he prefers *erleben* to *leben*.

Therefore the romantic "personality" is also something totally different from, say, the Kantian personality who confronts us as the bearer of the moral law and who finds himself, and thus his freedom, in being faithful to the commandment. The romantic, too, loves his own being; but he seeks this individuality in the fluid world of his feelings which, capable of the quasi miraculous, can enter into everything and mean everything. Only out of this emotional experience, which becomes for him the measure of all things, does he derive what is good and evil for him. It is not through ethical action and not through clear knowledge that he expects to find the way to himself. He believes that he can become certain of himself only in self-contained feeling, in emotional self-contemplation which does not give expression to the emotions but dwells on them and all-too-easily becomes sheer virtuosity of feeling, admiring itself in the mirror of introspection and preening its own beautiful soul. There is, therefore, no more unromantic remark than Goethe's when he says that man comes to know himself by doing his duty and living up to the demands of the day. The romantics say instead: experience yourself and revel in yourself.

It is for these reasons that romanticism is usually oriented backwards, that it has its ideal in bygone ages, in the paradise of the past. It does not want to create but to find again and restore. After all, whoever prefers to feel and dream soon sees himself surrounded by ancient images; and only those who direct their will toward fixed tasks know themselves to be standing in a living relationship to the future. Therefore it is also given to romanticism to hearken to the voices from former times. Romanticism is especially qualified for this because, with its abundance of emotion, it is capable of reflecting all the recesses and mysteries of the human soul and to feel its way into different individualities. It has discovered the poetry of transitions, also the poetry of the divisions and clefts of the soul; it has known how to comprehend the radiation that emanates from the individual phenomenon and has cultivated the devotion to what is minute. Man with his contradictions is its subject. Hence romanticism has produced the artists of biography and cultivated the kind of history which demands empathy. But only this kind; it has not shown much vision regarding over-all connections or the ideas of the centuries. Romanticism remains lyrical even when it contemplates the seriousness of great events, and history becomes for it a game in which one becomes absorbed. One will here look in vain for the great message of the past. The strength and weakness of emotion determines the power and the impotence of romanticism.

It is the same everywhere. It is always feeling that is supposed to mean everything. Hence the capacity for feeling defines the dimensions and the limits of romanticism. We see this at close range in its representatives of the last century with their merits and their weaknesses. In opposition to the exclusive rule of the sober understanding, romanticism had legitimately demanded another right and another value. But romanticism itself soon fell victim to the same fundamental mistake which it had arisen to combat; for almost immediately it, too, claimed exclusive validity. It elevated pure feeling above everything else, above all conceptual and all obligatory truth—and eventually not only above everything else but in place of everything else. It strove to drown in beautiful illusion more and more of reality with its commandment, and to let the profound seriousness of the tasks of our life fade into a mere musical mood, to let them evaporate into the floating spheres of existence.

It gave its name to a whole generation in the last century; and yet romanticism is not applicable merely to a particular epoch, to a mere period of history. Romanticism means much more: it designates one of the characteristic forms which have emerged again and again in the development of mankind—a certain type in which, from time immemorial, religious life in particular has manifested itself. To be sure, historical types, just like human types, never appear quite pure. Whatever exists is a mixture; nowhere does life know sharp boundaries and distinctions; it is never an equation without any remainder. There are certain romantic elements in every religion, no less than in every human soul. Every religion has its dream of faith in which

195

appearance and reality seek to mingle; each has its own twilight valley; each knows of world-weariness and contempt for the factual. But in one religion this is merely a quiet path alongside the road, a sound which accompanies, a tone which also vibrates. In another religion it fixes the direction; it is the dominant basic chord which determines the religious melody and gives it its character. Thus, depending on whether this or a wholly different motif is the decisive one, the romantic religion distinguishes itself quite clearly from the classical. And in this sense it may be said: Judaism is the classical religion and Christianity, compared with it, the romantic religion.

PAUL

Christianity accepted the inheritance of ancient— Greek and oriental—romanticism. At an early date, the traditional national religion in the Hellenic lands had been joined by a victorious intruder, probably from the north: another religion—darker, phantastic and sentimental—the Dionysian or Orphic cult of which much might be said, but certainly not: "What distinguished the Greeks? Reason and measure and clarity." It had all the traits of romanticism: the exuberance of emotion, the enthusiastic flight from reality, the longing for an experience. Holy consecrations and atonements were taught and ecstatically tasted with reeling senses. They aimed to relate man to the beyond; they aimed to make him one with the god and thus grant him redemption from primordial sin and original guilt. For this, it was said, could not be attained by mortal man with his own power, but must be a gift of grace which had to descend from hidden regions and to which a mediator and savior, a god, who once had walked on earth had

shown the way. Marvelous traditions told of this and
handed on the stories of the redeeming events and their
mysteries, that they might be renewed again and again
in the believers. Mystical music dramas, showy, phantastic presentations, seemingly removed into mysterious distances by the twilight, granted the weary,
drowsy soul the beautiful dream, and the sentimental
longing its fulfillment: the faith that it belonged to
the elect.

In the official religion, this wish of the individual to
be chosen and to stand before the god, this individual
desire to be important and attain eternal life and bliss,
had not found satisfaction. Now all this was offered to
him by this enthusiastic religion of moods. And thus it
was that this religion found its way more and more into
the souls; it became the new religion which gradually
decomposed the old naïve faith and the classical spirit
of the Greeks, and eventually destroyed it.

Moreover, it had received further strength from all
sides, wherever religious romanticism had a home:
from the oriental and Egyptian mysteries, from the
cults of Mithras and Adonis, of Attis and Serapis. In
essentials they were all alike: they shared the sentimental attitude which seeks escape from life into living
experience and turns the attention towards a phantastic
and marvelous beyond. What they proclaimed, too, was
at bottom always the same. It was the faith in a heavenly being that had become man, died, and been resurrected, and whose divine life a mortal could share
through mysterious rites; the faith in a force of grace,
entering the believer from above through a sacrament,
to redeem him from the bonds of earthly guilt and
earthly death and to awaken him to a new life which
would mean eternal existence and blessedness. The
roving yearning of a weary age was only too ready to

become absorbed in these conceptions of resurrection
and apotheosis, of instruments of grace and consecrations; and it even sought them out everywhere. From
all lands the mysteries could flow together in mighty
waves.

The tide moved along a free and wide course. The
region from the Euphrates to the Atlantic Ocean had
under Roman rule become the place of a matchless
mixture of peoples fused into a cultural unity. Just like
the ancient states, the old pagan religions, too, had
more and more lost their boundaries and their former
definiteness. A cosmopolitan yearning and hope gripped
and united all of them. The way was prepared for a
new faith without limits or boundaries. In the world-
wide empire it could become the world religion and the
world philosophy. Whatever it was that a human being
might seek, it promised everything to everybody—mystery and knowledge, ecstasy and vision, living experience and eternity. It was everything and took the place
of everything and therefore finally overcame everything. The great romantic tide thus swept over the
Roman empire, and the ancient world drowned in it.
Even as the old naïve poetry of the gods perished in the
sentimental myth of the redeeming savior, so what was
classical vanished, along with its sure sense of law and
determination, and gave way to the mere feeling of a
faith which was sufficient unto itself.

What is called the victory of Christianity was in
reality this victory of romanticism. Before Christianity
took its course, that through which it eventually became Christianity—or, to put it differently, whatever
in it is non-Jewish—had already become powerful
enough to be reckoned as a world faith, as a new piety
which united the nations. The man with whose name
this victory is connected, Paul, was, like all romantics,

not so much a creator of ideas as a connector of ideas;
the genius of seeing and establishing such connections
was characteristic of him. He must be credited with one
achievement—and this single achievement was of
world-historical significance and truly something great
—that he carried living Jewish ideas into the mysteries
which even then commanded the allegiance of a whole
world. He knew how to fuse the magic of the universal
mysteries with the tradition of revelation of the
secrecy-wrapt Jewish wisdom. Thus he gave the ancient
romanticism a new and superior power—a power taken
from Judaism. It was this blend, compounded by him,
that the world of the dying Roman empire—Orient and
Occident, which had become one world—accepted.

In Paul's own soul, this union in which romantic and
Jewish elements were to be combined, had prevailed
after a period of transition. Subjectively, this union
represented the story of his struggles which became the
story of his life. The images of his homeland, Asia
Minor, had early revealed to him the one element, romanticism; the parental home and the years of his
studies had presented him with the other, the Jewish
one. Then, in the land of his people, he had found those
who longingly awaited the helper and liberator of whom
the prophets had spoken—some hoping that he might
come, others waiting that he might return. Eventually
he discovered himself among those who were thus waiting—those whose eyes were fixed on the image of their
messiah, their Christ, who had died young and would
return when his day came—an image similar in many
of its features to that offered by his pagan homeland in
its mysteries. The pagans in those days were aware of
Judaism; and Jews, too, paid attention to the thinking
and seeking of paganism. Thus the promises and wisdom from here and there, from paganism and from

Judaism, entered into his unrest and doubts which
pulled him hither and thither, looking and listening
far and wide, in his craving for the certainty of truth.
He did not want merely to wait and hope; he wished it
might be given him to have and to believe.

Finally he had perceived an answer. It was a victorious and liberating answer to his mind because it did
not merely grant a coming, a promised, day, something
yet to be, but a redemption which was fulfilled even
then—as it were, a Now. This answer became for him
the end which meant everything because it contained
everything: both that of which the mysteries of the
nations had told him and that which the proclamations
of his own Jewish people had said to him. Alongside the
one God before whom the gods of the pagans were to
vanish, it now placed the one redeemer, the one savior
before whom the saviors of the nations could sink out
of sight: it placed the oneness of the savior alongside
the oneness of God. Thus he experienced it: paganism,
with its deepest aspirations and thoughts, was led to
Judaism; and Judaism, with its revelation and truth,
was bestowed on the pagans, too.

Now everything seemed to fall into place. What his
Judaism had let him find in the circle of those waiting,
in the proclamation of the messianic faith, as the fulfillment and goal of all prophecy, this faith in the final answer, in the final certainty, in him who had come and
would come—all this he discovered now in the quest of
the pagans; all this he perceived when he contemplated
the myth which the marvelous mysteries everywhere
presented to the world. And where confused strains out
of the pagan world had spoken to him of the mysterious
tidings of grace, in which a whole world had created for
itself the satisfaction of its yearnings, his own people's
faith in a messiah now permitted him to comprehend

200

quite clearly all that had till then seemed so dark. Now
he grasped it: not Attis or Adonis, not Mithras or
Serapis was the name of the resurrected, the savior,
who became man and had been god, but his name was
Jesus Christ. And the significance of Jesus, who had
become the Christ of his people, could not be that he
had become king of the Jews, their king by the grace
of God, their admonisher, comforter, and helper; but
his life and his power signified the one, the greatest,
thing, that he was the resurrected, miracle-working,
redeeming God, he that had been from eternity. And for
all who owned him, who had faith in him and possessed
him in sacrament and mystery, the day that was promised had become today, had been fulfilled. In him Jew
and pagan were the new man, the true Israel, the true
present.

The last veil now seemed to Paul to have been taken
from his eyes, and he saw the hitherto divided world
unified. In the messianic certainty of Judaism he now
recognized the goal toward which the seeking and err-
ing of the pagans had, in the depths of truth, always
aspired; and in that which the pagans had wanted but
not known, he now grasped the content and the answer
which was spoken, which was promised to Judaism.
Judaism and paganism had now become one for him;
the one world had arrived which comprehended everything, the one body and the one spirit of all life. That
Jewish and pagan wisdom meant, at bottom, the same
thing, was one of the ideas of the age. Now it seemed
to have become the truth. Now the Jews need no longer
merely wait, as the community of the expectant, for the
last day, which would then in turn become the first day,
when the messiah would come or come again; in a mysterious sacrament, the fulfilled time in which everything has been accomplished, the goal of the longed-for

redemption, was given to them even now, given in every hour. And now the pagans really could come to know him for whom they had from time immemorial looked, the named but unknown; and now they could comprehend the mystery which had since ancient times been present among them as their precious possession. Judaism and paganism were now reconciled, brought together in romanticism, in the world of the mystery, of myth, and of sacrament.

Precisely how this net of ideas took shape in the mind of Paul, how the different threads found each other and crossed each other, which idea came first and which one it then attracted—to ask about this would merely lead to vain and useless speculation. Beginning with his childhood, Paul had been confronted both with the possession of Judaism in the parental home and with the sight of the mystery cults in his homeland. In his consciousness both had their place, and they were woven together and became one. This union which was fashioned in him then emerged out of him into the world. And it became victorious in a world which had become weary and sentimental; it became the religion for all those whose faint, anxious minds had darted hither and thither to seek strength. It represented the completion of a long development.

For what had been most essential in the ancient mysteries is preserved in this Pauline religion. It, too, believed in the romantic fate of a god which reflects the inexorable lot of man and is the content of all life. What everything represents is not a creation of God and not an eternal moral order, but a process of salvation. In a heavenly-earthly drama, in the miraculous mystery that took shape between the here and the above, the meaning of world history and of the individual human life stands revealed. There is no other word but the defi-

nite word "myth," romantic myth, to characterize this
form of faith. With this, Paul left Judaism; for there
was no place in it for any myth that would be more
than a parable—no more for the new sentimental one
than for the old naïve myths of former times. This
myth was the bridge on which Paul went over to romanticism. To be sure, this man had lived within Judaism deep down in his soul; and psychically he never
quite got away from it. Even after his conversion to
mystery and sacrament, he only too often found himself
again on the old Jewish ways of thought, as though
unconsciously and involuntarily; and the manifold contradictions between his sentences derive from this
above all. The Jew that he remained in spite of everything, at the bottom of his soul, again and again fought
with the romantic in him, whose moods and ideas were
ever present to him. But in spite of this, if we are to
label him as he stands before us, the apostle of a new
outlook, then we can only call him a romantic. Trait for
trait we recognize in his psychic type the features that
distinguish the romantic.

THE EXPERIENCE OF FAITH

Paul, too, sees everything—to use Schlegel's term—in
the "phantastic form" in which the border lines of appearance and reality, of twilight and event, are lost; in
which he sees images which the eye never saw and
hears words which the ear never perceived; in which
he can feel redeemed from this world and its harsh-
ness, from what is earthly in him and from what desires
to cling to the soil of this earth. Thus he lives in the
beyond which transcends all things, beyond the struggle
between upward drive and gravity, beyond becoming
and perishing, where only faith can reach and only

miracles can take place. Therefore faith is everything to him. Faith is grace, faith is salvation, faith is life, faith is truth; faith is being, the ground and the goal, the beginning and the end; commencement and vocation meet in it. Faith is valid for faith's sake. One feels reminded of the modern slogan, *l'art pour l'art*; Pauline romanticism might be labeled correspondingly, *la foi pour la foi*.

This faith is so completely everything that down here nothing can be done for it and nothing may be done for it; all "willing or running" is nonsensical and useless. The salvation that comes through faith is in no sense earned, but wholly received; and it comes only to those for whom it was destined from the beginning. God effects it, as Luther later explained the words of Paul, "in us and without us."[1] Man is no more than the mere object of God's activity, of grace or of damnation; he does not recognize God, God merely recognizes him; he *becomes* a child of redemption or of destruction, "forced into disobedience" or raised up to salvation. He is the object of virtue and of sin—not its producer, its subject. One feels like saying: man does not live but is lived, and what remains to him is merely, to speak with Schleiermacher, "the taste of infinity," that is, the living experience; the mood and the emotional relation of one who knows himself to be wholly an object; the feeling of faith in which grace is present or the feeling of unbelief in which sin prevails.

The theory of original sin and election, which Paul formulated after the manner of the ancient mystery doctrine and then shrouded in a biblical-talmudic dress, serves only to demonstrate the completeness of that

1. *in nobis et sine nobis.* Weimar edition, VI, 530 (*de capt. Babyl.*).

power which makes passivity—or, to say it again in the words of German romanticism, pure "helplessness" and "absolute dependence"—the lot of man. A supernatural destiny which, whether it be grace or damnation, is always a *fatum*, determines according to an inexorable law that a man should be thus or thus. He is pure object; fate alone is subject. In this way, religion becomes redemption from the will, liberation from the deed.

Later on, the Catholicism of the Middle Ages softened this conception and granted a certain amount of human participation. But Luther then returned to the purer romanticism of Paul with its motto, *sola fide*, through faith alone; "it must come from heaven and solely through grace."[2] The image which he supplies to illustrate this point is, quite in keeping with Luther's style, harsh in tone, and yet thoroughly Pauline in its meaning: *velut paralyticum*, "as one paralyzed,"[3] man should wait for salvation and faith. The heteronomy of life is thus formulated: the life of man has its law and its content only outside itself.

This faith is therefore decidedly not the expression of a conviction obtained through struggle, or of a certainty grown out of search and inquiry. Seeking and inquiring is only "wisdom of the flesh" and the manner of "philosophers and rabbis." True knowledge is not worked out by man but worked in him; man cannot clear a way toward it; only the flood of grace brings it to him and gives him the quintessence of knowledge, the totality of insight. Knowledge here is not what instructs but what redeems, and it is not gained by think-

2. Weimar edition, XXIV, 244.
3. *Ibid.*, II, 420: *oportet ergo hominem de suis operibus diffidere et velut paralyticum remissis manibus et pedibus gratiam operum artificem implorare.*

ing but given in faith; it goes with the consciousness of absolute dependence. "Do not seek, for to him who has faith all is given!" This is the new principle, the axiom of romantic truth; and all wrestling and striving for knowledge has thus lost its value and, what is more, its very meaning. There is no longer any place for the approximation of truth, step for step; there is no longer any middle ground between those who see everything and those who see nothing. Grace now gives complete light where up to now only darkness held the spirit in its embrace. Grace places man at the goal, and he is the perfect, the finished man.

The conception of the finished man which appears here—truly the brain child of romanticism for which truth is only a living experience—became one of the most effective ideas in the entire Pauline doctrine. It has again and again attracted and even permanently captivated those minds who would like so much to believe in their entire possession of the truth and who long for the rest which such complete possession would afford. Since the end of the ancient world, the intellectual life of the Occident has in many ways been determined by this notion. It has established that orientation in which the answer precedes every question, and every result comes before the task, and those appear who quite simply have what is wanted and who never want to become and grow.

The philosophy appropriate to this conception of the finished man is that doctrine which considers truth as given from the outset, that scholasticism which possesses and knows the whole truth, down to its ultimate ramifications, from the start and merely needs to proclaim it or to demonstrate it *ex post facto*. Most of the thought produced by the Catholic Middle Ages shows the influence of this conception. And Luther's world of

thought is completely dominated by it; for Luther clings
to the rigid faith in such possession and, in that sense,
to the Middle Ages.

Only the age of the Enlightenment began to push the
conception back, but it really made a beginning only.
For when romanticism re-awakened in the last century,
the conception returned with it, and it has survived
together with romanticism. It has, indeed, created what
might be called racial scholasticism, with its doctrine
of salvation, with its system of grace, and with its faith
that this grace works through the dark abysses of the
blood—this modernized *pneuma*—and gives the chosen
everything, so that the finished man is once again the
goal of the creation. Wherever romanticism is found,
this conception appears by its side.

The much quoted *credo quia absurdum*—"I believe
because it is absurd"—is nothing but the ultimate formulation which results from this conception, almost as
a matter of course. What confronts the inquiring spirit
and his thinking as something opposed to reason, and
unacceptable, may be the truth for the finished mind of
the completed man, whether he owes his completion
to grace or another source. To this faith knowledge
must submit. Sooner or later, every romanticism demands the *sacrificium intellectus*, the sacrifice of the
intellect. Here, too, the best commentary for Paul is
found in Luther's words: "In all who have faith in
Christ," he says, "reason shall be killed; else faith does
not govern them; for reason fights against faith."[4]

Unquestionably, the romantic certainty which Paul
proclaims is derived from an original psychic experience. When a strong idea emerges out of the hidden
darkness of the unconscious, where it had slowly and

4. Erlangen edition, 44, 156f.

silently taken shape, and all at once enters consciousness, it is always at first distinguished by the suddenness of the unexpected and seems to possess the power
of a revelation. As if it had been fashioned by a miracle,
as if the path of thought had not in this case been
covered step by step, truth seems to confront the mind
finished and completed; it appears to speak to him, and
he feels that he does not have to do anything but listen;
and the person who has this experience may have the
feeling that grace has descended upon him and elected
him. This is, after all, also one of the forms in which
the seeking genius may find his solution; it is, in the
words of a modern thinker, the romantic type of inven-
tion. And it is the same which confronts us in Goethe's
epigram: "In very small matters, much depends on
choice and will; the highest that we encounter comes
who knows from where." Something universally human
is expressed here.

Romanticism has had this experience very intensely
—so intensely that this one thing has become everything for it. Romanticism considers this experience, in
which man feels as if he were a mere instrument of
a higher power, not merely a great experience, but
the essence, the *whole* and the innermost content
of our existence. Romanticism takes particularly the
initial instant of reception, the power of that moment,
for the quintessence and fulfillment of all humanity.
Romantic magic becomes romantic truth.

The first moving impression with its mighty effect,
with its suggestive capacity for multiple interpretations, here becomes everything, and there frequently
remains no significance whatever for anything further,
and especially for one's personal life's work. Instead of
any positive judgment, there is merely hostile melancholy which accuses life for not continuously furnishing

such high-pitched experiences. The relation is clear. Once the intoxication of this excitement has become the meaning of life, nothing remains, confronted with sober and harsh existence, except pessimism to which all reality becomes strange and hostile; *Welttrunkenheit* and *Weltschmerz*, this intoxication and this melancholy belong together.

This kind of absorption is dominant in every romanticism. Hence the jumpy and disconnected character of its thinking, the aphoristic, fragmentary style which is, for this reason, prominent in the Pauline exposition, too. And the stamp of this attitude which determines everything—this is a further misfortune implicit in it—can regrettably be of many different kinds: it can be ever so high and ever so shallow, most powerful or utterly hollow. It can be the strong impression of the hour, but also—much more frequently—a merely momentary, empty conceit of a mind eager, even greedy, for sensation. It can be genuine, but it can also be spurious; the psychic experience which overcomes a human being or the wish for artificial excitement with which those craving emotion spur on their feelings and senses. And here as there, this impression would count as everything and be received as a datum of faith, immune against doubt and rational examination.

It is the right of art to consider an impression valid simply as an impression and to accept it as something entire and complete without critical scrutiny. Art is, as Schopenhauer puts it, "everywhere at its goal." But for life, and hence surely also for religion, there is a danger, the romantic danger, in making the impression of an experience all-important. For then the sense for the content and commandment of life must all too soon evaporate together with any sense for reality with its definite tasks; and the place of all aspiration and exertion will be taken over by the sole dominion of the mood of faith which simply feels itself, and then finds it easy to deem itself, complete. This is faith for faith's sake.

For the romantic, the impression, the mood, that which comes over the human being, is everything. This determines his artistic bent, too. In the Pauline, as in any romantic religion we can clearly observe it. The component of faith and revelation, of transport and ecstasy—that which is, as it were, a psychic reception of religion, a religious consecration or even seizure— is here taken for the fulfillment of religion, for ultimate truth and perfection. No religion will want to do without openness to the profound, the hidden, the secret, the miracle of revelation, the experience of faith; this is the mystery of religion, that in it which gives birth. But for all it suggests and proclaims and bestows—and often this function could be found nowhere else—it still is not all of religion or even all of religiosity, any more than it is all there is to prayer, any more than mood as such supplies content, any more than birth is equivalent to life. The romantically pious, however, finds this suffi- cient and considers it everything. For he is a man of lofty sentiment who is capable of feeling and knows how to pray, but often does not get beyond feeling and prayer; the type which so easily remains on the thresh- old to receive everything there. His whole religion is merely a receiving; and therefore he finds it always so easy to think that he has finished his task. His faith remains purely passive; it is not faith in the challeng- ing, commanding law of God, but merely in the gift of divine grace. Activity fights for everything; passivity has everything. There demands are made; here every- thing is given; even the love of man which is glorified in romantic religion is merely the gift of grace which is the share of those who have faith. The only activity of the genuine romantic is self-congratulation on his state of grace.

One might characterize the Pauline religion in sharp juxtapositions: absolute dependence as opposed to the commandment, the task, of achieving freedom; leaning as opposed to self-affirmation and self-development; quietism as opposed to dynamism. There the human being is the subject; here, in romantic religion, the object. The freedom of which it likes so much to speak is merely a freedom received as a gift, the granting of salvation as a fact, not a goal to be fought for. It is the faith that does not go beyond itself, that is not the task of life; only a "thou hast" and not a "thou shalt." In classical religion, man is to become free through the commandment; in romantic religion he has become free through grace.

CULTURE AND HISTORY

It is therefore no accident that peoples with a live sense of independence have turned, consciously and unconsciously, toward the paths of classical religion—increasingly so as their sense of independence grew in strength. The history of Calvinistic, Baptist piety with its affinity to the Old Testament, its "legalistic" orientation, and its ethical stress on proving oneself, shows this clearly. And it was the same story wherever the social conscience stirred; it, too, had to effect this reversion, for it, too, runs counter to romantic religion. The social conscience finds romantic religion repugnant because it is at bottom a religious egoism; all passivity is a kind of selfishness, a desire for enjoyment; in it the individual knows only himself and what God or life is to bring him, but not the commandment, not the mutual demands of men.

In the religious activity demanded by classical religion, man finds himself directed toward others; in mere religious experience, in this devotion devoid of any commandment, he seeks everything in himself. He is concerned only with himself, satisfied with himself, concentrated on himself to the point of religious vanity, of a coquettishness of faith. Thus Nietzsche, in his superlative manner, once described this type: "He is terribly preoccupied with himself; he has no time to think of others." Nothing could be more opposed to the aspirations of a social conscience than this romantic piety which always seeks only itself and its salvation.

Romantic religion is completely opposed to the whole sphere of existence with which the social conscience is concerned. Every romanticism depreciates the life devoted to work and culture, that context of life which the active human being creates for himself and in which he knows himself in relation to others. Where life disintegrates into momentary moods, as in romanticism, and where living experience alone—the instant, in other words—is recognized as essential, while everything else appears merely as "the void between the instants," work will always be counted only as something lowly, or at least as something subordinate. Mere living experience, the instant, is the contradiction of work. Hence romanticism cannot gain any clear and positive relation to work. It is not a mere poetic whim but representative of the very flesh and blood of romanticism when Friedrich Schlegel sings the praise of leisure, of romantic sloth, and "sleep is the highest degree of genius" for him. All this is nothing else than that passivity of romanticism which would rather dream than work.

This defect has become most calamitous for romantic *religion*. As soon as it entered an area of cultural activity and was to be *inside* it and not just alongside, it had to find itself divided against itself: work was depreciated and yet had to be demanded. The history of medieval Catholic ethics with all its dualism, with its distinction between earthly and heavenly vocation, with the "commandments" and "counsels" it offered, manifests this contradiction. Nor was Luther able to overcome it. To be sure, he raised the estimation of worldly work. But to begin with, he got to this point only by the way of negation, through his opposition to an idle monkhood. And as soon as he looked for a positive appreciation of work, he was unable, here, too, to get beyond the Pauline conception of absolute dependence. For him the earthly sphere of existence and work, in which man is placed after all, is a decree from above, to which man must resign himself in humility and obedience; caste and guild represent a firm barrier which must not be tampered with, because it has been erected by God. For any upward social drive Luther lacked any sense or sympathy whatever: the conception of a God-given dependency and of the subordination of social classes as a divine institution is thoroughly Lutheran. Only Calvinism—in this respect, too, returning closer to Judaism—began to recognize more clearly that there is a liberating, ethical power in worldly work and that the rights and aims of civilian occupations manifest an upward drive.

Hence romantic religion also lacks any inner compulsion to approach political and economic life in order to make it more ethical and to drive it forward. Its indifference toward any earthly upward tendency has always made it easy for romantic religion to defend submission to every earthly yoke, even to preach it. From the Pauline exhortation, "Let every soul be subject unto the higher powers,"[5] one has always and with the greatest of ease got to the point of first tolerating every despotism and of then soon consecrating it. This Pauline doctrine, too, was taken especially seriously by Luther and those who followed him. Consider the silent coldness with which the Protestant Church of Germany endured, for example, serfdom and traffic in human beings.

Much as was demanded of the state ecclesiastically, little was asked from it morally. One did not have to ask anything. The romantic principle of the finished and completed was in any case opposed to any upward drive, and the romantic mood came to terms with everything that was low. One can have a strong faith and pious experiences without being disturbed by slavery, torture, and public horrors. The feeling of absolute dependence which is sensitive to sacred music is not disturbed by any of this. Already the ancient mystery religion got along very well with tyrants, and these in turn were very well disposed toward it, because they could easily see that the devotee of supernatural events is an obedient subject on the earth below. It has been ever thus, and episodes of Jewish romanticism attest it, too. The alliance between ruler and believer has been readily formed wherever romantic religion has held sway; every reaction has been consecrated and every forward drive been damned.

The problem of culture cannot be solved under a romantic religion. A romantic religion can either be *against* culture, desiring to recognize nothing beside

.

5. The passage (Romans 13, 1-2) continues: "For there is no power but of God: the powers that be are ordained of God. Whosoever therefore resisteth the power, resisteth the ordinance of God: and they that resist shall receive to themselves damnation." *Tr.*

214

itself—and this we observe in the history of Catholicism as also in the history of the Protestant Middle Ages which reach into the eighteenth century—or stand *beside* culture with a feeling of perplexity and a sense of being divided against itself. This second alternative we recognize in modern Protestantism, which must always cease to be Pauline and Lutheran as soon as it would truly enter the social sphere; and perhaps the clearest example of this is found in Naumann's *Letters concerning Religion.* Living culture always remains something extraneous to romantic religion—either because one fights it, as happens in the first case, or because no straight and clear-cut road leads to it, as in the second.

Many phenomena which seem to refute these assertions are merely the exceptions which confirm the rule; for they have grown on the Old Testament soil of Calvinism and Baptism. From there, too, came the Protestant social movement. The genuinely romantic Pauline faith with its heteronomy of life, with the passivity on which it is founded, can confront a culture only as an outsider without any real access to it—particularly a culture with a live social consciousness, one which finds inspiration and strength in the commandment which bids man not to stop short of cultural realization. This faith cannot as a matter of principle do justice to the tasks which the social conscience imposes on man; it can do so only *ex post facto.*

Nor are these considerations contradicted by the concept of Christian culture which has dominated so many centuries. This concept was a necessary result: for syncretism, the desire to fuse everything, is characteristic of romanticism. Romanticism wants to mean all things and hence seeks to blend all the areas of human and superhuman existence, to pull them together into a universal circle, a universal state, a universal art, a universal faith; hence, being unable to confront culture with religious tasks and goals, it always wanted to, and had to, merge faith and culture, or mistake one for the other. But quite apart from the harm done to the religious element, culture has thus always lost something of its individuality. Bereft of the commandment of freedom and of its own demanding worth, restricted within a faith which was to mean and determine everything, culture could often preserve very little of itself. Even as the relation of romantic religion to science became one in which the latter had to make the sacrifice of intellect, so the romantic union with culture gave rise to a situation in which the very task of culture, its right of development, its right to seek new possibilities, was taken away from it. In Christian culture, culture was deprived of much that belonged to it; and what prevailed under this name during the Middle Ages was—however great and wonderful—essentially an admittedly imposing ecclesiastical homogeneity, an unlimited expansion of the internal and external spheres of ecclesiastical power. All life was within the Church and its bright splendor; and only what could live there lived at all.

Only the modern age—that age which first began with the Renaissance, waned, and then re-awakened in the century of the Enlightenment—has once again restored to culture, at least in many countries, the rights which are properly its own. To be sure, it has often been claimed, even by Ranke, that the Reformation had brought this freedom about. But later, more exact research has shown this claim to be erroneous. However important Luther's work was, insofar as he destroyed the sole rule of the one universal Church over Europe, in his own thinking he still belonged clearly to the

Middle Ages. He still belonged to that age, not so much because of his scholastic theology, but above all because he shared the aspiration to dominate and shape culture ecclesiastically. The culture of the Reformation, too, was nothing other than the medieval Christian one, the extensive culture of constraint; it had a smaller sphere, both in space and in content, but the same ambition. Later, when culture faced a clear and open road again, it became worldly and hence also un-Protestant, both in its genesis and its character. It was able to prevail only by fighting the Church, the Protestant Church just as much as the Catholic. It was derived not from Luther and his work but from the men and tendencies against which Luther had contended most violently. Only when the culture which he had taught began becoming a thing of the past, could the new age commence.

Only then could the classical, ethical idea of history be regained—this idea of becoming, of the never-quite-finished, of the directed ascent. This idea, too, could have no place in the medieval, romantic sphere of thought; for it, too, depends on an understanding for the collaboration and community of aspiring, questing persons and on the recognition of human work and activity, as well as of human errors and failures as a path to the way which represents the commandment. According to this idea, the goal lies ever again in the distance at the end of a road. For romanticism, which repudiates any step by step progression, the goal is already given and perfected; it is only a gift by divine grace, not the task of human activity also; the fulfilled time corresponds to the finished man.

However much romanticism lives in the past and re-experiences it, it still cannot attain the idea of history as a power which makes demands on human life, nor can it do justice to this idea. One might put it this way, juxtaposing two German terms: romanticism does not know *Geschichte,* living history, but only *Historie,* dead history—a mere story. Romanticism deals with the past, not as something that is in the process of becoming, but as something finished which requires nothing but empathy. It knows nothing of the great message which demands further struggles for the days to come; it knows only what had been decreed as the universal end. It always feels as if it had been born belatedly. This alone would be reason enough why culture could not have any place in romanticism; it could only be a completed culture, and that is a contradiction in terms, for true culture must demand ever new possibilities.

It is thus typically romantic when the Christian Church claims that what is most essential in all events was terminated with a particular occurrence, the life and death of Jesus, and so lets the entire religious ideal be fulfilled once and for all in a single extraordinary existence. This one event becomes the absolute, the unsurpassable event in all history, and whatever comes later can be judged only in accordance with its attitude toward this one event. It becomes the quintessence of religion, that one becomes absorbed in the incomparable event which once occurred and tries to re-experience it. The past is turned into dogma.

This essentially unhistorical attitude toward history is particularly evident in modern Protestantism; indeed, here above all, because a completed story is almost all that remains to it. After it has given up most dogmas, a completed story remains almost its only axiom of faith. The question of the "unique" personality of Jesus becomes for it the question of the very existence of religion. All its exertions and aspirations must be directed again and again toward some kind of historical evidence for this one particular life, to counter

the ever new objections. All its striving and efforts are
thus a perpetual restoration, an ever renewed attempt
to present the one event of the past in a fitting style;
restoration is, after all, a romantic enterprise. The relation to religion becomes a relation to a story.

Thus a proved or contested sequence of facts—in
Lessing's sense, something accidental—becomes decisive for the fulfillment of religion; faith is made dependent on the certification of a story. To be sure, it is
also characteristic of the genuinely historical revealed
religion that it knows about the mystery of the beginning and picks a single event out of the past to determine the course of truth. Yet it makes an essential
difference whether, as in this case, a *beginning* is
posited or, as in the Pauline religion, the absolute goal
and the ultimate fulfillment. In the one case, the idea of
further creative activity is posited, or at least admitted;
in the other, it is rejected from the outset. In both religions we find a statement how things came about; but
in the one, what is thus given is a beginning which
points beyond itself into the future; in the other, what
is given is the end which meant everything and decided
everything. Classical religion knows living history;
romantic religion only a finished story.

The most that life can offer thus becomes for Pauline
religion a repose in the "fulfilled time." Movement and
becoming appears as an alienation from religion, an
alienation from the faith which is everything. What is
good is here characterized by repose; and what has a
history, is the ungodly and anti-godly. The Kingdom of
God which always remains the same may have some
sequence in time, a chronology, but no living history;
the latter appears only as the pressure of the demonic
which would gain dominion over the world and mankind. This, after all, corresponds also to the event which

219

stands at the beginning of this religion. Where a divine destiny is both the basis for and the answer to everything, the essence of history becomes a drama between below and above which really takes place beyond the human sphere which it enters only in the miracle of grace or in the victory of the demonic. Man ceases to be the will-endowed subject of history and becomes the object of a supraterrestrial struggle; and whoever would envisage reality may experience only the supernatural. Heteronomy thus conquers history, too; and the meaning of events is reduced to mere experience. Again it becomes apparent how everything in romanticism leads back to subjective experience.

THE SACRAMENT

But it is not only the position here conceded to subjective experience, it is rather this very experience itself which threatens romanticism as a dangerous cliff. The experience which "comes out of faith and becomes faith" is supposed to mean everything; it becomes the cornerstone of religion. Yet it is found in the soul only in rare festive hours. Man does not live on moods alone. And here we find the critical point of Pauline, as indeed of every romantic, religion: it can never do without the living experience, yet this experience does not want to and cannot come continuously, nor can it be brought to everybody; it "bloweth where it listeth." It is supposed to be the one and all of religion, that power without which religion cannot do; but the gates to it do not open every day, nor to everybody. Only one solution is possible: a way must be found for making the extraordinary constant; and the gift of the festive hour a gift of the weekday, too. The experience must be brought down to earth.

220

The history of religious romanticism tells of many
different phenomena in connection with this quest, nor
are all of them religious; the sublime and the vulgar
appear alongside each other. The Indian romantic mor-
tifies and hypnotizes his senses to attain this experience; he practices Yoga, the difficult art of achieving
absorption. His brother, the Persian Sufi, more cheer-
fully inclined toward sensual enjoyment, raises his cup
that "the fire of the tavern may consume the house of
the understanding"; through earthly drunkenness he
seeks the sacred intoxication. And in German romanticism, too, we encounter this word.

That romanticism, on the other hand, on which Paul
drew, had followed higher paths. It had taught the
sacraments—that is, the means of grace and blessedness, the sacred objects and rites, baptisms, anoint-
ments, meals which always produce a union of the deity
with the human being—so that the miracle of the experience can, by means of them, be made objectively
effective day after day. In them the phantastic form of
this religion becomes palpable and plain; they furnish
the ever-ready miracle, the *miraculum ex machina;*
they open the door through which the miracle enters
time and again, through which the spirit blows repeatedly: the living experience is to be made a guaranteed possession. Paul accepted these means of grace
almost unchanged from ancient romanticism, and there
is nothing which connects his religion more obviously
with the ancient mystery cults than his doctrine of the
sacraments. For him, too, they are indispensable, the
firm ground of existence in the faith, the necessary condensation of the living experience; without them, his
religion would float in the air.

This physical image from the natural sphere is no
mere metaphor here. No less than in the mystery cults,

the sacraments are for Paul, too, something entirely material and objective. Any attempt to see mere symbols in them, he would have vigorously repudiated as profane and shallow. They are something completely real, tangible; the miraculous divine energy dwells in them, and hence they are valid as such and productive as magical and sacred things through which the vital power of God is transmitted to man. Man himself is here, too, as indeed in the whole Pauline doctrine, an object only; he does not consecrate the action nor work it, but it infuses itself into him and works a miracle in him; and it is, in the words of an ancient Christian document, "the medicine of eternal life, the antidote against death."[6] The human conscience does not add anything to this action and does not subtract anything from it, at least nothing essential; it possesses its full and indestructible power within itself. Its significance is that of an objective event, of an actual process in man. Hence it is only consistent that the sacrament is said to work, too, quite independently of the human will and of anything a person might contribute—working simply by happening, *ex opere operato*. Without in the least impairing the miracle or diminishing it, the miracle can be obtained and carried out for a human being and in him by others—even for one who has died exactly as for those into whom the life of thought has not yet entered, such as newborn children. The human being in whom the miracle takes place need not participate either through action or through knowledge. That complete passivity, that absolute dependence in terms of which Paul conceives of human nature, and the heteronomy of existence which he teaches find unequivocal expression in these ideas.

6. Ignatius, Ephes. 20, 2.

But not only this; another essential point also finds expression here: the religion which began so spiritually becomes condensed and materialized. The sacraments accomplish the miracle and create the state of salvation; they join one to God precisely as the experience of faith did. But the salvation they bring is no longer something that relates purely to the soul, no longer something that works in the psychic realm and can be understood psychologically; it is something supernaturally material, something that works magic. Salvation here becomes a substance which enters man; a substance, to be sure, of a supernatural kind, and yet a substance. It is a heavenly water of baptism and a heavenly bread of communion that save from death for life.

The form in which the sacrament has prevailed is one in which it has retained its significance as a real thing: the Roman Catholic as well as the Greek Orthodox Church cling to this, and Luther, too, accepted it as a matter of principle. And gradually it pushed back the original state of faith more and more. Very understandably, for it offered no less: it gave everything and accomplished everything, it saved and redeemed, and was at the same time the ever ready gift of every day. Thus it gradually had to occupy an ample area in this religion.

To be sure, the Catholic Church has tried to remain faithful to its romantic origin and principle and has sought to preserve the experience itself, too, in all its extraordinary, immediate spiritual power. It has assigned a high status to those who turn their backs on this life so that they might have the full and immediate experience, and in consequence the Church has released other people from this obligation: in its monks and hermits it has created vicars of romanticism. For this was after all the meaning and idea of monasticism, namely, that there should be human beings whose existence would not merely be interrupted now and then by religion, people to whom the sacrament would not be the only thing to bring the moment in which the divine confronts and enters man—those, in other words, to whom the stream of the hours would again and again bring the experience as a whole so that it might arch over their existence and provide its dominant mood. To these persons religion is given in its romantic fullness, as the *vita religiosa.*

Some later movements in the Church, too, are best understood as efforts to restore its all-important place to the living impression of God. Luther's original striving and aspiration, the period of his "Methodist" piety, also aimed at this as did the enthusiastic Baptist movement and Pietism. In the same way, the Catholic Church has, as a matter of principle, clung to the original, extraordinary "miracle"; it has found the quintessence of sanctity only in those who perform this miracle, or in whom it is performed; and it has also time and again known how to discover such saints.

But however highly the solitary monks were rated as the true Christians and however highly the miracles of the saints were praised, the sacrament which at any hour transmitted a miracle and experience to every believer did not lose anything of its dominion. It was even bound to gain in importance the more secular activity and knowledge, which had originally been so severely depreciated, came in the course of time to press in all quarters their claims which were not to be denied and to demand the right of self-regulation. The more the pretensions to a "Christian life" had to be limited, and the less the faith of the Church remained an experience, becoming instead either political or philosophical, the more did the importance of the sacraments increase. Thus the sacrament remained as the ever-present miracle, the religious experience *par excellence,* the ever-secure gift from the higher world, and, in this sense, the determinate content of the romantic religion.

This, as has already been remarked, is what it still was without reservation for Luther. For him, too, it is that which supports the religion and creates the state of grace. While he decreased the number of the sacraments, he placed beside them the "word," which is for him the great instrument of grace in which the power of salvation dwells—that which by its sheer presentation effects the miracle of faith. It does not merely *mean* something, but it *is* something and is therefore effective solely by being preached, *ex opere operato;* its influence is not anything psychological, but supernatural, magical. Man stands before it absolutely dependent, purely passive and receiving. The affirmation of the word through faith comes over man without his action and without his aid, as a miracle; faith cannot be won, but only be given by grace. "That you should hear and receive the word is not by your strength, but by the grace of God which makes the gospel bear fruit in you that you may have faith in it."[7] In precisely the same manner Luther construes the meaning of the two ancient sacraments of baptism and communion: in them the miracle occurs which seizes man. "In, with, and under the bread and wine" is the wonderful substance, and the water of baptism is "a divine, heavenly, holy, and blessed water"[8] through which "the faith is poured

7. Erlangen edition, 10 (2), 12.
8. Great Catechism IV.

in and man thus re-created, purified, and renewed."[9] Man is always a mere object, and in the emphasis which Luther here accords this passivity of the believer he again goes even beyond the Catholic conception. In his earliest period, prompted by his opposition to the Catholic Church, he had attributed decisive power to the experience of faith; but gradually he ascribed, and had to ascribe, the true value to the sacraments until they became indispensable for religion and any true religion became impossible without them. As the Silesian reformer, Kaspar Schwenckfeld, reproached his master: he "will not let anybody become blessed without an external thing."

It was no mere stubborn whim when Luther eventually fought for this as a matter of life and death against the conception of the Baptists and of Zwingli who, closer to the Old Testament in this respect, considered the sacrament essentially a symbol. To Luther this must have meant a devaluation of the most sacred, and to accept this view, he would have had to abandon his guide to truth, Paul. His Pauline principle, *sola fide,* "by faith alone," stood and fell with the claim that man is absolutely dependent and that salvation can come over him only through a miracle. This complete passivity demanded a sacrament that, being no mere symbol to which man must give meaning, is a supernatural reality that gives man everything as a gift. The romantic faith cannot in this world do without the designated instrument of grace. Luther could not do without this any more than John, the Evangelist, or Origen had been able to do without it. Like them, he tied God to an "external thing."

9. Weimar edition VI, 539 (*De captiv. babyl.*): *fide infusa mutatur, mundatur et renovatur.*

Because it is romantic, the religion for which Paul had laid the foundations was bound to become a religion of sacraments, and with this it became—one might almost say—a religion of ceremonies. Something ceremonial—for that is after all what the performance of the sacrament is—is moved into the center of the life of faith as indispensable for the occurrence of salvation. Judaism, too, has created its ceremonies, perhaps even too great a profusion of them; but here they were erected only as the outworks of the religion, as a "fence around the doctrine," as the ancient saying puts it: they are symbols and signs which point to something religious, but their observation as such was not yet considered true piety, not yet a good work. Through Paul something of twofold significance triumphed: a ceremony was conceded a central place, and this ceremony enclosed something real, a work of magic, the occurrence of a miracle. It had been the way of Judaism to overcome more and more an abundance of miraculous notions which had originated in the days of its childhood. Now in Christianity this abundance emerged again as a constant—every flowering of romanticism has involved a flourishing of the faith in miracles—and it here becomes a principle, a dogma, a central concept of the religion. Now religion exists only where the miracle is to be found; and only where this takes place is there a divine service. The religion of the sacraments has its place in the Church of the miracle; and its cult with its ceremonial is the drama of the miracle.

THE ROMANTIC CHURCH

The position thus won by the sacraments had to lead to a heightened conception of the Church. If the miracle is the essential and everything depends on it, then it must endure uninterruptedly and gain a continual and permanent miraculous existence; and this can be guaranteed only by a Church which itself has been established by a miracle and which is infallibly active in accordance with a divine right—a Church which is itself a miracle, a never-ending miracle. Thus the romantic Church came into being—and the Lutheran Church, too, must be included in this—the Church which, by virtue of supernatural right, embodies the kingdom of God and in whose existence and through whose existence alone the miracle is ever present. Outside of this Church there is now no longer any faith or any salvation; for only within it does the experience occur, and it alone dispenses the miracle and thus effects redemption. It alone has faith and it alone makes blessed; it is the vicar of God on earth, and only those are with God who belong to it; it shuts and opens the gates to the Kingdom of Heaven. It is everything, and the individual in his striving and searching is nothing; he is absolutely dependent on it and can only share its faith. Whatever would be different and independent, is denied salvation and turned over to the abyss. Religion becomes the faith of a Church, a denomination whose articles of faith circumscribe piety once and for all. What the ecclesiastical sphere gains here, the religious sphere loses.

In this denominationalization, humaneness is narrowed down. The glory of God no longer fills the world but only the Church; everything outside the Church is the realm of the devil, given over to his dominion. Mankind is cut in two; the deep abyss passes right through it and separates the elect and the damned unbridgeably: as far as the world extends, everything falls apart into heaven or hell. The conception of the unity of mankind is thus broken up. Ahead of man is placed the believer; and ahead of love, the denomination.

Much could establish itself upon the sentence of the Fourth Gospel, "no man cometh unto the Father, but by me"[10]—the harshest and most denominational sentence ever spoken. It furnished the basis for much mercilessness which later carried its own judgment of heretics into the very conception of God, and for much pious cruelty which brought its earthly and eternal sacrifices to the greater glory of God. This sole way of loving God has often left little room for loving man. The Church could unfold within this particularistic narrowness that self-assurance with which it praised itself as the *ecclesia possidentium,* as the owner of salvation, as the realization of that future in which all is fulfilled. Corresponding to the finished man of romanticism there was the finished mankind, the Church. As such it became the object of faith and that which is holy; the faith of the Church became the faith *in* the Church.

This development was necessarily continued. To appear in the sacrament, the miracle requires its personal mediator every time; therefore the Church must impart something of its continual miraculous power to individuals and consecrate them to wield miraculous power. By means of the permanent sacramental power that dwells in it, it must create those capable of administering the sacraments, those who serve the sacraments. Thus the romantic Church becomes a Church of priests. This was the natural development of the original idea. The religion which, for the sake of the fundamental miracle, based itself on the idea of the savior as mediator, and which, for the sake of the perpetuity

10. John 14. 6. *Tr.*

229

of the miracle, gave itself a general mediator in the form of the Church, now had to see to it that every day should manifest this miracle and hence it had to create particular mediators in the form of consecrated priests. In them the experience which emanated from the savior, which became tangible in the sacrament, and which was guaranteed by the Church, was now offered personally. Alongside the men of complete romanticism there appeared the men of the prepared sacraments: alongside the saints and monks, the priests. The profession of the experience is thus created; the experience is made into an office and thus into a privilege. The priest grants and the laymen receive, being directly dependent on the priests, and not only on God. Where the priest is, there alone is religion; the office has become an essential component of the faith.

The faith which at first wanted to base itself on an experience which was to be most intimately one's own, now is content to be merely the faith in the experience of others. It permits itself to be represented by others and believes because, and whatever, the Church believes. The place of the *fides qua creditur*, the faith *with* which one believes, is taken over by the *fides quae creditur*, the faith *in* which one believes. In other words, the place of one's own faith is taken over by obedience of faith. Obedience becomes the substitute for experience—to be sure, an indispensable substitute in romantic religion. Man now merely has to accept what is offered to him, passive in this respect, too: he believes in the faith of another.

This is the obvious development of Paulinism; the phrase "obedience of faith" was after all coined by the apostle himself: it begins and concludes his most important epistle.[11] The heteronomy of life which he had

11. Romans 1.5 and 16.26. *Tr.*

taught, eventually had to create this heteronomy of experience, too. And with this, dualism came again which always haunts the exuberance and exclusiveness of the romantic experience. Piety splits into two modes, one immediate and one mediate. Around those, on the inside, who believe are those on the outside who believe them; each group has its own ideal. The unity of faith and of all believers is gone and gives way to a religion of the first and second degree; and between them there is the border line which separates priest and layman.

The significance of the change which Luther effected in the history of Christianity is that he sought again to establish a priestless Church; together with the fact that he broke the sole dominion of the one Church in central and Western Europe—this is his most important achievement. Here he took up again the Old Testament idea of a universal priesthood, although prompted by motives quite different from those of the Old Testament. He did it precisely for the sake of the original romanticism; for he wanted to give complete sway to the basic mediator, the savior, and to utter dependence on him, and it was for this reason that he rid the community of the other mediators, the priests. But however decisively he demanded this equality of all believers during his first, revolutionary period, he did not remain quite faithful to it. He could not, because the instrument of grace to which he clung required its legitimate, consecrated keeper, and the word needed its appointed preacher. Where the existing Church claims that—as the Augsburg Confession puts it—"in it the Gospel is taught right and the sacraments are administered right,"[12] there the minister who is entrusted

12. Article VII: *Est autem ecclesia congregatio sanctorum in qua evangelium recte docetur et recte administrantur sacramenta.*

with these must eventually become again some kind of mediator of salvation; and the ecclesiastical office, a road between God and man.

Here, too, dualism again enters the community; piety again becomes twofold and splits in two: there is the perfect piety of the consecrated and the adequate piety of the laymen. The ecclesiastic emphasis again had to become more and more decisive the more hierarchical needs and hierarchical wishes awakened in Luther and gradually grew stronger; for such was after all quite generally the development of his soul and his life that questions of faith became for him questions of power. The state Church which he created required its certified ministers of priestly cast; and the universal priesthood which he had once taught now found refuge only among the outcasts of the Reformation, the Baptists. To Luther, the guardian of the state religion, any talk of universal priesthood now appeared as the ravings of zealots.

The alliance between romanticism and external authority was thus forged in his Church, too; and this alliance is a perfectly natural one, such as only an elective affinity can form. Whichever one comes first, eventually they have to find one another. Every strong authority in matters of faith, if it would possess and administer and provide everything itself, can permit and proclaim only that kind of faith which is merely accepted and remains purely passive. The only freedom which it can grant is that of moods and experiences, such romantic freedom as has wholly subordinated the individual's own aspiration and thinking, while seeking compensation in the consciousness of the finished man.

Conversely, the more romantic the faith and the more passive it therefore feels, the more it must feel the need to lean against something established and firm in order to find tangible certainty in it, this being the only source of security for those who find nothing of the sort in themselves. Romantic faith requires established authority as its necessary complement in this world. It is like an internal balance, but also like a psychic retribution, that this romantic faith, which began by repudiating any definite law so that it might follow unrestrained feeling, must in the end get to the point where it seeks an authority in matters of faith.

In his brilliant characterization of Augustine, the founder of the philosophy of authority, Harnack points out that "the world has never yet seen any strong religious faith which did not at some decisive point have recourse to an external authority." In its all-inclusiveness, this statement is immediately refuted by the faith of the prophets which did not, like romanticism, seek to connect but to remake, to create the break where something new could be built; the prophetic faith shows that the statement does not apply to classical religion. But regarding romantic faith, the statement is surely correct: it does, indeed, by its very essence, demand an established authority and hierarchy. Romantic faith has always been, or become, papal; that is, to become truth for it, something always had to be prevalent truth, guaranteed by a firm authority; it is here of the essence of faith that it is guaranteed. A thinker like Augustine experienced it this way without reservation, with the strong and proud feeling of one who knows his religion to be assured; and this assertion was basic for his life: "I should have no faith in the gospel if the authority of the Catholic Church did not induce me."[13]

13.   C. epist. Manichaei cp. 5: ego vero evangelio non crederem, nisi ecclesiae catholicae me commoveret auctoritas.

It was the desire for repose that led him here. There is no more soothing goal for a tempest-tossed spirit than a strong authority. It offers a secure haven for those who would seek refuge from the winds.

ROMANTIC TRUTH

In the Church, authorities were created quite early: personal ones in the hierarchy of a miracle-working priesthood and objective ones in the propositions of the *dogma*, the profession of the miracles. These belong together and complete each other. The dogma comprehends and grants the knowledge of faith, even as the priesthood with its sacraments possesses and dispenses the experiences of faith. Both of them embody, and transform into a body, an originally spiritual content of faith. If romanticism began by finding knowledge in such seizure and transport as come over man through meditation and ecstasy and let their waves close over him, now all this floating and flowing became condensed. Dogma is frozen feeling; clotted, petrified mood. Billowing knowledge becomes firm, tangible acknowledgment. Just as in the sacrament, the process of materialization also reveals itself in the dogma. Sooner or later, this process takes place in all romanticism.

The desire for dogma appeared quite early. The miracle of the mysteries in which faith seeks knowledge is, by its very nature, something fluctuating and unstable and therefore calls for a standard determination which can always be pointed to and handed on: its symbol, its "mark of recognition" which discloses its true significance and effect. The Greek mysteries already had their sentences which were to proffer the saving truth, their passwords which opened the gate of redemption. What such formulations grant to faith is that it need no longer be ecstatic or seek transfiguration. The faith which had wanted to drown, to sink down in the infinite, amorphous, now has its firm complex of ideas, determined once and for all, which can simply be accepted. Now the believer finds it still easier to be a finished man in his own eyes and to remain assured of the fulfillment of his knowledge. This calm conviction will be even stronger in him insofar as it is a wide-spread conviction. It may be nourished as a catholic, all-embracing conviction, with the powerful consciousness that one possesses what is valid without exception "always, everywhere, and for all." Though this dogmatic certainty is created by the Church, it in turn fortifies the idea of the Church.

But this power of certainty still has to be paid for dearly in the end; for in this universal faith which the individual merely shares, any individual or personal faith is easily lost, as has been shown. The faith now is no longer that which has been revealed and experienced, but what is formulated and published. It becomes faithfulness; the experienced becomes something learned and spoken, a systematic doctrine of faith whose propositions have to be accepted. Since it is no longer the individual as such who believes but the Church, the individual merely stands within the faith of the Church. And the Church, in turn, confronts everything personal with mistrust and must repudiate it and reject it as raving enthusiasm and addiction to innovations.

In its basic idea, all this is quite logical. If human knowledge is absolutely dependent on divine grace, then it is also unconditionally dependent on the Church; for the Church alone, with its sacraments and the theology of sacraments which it administers, guarantees the divine grace which bestows knowledge. Thus the mystic certainly could, and had to, be an obedient son of the Church with faith in its dogmas; and the doctor of the Church, the teacher of its dogma, could share in the ardent feeling that he was seeing God. Mysticism and scholasticism do not signify any tension or any opposition in the Church. Meister Eckhart here belongs alongside Thomas Aquinas.

Along with dogma appeared also its corollary, orthodoxy—that bent of mind which would cultivate respect for the answer but, in the process, often loses respect for the problem. The history of classical religion also tells of this; but here it appears only as the claim of a party, not as the manifestation of an original, native tendency. In romantic faith, on the other hand, it is an essential quality, something grounded in this faith from the beginning. There is, therefore, no Christianity without it. However protestant a movement may here be at the start, in the end, if it would remain Christian, it must assume the form of orthodoxy. Precisely in Lutheranism, the religion of the Word To Be Preached, orthodoxy appears as a dominant concept, as the condition of all piety; the profession of the creed occupies here also the place which the cult occupies in Catholicism. Orthodoxy here gains what the sacrament has lost—lost, to be sure, not in miraculous significance, but in breadth—it gains, above all, in voice and pathos. It had to become more pronounced, more emphatic, because it could not base itself on the popular conception of infallibility, that Catholic consciousness of what is valid "always, everywhere, and for all"; it became a professing orthodoxy, *fides explicita*. But whether it is this orthodoxy or the quieter one of Catholicism, its *fides implicita*, it always amounts almost to stripping the individual believer of the rights of majority; he now appears only as the lowly subject who accepts, whose first virtue is obedience, and who has done enough for himself when he believes the authority and resigns himself to the finished propositions of the dogma. The heteronomy of this kind of religion manifests itself in this, too.

Whenever romanticism determines the way of thinking, there is a change in the meaning of truth: truth is, as it were, frozen. In romantic antiquity we find an example of this even in the very movement in which one might be tempted to find the diametric opposite of Pauline religion: the philosophy or, as could be said just as well, the religion of Epicurus. At bottom it has something romantic; and therefore it, too, has its final axioms which are, in spite of their scientific appearance, mere dogmas. Epicureanism, too, displays a certainty of possessing truth and lives in the secure feeling of resting in the right faith. The skepticism which used to exist alongside this attitude was no more than the sharply outlined shadow cast by that which is rigid: it was the romantic irony of those days. Romantic dogmatism lived also in the garden of Epicurus. There it led its unworldly existence; in the Pauline Church, however, it became a dominant power.

Here dogma received its full, all-embracing significance; for here knowledge, *gnosis*, does not merely instruct—it redeems. The salvation of man, his eternal bliss, depends on it. Thus the dogma becomes the one and all to which a man "must hold fast"; in the dogma we have the very essence of the religion. Dogmatic exactitude becomes the guarantee of the possession of the eternal good. Deviation from the confession is the road to damnation; error becomes abyss.

With this, the concept of truth loses its ancient value and is altogether annulled; and the concept of the dedication to truth, truthfulness, suffers the same fate: it, too, is now understood in terms of the confession and receives its true place only in this context. It is a psychological law that concepts strive to be univocal; and any powerful new meaning assigned to a concept will only too soon crowd out the old meaning and monopolize the concept. Thus the new dogmatic content interfered more and more with the force of the older ethical meaning. Truth and lie now receive their pre-eminent meaning from the finished ecclesiastical doctrine and not from any infinite ethical duty; they are no longer a matter of conscience, but rather a matter of dogmatic definition; they no longer constitute an obligation for man, but are simply what he receives once and for all as his fate. Love of truth now becomes love of the ecclesiastical truth, and a lie now becomes a deviation from the dogma. "Who is a liar, but he that denieth that Jesus is the Christ?" (I John 2.22). In every confessional zeal we encounter an inclination to dispose of any alien faith as untruth; but here this inclination is made a principle which, in the end, does not care any more whether the heterodox live in the noblest purity, or whether the orthodox pursue crooked paths: the latter is, for all that, the man of truth, and the former the slave of a lie. The ethical Yes and No recedes behind the Yes and No of the confession.

It is no mere accident that the command of truthfulness so rarely finds expression in the Pauline and the subsequent Christian literature. The precepts of faith and humility, of suffering and hope, of pity and charity occupy a spacious sphere, but our simple virtue generally disappears behind them. And it is lacking not only in the literature; the turning away from it is one of the chief traits of the entire romantic Middle Ages.

For this, too, the deeper cause is to be found in romanticism. From a purely objective point of view, a lack of truthfulness is manifest in the importance as-

signed to appearance and dream and in the indifference
—really aversion—to reality. Moreover, romanticism
negates and repudiates an essential part of that honesty
which man owes to himself: the test of criticism and
the standards which it would apply. When Novalis
found that "all doubt, all desire for truth," was nothing
but dissolution, and considered the striving for knowledge a kind of "brutality"—this was admittedly somewhat superlative, but thoroughly romantic. Luther had
said much the same thing in the language of his own
time.

Romanticism is bound to spurn objective content and
the discipline of thought, as both would limit and re-
strain the ego or—as romanticism prefers to think—
violate the ego. Sooner than admit either of them, romanticism flees into the protection of external authority, or indulges in irony which affirms nothing and
transposes everything. From all seeking and inquiring
doubt romanticism keeps its distance.

In this respect, the Church has for the most part remained thoroughly romantic. Criticism and examination, wavering and scruple in matters of faith have
been, to its mind, the path on which the evil spirit approaches, the path that leads to lies. That subordination
to authorities, on the other hand, which neither questions nor inquires, but lives in pure passivity under
the axioms of faith, has been identified with the understanding to which the very depths are opened up,
with the knowledge that spells salvation, with the finished life. The logic for all this was easily devised. One
elaborated that syllogistic which only requires the first
proposition and then can prove and derive everything
from that: the logic of obedience which first captivates
and then shows the captive how perfectly the links of

his chain fit together. In its sense, this logic has made true the sentence: *et cetera adjicientur vobis.*[14] In this manner, a self-enclosed system was created and by means of a truly impressive feat of intellectual labor everything was fitted into it and all was arranged neatly. Whoever enters into the circles of Thomas or, for that matter, Melanchthon, needs but admit the axioms at the beginning, and then everything else follows necessarily and persuasively, often with impressive consistency. And for those who desired this by all means, even romantic irony was admitted by way of the doctrine of double truth: if only the obedience of faith was not compromised in any way, everything else was gladly permitted. The truth remained fixed and finished.

THE COMMANDMENT AND THE DEED

What thus happened to truth is merely a single instance of a more general development. Those with a romantic faith always dwell beyond all things and beings. Since they want to remain within the realm of passivity, they dwell beyond the direction and the demands of reason —beyond its logic and also beyond ethics. The old-fashioned justice, too, is preserved here only as an old-fashioned word: the content is completely different. Veracity and justice as active virtues no longer have any place in romanticism.

For the believer there is no command to do anything. "Christ is the end of the law";[15] the new justice annuls the old: thus Paul formulated it. But the idea is older than Paul: it is that romantic notion which recognizes man only as an object and considers valid only what

14. ". . . and the rest shall be added unto you." Matt. 6.33. *Tr.*
15. Romans 10.4. *Tr.*

240

happens to man, what he experiences. Paul merely gave this notion its most exaggerated formulation by finding justice altogether in *not* willing, in passivity; he not only measured the value of activity by the standard of romantic aimlessness, but placed it in the category of unbelief, of godlessness. Justice is for him exclusively something that happens to man: man therefore need not exercise it; he only must believe in it. Thus it presupposes as its very condition that the will to be just, and indeed any active striving and willing, is negated. The whole theology of Paul revolves around this negation.

That this became the pivot of his romanticism is connected with the climate of thought in which he lived. An old Jewish saying has it that in the ideal days of the future, when the spirit of God will dwell in the hearts of men, every commandment, every "ought" will cease. One felt that all fulfillment of duty was based upon a tension; the tension between will and obligation, between inclination and duty. The ideal is for this antagonism to give way to a higher unity: duty should become one with our inmost nature; what we ought to be should become one with what we are; or in the words of a saying current in those days, God's will should become our will, and thus our will would become one with the divine will. The idea here is precisely the same as in Schiller's remark: "Accept the deity into your will and it will descend from the throne of the world." The language of Paul's time had also expressed this idea by saying that in the messianic days there would be no more guilt or merit, neither commandment nor law. Seeing that the community founded by John had considered Jesus the messiah and had waited for his return, it might well have been said here already that the Law would come to an end as soon as he appeared again, and with him the expected time in which "all has been fulfilled."

For Paul, this time had come already. In the sacrament all was "fulfilled," and salvation, the life of eternity, was given. Hence the Law had to be finished and annulled. If it continued to be valid, then the redemptive mystery could not be what it should be. That the Law should cease for the baptized was therefore for Paul the crucial question on which the very existence of his religion depended, from his Jewish messianic point of view, too. Any recognition of the Law meant the denial that salvation had come and that the redemption had occurred. Sacrament or Law—the decision between these two had to be made. Paul could not get away from this. Thus the old ideal was romanticized: the wish begotten by longing was transformed into the secure possession granted by grace. For the finished man the Law is annulled.

Justice was thus deprived of its old meaning. It was no longer a matter of work and achievement, connected with the idea of duty and the striving for the good; instead, "whoever believes in him is just." Justice is now only an act performed *on* man, a work of the miracle of grace, a gift, something finished—not a task involving an endless demand. From the start it precludes anything individual and personal, any independence or spontaneity or will of the self. Whoever would become just by his own effort, is on the path that leads away from justice—or as Luther put it, "befouls himself with the Law."[16] Man can only be made just; in this, as in everything else, he can only be an object, according to romantic religion. That is the meaning of the fre-

16.   Erlangen edition, 51, 284.

quently cited dictum that he can become just "solely through faith—*sola fide*."

Although one has at times wishfully read such an interpretation into it, this dictum does not by any means refer to an attitude or mood which alone confers value on a deed. No construction could possibly be more remote from the true intention of this dictum: it fights, to cite Luther again, against the Law as such and the Law as a "whole";[17] it has nothing whatever to do with ethical motives. It means entirely and only one thing: you are absolutely dependent, you are nothing by virtue of your deeds or achievements; whatever you are or become, you are only through the destiny of faith, you become only by virtue of a miracle.

The strictness of this romanticism was admittedly attenuated before long; the human desire for deeds made its demands. Even in the scriptures of the New Testament we encounter the word of James of "faith *and* works," and the Catholic Church was glad to follow him; here, too, as elsewhere, it granted human aspiration a legitimate sphere. Through the sacrament of penance the Church made a place for it; and, for its sake, the Church even adopted a certain ambivalence and the danger of an ambiguity for which it was to be reproached frequently. Luther, however, later returned to decided and uncompromising romanticism, and "solely through faith" became for him what it had been for Paul: the sole meaning of justice. Again, justice becomes nothing but the consciousness of absolute dependence on the grace of God in Christ; all spontaneous

17. *Ep. ad Gal.*, ed. Irmischer, II, 266: *"Credentibus in Christum tota lex abrogata est*—For those who believe in Christ, the whole Law is abrogated." In the same place it is emphasized that this abrogation applies particularly to the moral law.

243

willing is again identified with sin. Luther says this expressly: "The Gospel is a doctrine which admits no Law."[18] "The Law has been fulfilled—by Christ; one need not fulfill it, but only adhere with faith to him who has fulfilled it and be made like him."[19] "We are called just, not when we do what is just, but when we believe and trust in God."[20] "Christian justice is faith in the son of God."[21] "All that you begin is sin and remains sin, however prettily it may glisten. You can do nothing but sin . . . All is sin that you do alone from free will."[22]

"You can do nothing but sin": that is indeed the necessary complement of this new justice. If man is not the free subject who can decide in favor of the good, neither can he be the person who originates and causes sin; sin can only be something that has overcome him and compels him: it is original sin. The Orphic mysteries already contained this idea; Paul found a place for it in the biblical narrative and clothed it in biblical language; Augustine gave it philosophic form; and the Reformers again restored its full force. Original sin is that sin which is above and beyond the ability of the individual human being who is born in time; it is the sin that belongs to the drama of destiny which embraces heaven and earth. Like that justice which comes to man from the super-terrestrial region, in the miracle of

18. *Ibid.*, I, 113: *Est ergo Evangelium doctrina talis, quae nullam legem admittit.*
19. Weimar edition, I, 105: *quod lex est impleta, scil. per Christum, quod non sit necesse eam implere, sed tantummodo implenti per fidem adhaerere et conformari.*
20. *Ibid.*, I, 84: *Non enim qui justa operatur, justus est, ut Aristoteles ait, neque operando justi et dicimur justi, sed credendo et sperando in Deum.*
21. *Ep. ad Gal.*, ed. Irmischer, I, 334: *Justitia christiana est fiducia in Filium Dei.*
22. Erlangen edition, 10 (2), 11.

grace, this sin, too, is at bottom something supranatural to which mortal man is abandoned without any power of his own. The prophetic doctrine of individual sin is thus annihilated, and in its place the ancient Greek myth of blindly working guilt lives on. What is personal is again supplanted by fate; and in place of the sin which man has committed, and which man should therefore conquer, we have the fate of sin which man himself cannot overcome.

This Pauline doctrine would be deprived of its very essence if it were taken to mean no more than this: that there is a great continuity of guilt in the succession of generations and that the sin of the individual must be understood in terms of this great chain of which it is a mere link. Nothing of any such psychological, social, or ethical significance is to be found in the doctrines of Paul, Augustine, and the Reformers. With them, sin is not something that develops, something of which one seeks out the individual roots or traces the growing calamity; sin is rather the determinate and rigid definition of the human race and of that life out of which and into which man, as man, is born. It is not in him, but he is in it; it is his essence, and all his knowledge of himself can never amount to more than to consciousness of sin.

The Pauline conception of guilt has no more social than personal orientation. Neither the individual nor the group is held responsible for having introduced sin by its own striving, nor is either considered capable of annulling it. All such claims have always been condemned as Pelagianism by the Church—both Catholic and Protestant. Sin resides in mankind by nature, and it can be destroyed only by the annulment of nature; that is, by a miracle, by grace which works in man. Even as its existence is "radical," its abolition, too, must be "radical." In the words of Augustine: "All sins have been annihilated with the sacrament of baptism: all of them, entirely—*cuncta prorsus.*"

Sin and justice thus confront each other in a harsh dualism, abruptly, without any mean or transition. They are manifestations of two fates, two worlds, that of grace and that of guilt. Man belongs to them not by virtue of any active capacity, but only passively. They represent the two destinies; and in the characteristic phrase of the Epistle to the Ephesians, man is "lotted" for one or the other. The die of fate is cast for him and he is the finished or—and this is the same thing—the mythical man. This dualism was from the beginning conceived dramatically as a fight between the forces of destiny. The great adversary of God, the devil, appears; he is the originator of sin, and sinful men become his instrument. The doctrine of the devil occupies an important place in the epistles of Paul; and these could hardly be given a more apt title than: The Book of the Devil and the Redeemer.

Faith must assume its place here. Since sin exists but is not supposed to be of human origin, and hence must be derived from the beyond, there must be a supernatural agent for it, even as the Redeemer is the agent of the good. Each entails the other. Where man is the father of his own sin, he can also liberate himself from it. But where sin represents the work of a supernatural power, where an adversary of God has fashioned it, it becomes necessary for a divine savior to appear in order to vanquish it. It was with good reason that the Church taught: if there were no devil, there would be no need for a redeemer. The doctrine of the devil is no mere curiosity in the Christian religion; devil and savior have the same root. Therefore Luther believed in the one as much as in the other, with all the strength

246

and sincerity of his soul. And when men like Vilmar and Martensen have confessed the same in modern times, that was no mere romantic eccentricity; it was genuine faith—the same which was alive in Paul and those who followed him. *Nullus diabolus, nullus redemptor:* no Devil—no Redeemer.

In the doctrine of the devil, man's deprivation of his right as a subject gains its ultimate and most pregnant expression. It is no longer man that seeks and strives, wins or succumbs; the contest is carried on in him and over him. The psychic struggles he experiences are really struggles in which supernatural powers fight each other. The history of the soul is the drama between heaven and hell. The doctrine of man is transferred into the supernatural realm and thus really ceases to be psychology, the doctrine of what is human. The dogma determines it rigidly and fixes the stages of sin and grace. To be sure, in the Church the science of the soul has been pursued, too, to investigate the nuances of light and shade; and Augustine even became a master in this. But this, too, easily became no more than a brooding upon sinfulness; and above all, the dualism of guilt and grace, of the work of the devil and the work of the Redeemer, remained and cut through the human soul. The good and the true were finished facts. Of course, attempts were made—for example, by Duns Scotus and his school—to concede some right to individuality and to personal character traits; but the Catholic Church—and the Protestant, too—in the end rejected them mistrustfully. It did not want any breach in its closed system, and the impressive force of this tightly knit structure could be guaranteed only as long as man was reduced to a dogmatic concept—not if man was considered with his contradictions, in accordance

247

with the full rights and demands of his individuality, in the perspective of his search for his task.

ETHICS

The Pauline dogma removes the very ground from under man's rights as a moral subject, as an ethical individual. That which could and should unfold into a personality, that which is unique and individual, must give way to the concept of the species. Man appears merely as one of the manifestations of sin or grace; in Spinoza's terminology one might say: he is merely a mode of one or the other. It is clear why Schleiermacher could suppose that he was somehow close to Spinoza. Moral freedom—the freedom revealed in the fact that the good is possible for man and should become actual through his agency—is rejected. There is only a freedom that has been granted, predestined, "lotted"—a freedom which consists in being free from the devil and the demons.

The point must be stated still more comprehensively. The Pauline faith deprives ethics itself of its basis. The sacrament had already rendered ethics all but superfluous: the mystery alone meant something and the moral sphere lagged behind. Moreover, baptism has become decisive, and the great work of grace is finished: what could any human achievement mean after that? The Church, especially the early Church, always found it difficult to say what could happen to and through man after the sacrament. Ethics was from now on reduced to a subordinate, if not altogether superfluous, position. The new justice seemed to annul it altogether. Where the will that decides for itself is considered the path of destruction, no place is left for ethics; indeed, it is expressly repudiated. Religion now becomes the opposite, the contradiction of ethics; each excludes the other in principle. Either faith or ethics! That is the innermost meaning of the fight which Paul and Luther waged against the "Law." They did not merely oppose something ceremonial; "Law" is for them any valuation of human activity, even the most moral. Man becomes good only through the miracle which has been accomplished. Whoever expects the good from the fulfillment of the commandments and duties, still lives under the yoke of the Law. Law and miracle cannot be reconciled. Either the one or the other; either will or grace, deed or mystery, ethics or religion. However one chooses to put it, it is always the same opposition that defines the essence of religion, first for the apostle and then for the reformer.

What we have here is a unique approach to religion that has not only historical significance but also some psychological justification. It is justifiable as something peculiar that should not be obliterated. The romantic experience in which man is purely receptive is indeed the contradiction of the deed. The deed confronts it as something strange, almost as a disturbance and an obstacle which must be removed. If religion is to be exhausted by the miraculous experience, as Paul would have it, then no place can be conceded to this strange element, for activity and this receptivity preclude each other. Where the Pauline doctrine is ethicized, as happens at times today as a concession to what is felt to be modern, the doctrine is deprived of its very essence, loses its own character, and ceases to have its own path. The demands of ethics have a place only outside the sphere of this faith; at best, alongside it. The commandments of ethics can at most constitute a supplement to the doctrine of salvation, an appendix to that which alone is of vital significance. Ethical religion is in this context a contradiction in terms, *contradictio in adjecto*. Romantic religion says in effect: religion must supplant ethics.

The anarchical principle of Gnosticism, "everything is permitted," is therefore only the new justice carried to its logical conclusion. In principle and theoretically, it is a matter of indifference for the Pauline doctrine how man behaves in action, whether he does good or evil. For deeds are deeds and have nothing to do with religion; they always involve a valuation of the human subject and a denial that only faith in grace remains. Already the Epistle of Barnabas proclaimed: the tablets of Moses are broken.

Paul himself was still too deeply rooted in Judaism and hence made moral demands time and again. These demands are genuine insofar as they proceeded from his honest and deeply ethical personality and from his living past from which he could never disentangle himself entirely. But they are not genuine insofar as they did not proceed from his romantic religion which he proclaimed as that which was most truly his own: they are merely mounted on it as something extraneous and essentially different. They proceed from his personality but not from his faith, and they constitute the contradiction of his character; the human being here was stronger than the form of his faith. The Gnostics, however, were no longer rooted in Jewish soil nor disturbed by "fruitless remembrances" or "futile struggles"; so they took up the idea of romantic anarchy in earnest. Paul and many of his followers soon shrank from this development in horror; but this was merely the horror they felt at seeing their own ideas carried to their logical conclusion. Gnosticism is Christianity without Judaism and, in that sense, pure Christianity. Whenever

Christianity wanted to become pure in this way, it became Gnostic.

When the Church entered into the state and needed morality, it had to reject the Gnostic path more and more decisively. But even then it was unable to develop any univocal and clear relation to the ethical commandments: this would have contradicted its character. The Church was unable to give these commandments a goal of its own. The demands were made, but they always retained an inferior position as something that is merely natural as opposed to that which is truly religious. Although Catholicism included them under the "law of Christ" in line with its principle of "faith *and* works," they still remained a mere appendix of religion, something that accompanies religion. The high rank they are assigned is no more than this: they are placed on the same plane and in the same category as the rites of the sacramental cult, the ceremonial practices. They are not inferior to these, but not superior either: they are like them "good works."

In Protestantism the relation is again exclusively one of side-by-side existence. The moral commandments were relegated to the civic sphere, and only too soon the magistrates were conceded a moral mandate. The prince became, in Melanchthon's biblical formulation, "the custodian of the two tablets of the law—*custos utriusque tabulae.*" He must look after legality, after the external fulfillment of the moral commandments. Morality becomes his province and thus part of the sphere of the police. What was to be conceded to ethics was thus in fact gained by the absolute power of the autocratic prince. And this power has therefore been defended far more often by Protestant writers than by Catholics. Again it becomes manifest how romanticism leads on all its paths to the compulsion of authority.

As a matter of principle, the moral as such remained without religious significance.

This is of the very essence of Paulinism. Luther, above all, understood this clearly. Here, too, his words furnish us with the best explanation of the doctrine of the apostle and show how decisively the opposition to ethics is implicit in it. "Let life be the earth, and the doctrine, heaven—*vitam sinas esse terram, doctrinam coelum*":[23] that was the principle from which Luther started. From this, the rest followed without difficulty. "I live as I live; that does not make the doctrine false. We must not consider and judge the life, but the doctrine."[24] "Even if the life is not so pure, the doctrine can remain pure nevertheless, and one can be patient with the life."[25] "You do not owe it to God to do anything except believe and profess. In all other matters he releases you and leaves you free to do as you please without any danger of conscience."[26] "A Christian should know that it does him no harm whether he keeps the law or not, even if he does what is otherwise forbidden or does not what is otherwise commanded: it is no sin for him; for he cannot commit one since his heart is pure."[27]

That which is said in these and similar statements of Luther, however exaggerated it may sound, is yet nothing other than the very claim of the Pauline doctrine. Even his oft quoted word "*fortiter pecca*—sin bravely," which he wrote to Melanchthon in 1521, does not by any means stand alone as if it were an expression of casual irony. It is purely Pauline in its essence;

.

23. Weimar edition, XIV, 464.
24. Weimar edition, XXIV, 606.
25. *Ibid.*
26. Weimar edition, XII, 131.
27. Erlangen edition, 51, 284.

and it is typically romantic. Modern romanticism developed exactly the same attitude.

The more sin there is, Luther thought moreover, the better can divine grace prove its power. In the demand for good deeds as something decisive, he perceived the tempting voice of the devil who would pit human activity against grace; and opposition to, and even transgression of, just conduct therefore had to appear to him as a bold defiance of Satan. Ethical demands versus grace! "At times one must . . ." he therefore advised, "commit some sin out of sheer hatred of and contempt for the devil, so we leave him no room at all for making petty things matters of conscience; otherwise we shall be vanquished if we would guard too anxiously against sin. . . . Being so threatened and vexed by the devil, we must banish the whole decalogue completely from our sight and mind."[28]

Opponents of Luther have tried to make it appear as if such sentences were typical of one of those philosophies which men devise as theories of and justifications for the manner in which they have conducted their own lives. This would certainly be unjust to Luther. These statements are merely the logical conclusion—or, if one wants to bring out the roughness of Luther's character, the stubborn results—of the basic idea which he had learned from Paul: "*sola fide*—through faith alone." He was forced to these conclusions if he wanted to remain faithful to this conviction. Through faith alone—to him this could only mean, without deeds and even in spite of deeds.

The Reformer is misunderstood no less when he is modernized and when, for example, one attributes to him the view formulated by a religious thinker of a

28. *Dr. Martin Luthers Briefwechsel*, ed. Enders, VIII, 159f.

later age who once suggested: "Sometimes it would seem as if man had a volcanic need for occasional ruthless transgressions against all propriety in order to clarify, liberate, and soothe his soul." It is not an explosion of the soul that we hear in Luther's statements concerning the indifference of sin nor the breaking of ancient fetters, though all this, too, had taken place in his life. It is only the unyielding constancy of his fixed basic idea of faith. This alone finds loud expression in these statements. His character, on the other hand, manifested far more the opposite of all this, the strict ethical demand. His conscience and his life condemned sin in spite of everything and exalted man's duty to be virtuous and ethical. Only his faith was ruthless and amoral. Herein, just as in the case of Paul, was rooted the contradiction of his personality. However much his disposition demanded, and even illustrated, something else, he clung to the faith that we, as human beings, are mere objects for God's work, and that our conduct is therefore a matter of indifference. At times he was even terrified by those who had, as it were, issued from him, the so-called antinomians, "Jäckel and Grickel"; but this was the same fear which Paul and his followers had felt when they were confronted with Gnosticism: the terror before the logical conclusion of one's own ideas. In truth, these men were his consistent, and in that sense, his most faithful disciples.

It becomes quite evident at this point how impossible it is to derive Kant from Luther, as a certain construction of history suggests from time to time. For Kant the liberating and redeeming power comes from the Law. Nothing is good to his mind "except only a good will." And he affirms the principle: you can because you ought to. For Luther, on the other hand, the Law oppresses man and "befouls" him. The will can, to his mind, only be the will to sin; a regard for the will is for him godlessness itself. And beginning and end is for him: You ought to, but you cannot. A more extreme antithesis than that of Kant and Luther is scarcely conceivable. Whoever places them together does not know enough of either the one or the other. Kant's ethics, almost still more than his critique of knowledge, represents the most extreme antithesis of that which was Luther's certainty.

Another attempt to establish an affinity between the Reformer and the philosopher will not do either: the claim that Luther repudiated all eudaemonism and any thought of reward for human conduct and must therefore be considered an ancestor of Kant. For the idea of reward—which, incidentally, was not by any means altogether unknown to him—remained a matter of indifference to him only insofar as ethics was a matter of indifference to him. Because man cannot *do* anything decisive to become just or to be saved, nothing significant can, of course, be granted to him for what he does. Eudaemonism is thus surrendered here for the price of ethics. This may be considered a high price or a good bargain, but it certainly is not Kant's purism that is purchased here. If Luther, too, speaks of a man's disposition, it is only the word that he has in common with Kant. A disposition is for him merely the disposition which has been received as a gift, granted by grace, and of which one may justly boast. It is utterly opposed to Kant's pure consciousness of duty.

Kant's philosophy of the Law is the very antithesis of all romanticism with its opposition to whatever imposes limits and obligations. At first glance, this may seem rather far-fetched, but in truth there is a close connection between the following two phenomena. On the one hand, there are the German romantics of the last century who scolded and declaimed against the "virtue-pedants and maxim-grinders," against Kant, this "genius of a pedant" with "his intricately crooked steps," or against the "leaden, moralistic Schiller." On the other hand, there are Paul and Luther who at bottom say exactly the same thing when they give vent to their wrath against the Law because it fetters, oppresses, and kills. It is in both instances the same romantic mood, with its repugnance for the commandment which sets limits.

THE SENTIMENTAL

In the Church, ethics has basically always caused embarrassment. It was there—it had been introduced by the Old Testament which had been accepted as part of the Bible—but the faith lacked any organic relation to it. For the purposes of historical contemplation one had recourse to the Epistle to the Galatians and followed it in designating the "Law" as "the tutor of those not of age unto Christ." But in this way, ethics had been designated as that which no longer speaks to the believer. It was considered antiquated and outmoded, a truth no longer valid, something to which only a relapse to a lower stage could lead back.

In spite of all this, the religious desire for ethics has of course not vanished in the Church; the longing for its value has always remained awake. But as long as the faith kept faith with itself, this quest was vain, and the lot of ethics here has always been twofold: either the path to it—not to piety—got lost in mere enthusiasm which took the form of a pious prayer in some, while in others it amounted to no more than a hollow sentimental pathos; or this path led to the collecting and classifying activity of the casuists. Ethics—

not piety—evaporated into empty feeling or into a game of classifying concepts. We can see this in the many masters of the Catholic and the Lutheran Churches who were in their religious ethics either ecstatics who reveled in enthusiasm, or ingenious subtilizing fathers confessor, or both in one. We see it most closely and clearly, combined in one person, in Schleiermacher, when we consider the false emotion of his *Monologe* and the advocatory art in his *Christliche Glaubenslehre:* things which people have discovered in the *medulla theologiae moralis* of the Jesuit Busembaum can be found in this case just as well and no less openly.

This kind of enthusiasm and casuistry in ethics have a common root: one as much as the other is characteristic of a merely external acceptance of ethics. They get along together just as harmoniously as the rapture of the mysteries can coexist with subtilizing, or ardent piety with frivolity. Many a pious church hymn and many an insinuating amatory song have the same author. Romanticism has no difficulty in bringing such extremes together.

Romantic enthusiasm lifts the good aloft and removes it into the dim distance of the incomparable and unattainable; at the same time it portrays the good in a human countenance out of which it looks at us and we can look back at it, face to face, in admiration and ecstasy, and stretch out our arms toward it. Thus the moral good is represented in human, and at the same time superhuman, form; it is of our own kind, and yet above our kind; it confronts us, but makes no demands. It is not really a standard and lacks the power to issue commandments. Both are given at once: the ethical which one would like to love; and the passive, the romantic, in which one wants to live. As a substitute

for constant activity demanded by the ethical commandment, we have adoration in which the romantic
impression of the moment is vented, and yearning
which need only admire and enjoy but not achieve anything. This romantic enthusiasm always feels that it
has done enough when it has beheld the object of its
rapture and exclaimed fervently: *ecce homo!* In the
Gospel according to John, where Pontius Pilate speaks
these words, "Here is the man," Pilate is represented
almost as a romantic; and Luther showed a fine understanding of the romantic manner when, in translating
the Bible, he deviated from the real and literal meaning
to introduce a sense of admiration: "Behold, what a
man!"

There is a vast variety of subtle shades all the way
from gentle longing to sentimentality, this sad-sweet
joy at being so lowly and weak oneself while ardently
adoring something that is so ideal and perfect. And this
joy will only grow in pain and rapture, the more ecstasy
aspires to ever loftier and more miraculous features
which are sought and seen in the ideal. The boundless-
ness of feeling exalts it beyond this actual world with
its defects and attributes all transcendent qualities to
the ideal. A radiant nimbus crowns it. Absolute man
is thus created: the man who has become a dogma.
Ethics evaporates into exaltation. The place of the determinate ethical commandment is taken by the aureole-
surrounded image which is to be adored. Fichte called
it the "over-real"; Schlegel said, the "over-holy."
Modern Protestant theology had its own favorite word
which was meant to convey everything: *unerhört*—
"tremendous."

The ideal here is no longer the ethical personality
which man should embody as he strives and struggles,

but the superhuman and thus after all mythical personality: the saint, the hero, the god-man. Enraptured, one feels seized by him—and has satisfied oneself as well as him. And because the ideal here is "over-holy" and "tremendous," people like to praise all this as a heroic ethic. As a matter of fact, it is merely a heroic landscape with a castle built right up into rosy clouds where phantasy loves to alight from time to time without obligation.

To this romantic idealism, Feuerbach's well-known explanation of religion is indeed quite applicable: at least insofar as it tries to be ethical, this kind of religion really offers a magnified reflection of man; man beholds the artifact of his own feelings—something born of the union of phantasy and emotion. The development is really obvious. When the pious ego has high aspirations but is denied any creative ascent, its desire must lead it into the remote regions of transfiguration. Romantic enthusiasm follows from absolute dependence. The psychological motivation here is the same as that which invoked authority as the support and complement of the passivity in which man is supposed to discover his essence. The authority gives the dependent creature the prop he requires, and romantic enthusiasm gives him the scope for which he longs.

This enthusiastic veneration of the radiant human image is a typically romantic trait and therefore by no means confined to the Church. It is equally characteristic of the whole of antiquity in its decline, particularly the later phases of Stoicism, and of similar ages during which the cult of personality has its history. The romantic always needs a person to worship, whether it be as an object of religious fervor or merely of aesthetic feeling. That this trait has won greater significance in the church is simply due to the fact that the absolute man here became the historic point of unity for the religion.

It had been Paul's work to substitute faith in Jesus for the faith of Jesus. He had implanted the savior of the mystery religions who redeems by grace into the person of the Jewish messiah: the latter had furnished the name and the figure, the former the content. Now the Gospel, the tidings of the messiah—of his life, his preaching, and his death—was romanticized and transformed into the tidings of the god-man. In this form, the Gospel could be placed alongside the Pauline epistles, the book proclaiming the victory of the redeemer over original sin. A certain unity had been achieved, even if in spite of everything, it remained artificial.

There was one factor which facilitated this union: the sentimental mood which pervades the Gospel. This mood is not confined to the Gospel: a large portion of the Jewish literature of that time is characterized by this tone of world-weariness and *Weltschmerz*. But it is most fervent in the Gospel. And it is notable how we perceive it here even in the words about nature. There is nothing left here of the ancient biblical naiveté which had simply listened to the songs and sounds outdoors and looked out into the green and the blossoms, now gay, now sorrowful. The simplicity which saw and heard quite without affectation has developed into a sentimentality which seeks and desires only itself in everything that is outside—that melancholic poetry of the city-dweller who can grasp nature only with the yearning which impels him toward that which is distant and different. Only the mind and thought of a sentimentalist could have found expression in such emotion-laden expressions as those about the fowl of the air which neither sow nor reap nor gather into barns, and of the lilies of the field, how they grow and neither toil nor spin. That would hardly be the song of the unsentimental peasant.

But in spite of this sentimentality, in spite of all the points of contact with romanticism, the Gospels constitute, at least as far as their original content is concerned, a thoroughly unromantic book—or, as we might say just as well, a book in the spirit of the Old Testament, a thoroughly Jewish book. For the determinate commandment has its place in them; the demands of the Gospels do not lack the ancient prophetic decisiveness; and the Law they put up is unconditional. This is what is most essential and most genuine in them, and by virtue of this they stand, to be precise, outside the Christian sphere, if we use the word "Christian" exclusively in the sense which its whole history has given it. Christianity is, ever since Paul created it, a doctrine of salvation, the doctrine of grace which redeems through Christ; and of this, which alone is truly Christian, the old, the real, Gospel has nothing at all. Whatever of all this is to be found in the Gospels, in the form which they eventually assumed, has merely been added to them to fit them for the New Testament; but for the original Gospels this is an accretion, something alien and opposed.

History proves it by experience. The real Gospel has always been something of an embarrassing reproach in the Church, as long as it could not be reduced to a mere image for romantic exuberance. In a literary sense, one possessed it and praised it loudly; but in any other sense, in practice, one did not take it seriously. The Christian attitude toward it was nothing but a continual attempt to get rid of its essential core and to interpret away its power to command. One often spoke and wrote of the imitation of Christ; but one guarded against understanding it in its original sense as a demand made upon all men.

The Catholic Church, to be sure, has in this case, too, as elsewhere, contrived a way out. In much the same way in which it dealt with pure romanticism, it took the Gospel also off the shoulders of the community of believers and handed it over to a few chosen persons. It was removed from the sphere of duty, and faithfulness to it was declared to be a supererogatory accomplishment, *opus supererogationis*. Thus it was circumvented and still left intact. Catholicism never lacked men and women of such evangelical piety. It had its Francis of Assisi, this most moving figure of the Middle Ages—moving in its cheerful purity and infinite longing—and though he had no peers, there have been a number who were of his kind. But the decisive influence he had within the world of the Church was really due less to his fulfillment of the ideal, than to his ready obedience to the authority of the Church. Essentially, he himself belongs to the group that had followed John the Baptist and then found their messiah in Jesus. But those who followed him and called themselves after his name were men of the Church for which Paul had laid the foundation. In spite of everything, however, a place had been left for the Gospel within Catholicism, even if such a place was purchased at the price of a division between ordinary and extraordinary religion.

Protestantism, on the other hand, became utterly helpless at this point. Apart from occasional possibilities in Pietism, it had no room at all for the real Gospel. Here it has always been pure literature. It offered a beautiful text for sermons; but the sermon which followed the text generally said something completely different. People were not told that to be a disciple of Jesus and a Christian one had to live up to the com-

mandments of Jesus. Instead, the sermon generally
proclaimed clearly and loudly that a Christian need not
fulfill them, or at least not always, or not entirely, and
could still be a good Christian. All eloquence was devoted to this theme. The determinate demand is interpreted away, the commanding force is annulled by some
demonstration, and the essential message and the
enduring significance of the Gospel has again and again
been summarized in this way: its value remains great
and exalted, but it is not meant so precisely and seriously that one should also fulfill it. This was called the
interpretation of the Gospel.

Modern liberal Protestantism, finally, has turned this
romantic irony into a romantic play—one might almost
say, a romantic comedy. It wanted to make room again
for the evangelical ideals. The ancient Church had
assigned them a place in the sacrifice entailed in pure
monasticism, but modern liberal Protestantism grants
them a more comfortable and eloquent place—in the
wide and windy expositions of the New Testament
handbooks. Here alone this evangelic piety has its field:
here it sows and reaps. It brings in abundant sheaves
of words and thus satisfies itself. In the commentaries
to the New Testament, poverty, for example, and self-
denial, and renunciation of all earthly aspirations and
cares are exalted, though very soon thereafter, in the
theory and practice of the Christian life, the very opposite of all this is taught and demanded. In the commentaries, any invoking of God in an oath is repudiated as
a typically inferior show of faith; but in life oaths are
defended and even demanded. There it is considered
pious and noble not to resist evil, while here it is accepted as a duty for a man to fight all injustice. There
one speaks of moralism with the scorn of those who are
elevated far above it, while here the blessings of sober

civic morality are praised and inculcated. This commentary idealism, this textbook holiness—what else
can one call it but romantic comedy? That those per-
forming it do not at all experience it as such, can perhaps be explained only by remembering that the real
Gospel could not at any time be taken seriously in
Protestantism.

But at bottom, this is true of the Church altogether:
it has scarcely got around this difficulty. What confronts us is not a contradiction between ideal and
reality—that is essentially human—but the romantic
discord of text and sermon, of word and will, the triumph of romantic irony over the ideal. From Joachim
da Fiore and Savonarola down to Kierkegaard and
Tolstoi, men have frequently protested with agony and
scorn against this condition, but always in vain. It was
bound to be in vain, because all this is of the very
essence of romanticism which is, after all, the essence
of the Christian Church; and the Church therefore
could endure this condition so easily, in spite of everything.

Romanticism does not know imitation, but only
admiration. The life of the heroes is experienced as a
spectacle for God and man. Characteristically, this designation is first encountered in the romantic phase of
Stoicism, then in exactly the same way in Paul and,
after him, frequently in the Church; and it is no less
common in modern romanticism. This expression is not
designed to suggest a mere comparison: for the romantic enthusiast, the ethical is in fact something that
is exhibited and can be seen or heard and thus experienced and enjoyed. It is an edifying proclamation, a
touching story, a word spoken from a stage—a poem,
but no demand made of man; an experience, but not
something that determines one's life. The place of the

enthusiasm, this feeling that feeds on itself, often finds expression in sentimental flaccidity: emotion blurs all outlines and lets everything human coalesce. Such gentle melancholy can be pure and noble: it can take the form of that graciousness which comprehends and forgives all. But much more often it means forbearance of a different sort: forgiving and transfiguring all our own faults and responding with silence toward our own guilt. The result is a calm, an almost serene, consciousness of sin—the lovely melancholy of religion. At this point it is again accompanied by the danger of irony, the danger of casuistry.

A good illustration of this tendency may be found in the development of German romanticism, which was so sentimental in its beginnings, but eventually, in its final phases, became identified with that affected mockery which would be above the Law, and with that frivolity for which the whole of ethics is a mere play on words, a mere artistry of concepts. Romanticism claims that the individual has the right to have, in every particular case, his own feeling and his own mode of expression—and, in the end, his own morality. Moral questions become occasions for jokes. Often, sentimentality and frivolity have the same root.

Casuistry has its place even in the poetic imagination and in revery, and from these, too, it enters romanticism. But it becomes most pronounced where the romantic mind has come into sobering contact with prosaic life. The higher all this romantic exuberance has worked itself up into the "over-real" and "over-holy," the less significance it leaves, with its sublime expressions, to the reality of this life. No matter how much it seemed to mean, it means little now. Again and again it must be adapted to this lower world and interpreted for it; and in this way, moral tasks easily

become a matter of calculation, a suggestion of possibilities—subjects fit for negotiation, rather than commandments. Casuistry is usually nothing other than the
precipitate of exuberance which has come into contact
with cold and hard reality—even as the sacraments and
dogmas are the result of the same kind of condensation.
The process is the same in one case as in the other. The
feeling evaporates and the word remains—as a subject
on which both worldly wisdom and unworldliness can
test their skill.

For romanticism this technique is almost indispensable: how else could ethics be approached in its context? Morality has for it the character of a mere *modus
vivendi*; it is something provisional and essentially inferior; and as something that is externally added and
commanded, it naturally requires an external construction. In the romantic context, the ethical commandment
does not arise organically, as it does wherever men
affirm the unity of the independent moral person with
his obligation to act freely in order to realize justice
and perfect himself. Romanticism repudiates all willing
and acting that originates in the self; and the moral
law and the individual conscience are denied any decisive significance, any value or right of their own. Any
judgment or decision regarding what is right or good
must therefore come from outside as a matter of mere
technique. Moral demands are thus no longer commandments or categorical imperatives, but mere directions:
either decrees of the constituted authorities or "counsels for the conscience" of those who have heard a call.
As the sacred "ought" which manifests itself in man
becomes less and less decisive, external factors, circumstances and considerations, become more and more crucial. The doctrine of morality becomes a doctrine of
individual cases, and the study or science of it approxi-

mates jurisprudence and becomes a matter of interpretation and legality. All this was long familiar to romantic religion from elsewhere. Dogma and Law had gone hand in hand in occidental Christianity from the very beginning, and Doctrine enjoyed the dignity of the law of the state.

The only thing categorically demanded is therefore, once again, submission to an external authority. This serves as the sanction, and this alone can define and guarantee, and thus grant certainty and security. It can make up for everything else; hence absolution is so easy. It covers everything; and corresponding to the doctrine of double truth, we now have a manifold morality. Since the demands which are made come from the outside, dispensations can also be granted from outside: the authority which commands also absolves. It could scarcely have been otherwise. An authority which decides everything must also have the competence and the power to acquit, to pardon.

The forms and effects of casuistry have varied according to ages and regions. But whatever its extent may have been, it has always belonged to romantic faith. Though not always desired, it is the ever-ready mentor of romantic ethics, which is the ethic of absolute dependence; casuistry invariably attends the moral law, which is assigned no intrinsic value of its own. It would therefore be a mistake to assume that casuistry developed only among the fathers of the Society of Jesus or, somewhat earlier, among the Scholastics. It can be found in the ancient Church, too, and, still earlier, in the romantic phases of Greek philosophy; for example, in the thought of Chrysippus and his disciples. And it is no less erroneous to associate it exclusively with Catholicism, as if it did not also have its place in Protestantism.

Protestantism has of course limited the area of the application of casuistry: we need only recall Protestantism's fight against the sacrament of penance and the power of absolution. But in the first place, the very essence of indulgence and absolution is found in baptism which the Protestant Churches, too, dispense as a liberating sacrament and a guarantee to blot out sinfulness. What is really decisive, moreover, is that here, too, the moral law is brought to man merely from the outside. In Protestantism, too—and, as a matter of fact, still more decisively than in Catholicism—ethics is not an essential part of religion, but can only be added to it; the positive appreciation of the moral idea and the moral will is lacking. Therefore, casuistry with all its dangers is present in Protestantism also; and in the history of Protestantism, morality is considered for each case separately.

The air of superiority with which some modern representatives of Protestantism like to depreciate the "moralism" of the Old Testament is really an expression of their embarrassment: fresh from Kant's philosophy, they look for an ethic which their Pauline faith does not permit them to find. If a romantic religion wants to become ethical, it has only two alternatives: romantic exuberance or casuistry. Via the first, it seeks to escape from the definiteness of the Law into the expanse of heaven; and it has no other way but the second when it wants to return to the narrow confines of the earth.

Everything that is characteristic of romantic religion makes a united front against the idea of a moral law. All its multifarious tendencies coalesce in this opposition. Justice is to be reduced to a mere feeling and experience; the good deed is effected, not by human will and action, but by divine grace; man himself is a mere object and not a personality; and the conception of the finished dominates everything. The essential ethical dignity and value is ruled out by everyone of these factors. The will becomes supernatural, and only *concupiscentia,* concupiscence, remains to man. Ethics here lacks the foundation and the carrier as well as the ideal and the goal. Something more diametrically opposed to ethics than romanticism would be hard to find.

HUMANITY

We may deem it further proof of these considerations that the universally human, the humane, cannot be freely appreciated either. It is encroached upon from all sides. The value of the right act, created by the human will and hence possible for everybody, is blotted out or overshadowed by the significance of that supernatural providence which elects one man and rejects another. The ideal of the baptized believer, which goes hand in hand with the sacraments, interferes with the growth of the ethical ideal of the good man. In addition, there is the feeling of contentment and self-righteousness. This feeling that one has been redeemed without having done anything to merit it generally rules out any feeling for those who are merely human but who live in a different world, without salvation. They are considered men set apart, and no connecting link establishes a bridge to them.

What is thus taken away from humanity is at the same time a loss for universalism. It had already been narrowed down considerably by the conception of the Church, which had done away with the unity of mankind and all but reduced the God of all men to a God of the Church. To be sure, within the Church the equality of all believers was claimed at least in principle. But

270

the price for this is that all who stand outside the circle
of the elect are placed immediately and absolutely in
the realm of depravation and become *massa perditionis*
—the multitude that is destined to perish. When the
Epistle to the Galatians, and similarly also that to the
Romans, exults, "here is neither Jew nor Greek, here
is neither bond nor free," the full emphasis falls on
the word "here"; and Luther's translation brings this
out very well.[29] Between "here" and "there" lies a deep
cleft, and the unity of mankind is thus destroyed.

What romantic religion takes away from the worth
of man and his freedom is not compensated for by the
fact that the ideal and commandment had their place
in the original preaching of the Gospel. In this case, too,
the essence of the Gospel has been without lasting effect
in the development of the Church doctrine. This is
understandable enough when we consider that the
Gospel is in this respect at one with the Old Testament,
which is also attested by the fact that the commandment to love one's neighbor appears in the Gospel as a
quotation from the Old Covenant. Hence this humane
word generally required interpretation in the Church;
and theoretical and practical intolerance had an oppor-
tunity to test their skill on it.

But for all the triumphs that this particularism won
in the Church, it did not owe its existence to the
Church: it always attends romanticism. Diogenes the
Cynic already had been able to mock that "an Agesilaus
and an Epaminondas, because they were not initiated
in the mysteries, are supposed to be among the repro-
bates in the underworld, while the most insignificant
wretch is granted an abode on the isle of the blessed if
only he was one of the initiated."

29. Galatians 3.28; Romans 10.12. *Tr.*

It is no more than a consequence of such narrowness when a man like Augustine claims that any supposed excellence in a pagan or unbeliever has merely borrowed the semblance of goodness and is, in reality, "sooner a vice."[30] And it is another such consequence when the literature of the Church asserts for centuries, whenever the question of human virtue is brought up, that virtue does not exist where the right faith is lacking. This, of course, is quite consistent: where the strength of moral action is gained only through the miracle of grace, and the non-Christian stands outside and has no part in this gift, he must also be lacking in any true moral capacity. A capacity for good in a pagan or a heretic is, in this context, almost a self-contradiction.

In the self-assured consciousness of its strength, the Catholic Church has often exercised the virtue of inconsistency and built bridges. Even as it was always inclined to make some concessions to the sphere of human activity and its value, it did not hesitate at times, especially in the age of the Renaissance, to circumvent this principle of narrowness. Later, when a day came that demanded it, the Church even repudiated the principle expressly: Jansenism seems to have risen against the Church in the name of Augustine and was proclaiming this ethical particularism in his name. The Church had to fight this position. At the same time, it also wanted to define its position as against Protestantism. For in the Protestant doctrine, too, this principle of exclusiveness had again become more prominent —not simply as something more or less accidental or

.

30. *De civitate Dei* XIX, 25: *Proinde virtutes, quas sibi habere videtur—sc. mens veri Dei nescia—, nisi ad Deum retulerit, etiam ipsae vitia sunt potius quam virtutes.*

occasional, but as a clear consequence of the central and decisive phrase "by faith alone." It is part of the new romanticism that morality, too, can be born only of that faith which is received as a gift. Melanchthon merely gave this doctrine the characteristic imprint of his dry, cold manner. In the *Loci Communes,* in the chapter on "The Power and the Fruits of Sin," we find the soberly and rigidly stated proposition: the excellencies of a Socrates or a Zeno are the attributes of pagan, hence of "unclean," souls, and as such mere "shadows of virtue"; they "must not be considered true virtues, but are to be regarded as vices."[31] These harsh words are aimed, above all, at humanism; for this movement had sought piety outside the Church, too. Nor was this the only point at which humanism, after preparing the way for Lutheranism, was dispossessed and displaced by the latter.

Assuming the presuppositions of Paulinism, the repudiation of the merely human was entirely consistent. Augustine and Luther were merely the faithful disciples of the apostle; they took seriously the word of the Epistle to the Romans: "Whatsoever does not issue from faith is sin."[31a] Or, to cite Melanchthon again: "By virtue of the forces of nature, all men are truly and

31.   *Loci Communes,* ed. Plitt-Kolde, p. 86: *Esto, fuerit quaedam in Socrate constantia, in Xenocrate castitas, in Zenone temperantia, tamen quia in animis impuris fuerunt, immo quod amore sui ex philautia oriebantur istae virtutum umbrae, non debent pro veris virtutibus, sed pro vitiis haberi.* [Both here and in the quotation from Augustine in the preceding footnote, Dr. Baeck translates *vitium* as *Fehler:* fault, error. But the word also often means "vice"—particularly when coupled with *virtus* in discussions of moral matters. *Tr.*]
31a.   This quotation, from Romans 14.23, is reiterated time and again in Kierkegaard's *The Sickness unto Death* and represents one of the central tenets of that book. *Tr.*

always sinners."[32] This principle was certainly helpful for the missions. Their success could be assured if the unbeliever was denied everything and the convert could thus be promised everything. It strengthened the missionary tidings that all those who were addressed could be considered as lacking in everything. The affirmation of the dignity of man certainly brings men together and teaches them to understand and respect one another; but for this very reason, any missions based on this idea cannot equal the compelling effect of the threat of damnation. Where the dignity of man is affirmed, heaven is not set off by the frightening image of hell in the foreground. The conception of a Church "which alone makes blessed," completely excluding all outsiders, seems to offer the potential convert a greater bargain.

The next step to active intolerance is small indeed. Where everything is denied to those outside the Church, while everything is given to those who are within it, it is easy to see how the Church would soon claim the right to drive out whatever remains outside it as being void of value. Gradually, such a Church becomes convinced of its competence, even its duty, to annihilate that which it cannot acknowledge. Whatever is apart from and without it is null and void and hence should be annulled. The Church possesses salvation and has been gifted with perfect justice which, to be complete, must include this office of passing judgment by virtue of which it abolishes whatever contradicts it. In the desire for such full judicial power, there has been little difference between the Papacy and Lutheranism.

Another development has been no less calamitous and

.

32. *Ibid.*, p. 87: *Et ut rem omnem velut in compendium cogam, omnes homines per vires naturae vere semperque peccatores sunt et peccant.*

no less frequent. This finished perfected justice, this
self-assurance of the possessing, has also often found
expression in a tranquil, comfortable, almost smug
indifference. Being satisfied with itself, the Church
was capable of beholding a great deal without being at
all upset. Since it considered itself a world apart, it
could leave many matters in this world to take care of
themselves. Having issued from divine grace, the pious
faith was superior to everything impermanent and
human; hence it could regard earthly deeds, of whatever character, as something inferior and indifferent,
as beneath it. So one was prepared to overlook and dis-
count and indulge anything: the correct faith was
easily satisfied with itself; for "whoever believes in
him is just."

A good deal of Church history is the history of all
the things which neither hurt nor encroached upon this
piety, all the outrages and all the baseness which this
piety was able to tolerate with an assured and undis-
turbed soul and an untroubled faith. And a spirit is
characterized not only by what it does but, no less, by
what it permits, what it forgives, and what it beholds
in silence. The Christian religion, very much including
Protestantism, has been able to maintain silence about
so much that it is difficult to say what has been more
pernicious in the course of time: the intolerance which
committed the wrongs or the indifference which beheld
them unperturbed. Perhaps such indifference is even
more romantic than intolerance, for it is more passive.
It is wholly fitting for the faith which does not want to
wrestle and act, but is content to wait and experience;
it is entirely commensurate with the repudiation of the
Law. The moral duty of justice and the fight for justice
are associated with the phase that lies in the past and
has been overcome.

REDEMPTION

The ideal of the romantic looks altogether different. For him the highest aim is the achieved redemption, the quintessence of being beyond the Law, of pure abandonment of self. This is the end of romantic religion. All romantic faith is faith in such redemption. It is the fulfillment of the longing for passivity, of the desire to be rid of the commanding will, of the craving to be seized and to experience absolute dependence.

This is what Paul taught quite clearly. Redemption is the fact of salvation which has been consummated in man; man does not bring it about, nor does he contribute to it: he merely experiences it. On human paths and in the framework of human duty there is neither atonement nor reconciliation. Even as man does not create sin, but is born in sinfulness in accordance with his lot, man himself cannot get rid of sin—he can scarcely even fight against it. He does not rise up against his guilt; but a Higher Power, which elects some men, raises him entirely out of his guilt. He is pulled out without doing anything himself, without any achievement of his own; someone else has achieved it, acting in his place. "Christ's justice is our justice, Christ's expiation is our atonement." No road leads to the goal, and no human strength is here confirmed: something supernatural and finished takes place; redemption is something that happens to man; man is only the object.

Redemption has nothing whatever to do with the exertions and tasks of the inner life, with the struggles and responses of conscience, with the wrestling and ultimate peace of the soul, with ethical striving and ethical freedom. Redemption in this sense does not signify any unfolding of human nature, any arduous ascent, any triumph over sin—altogether nothing that can be commanded—it is a supernatural process, determined by the chance of fate and accomplished by a miracle. What this redemption signifies is a metamorphosis in which the substance of man is changed: he is liberated from his "mortal body," from transitoriness and sinfulness, and made godlike and eternal. Redemption is granted from the beyond as a gift of grace, and its essential nature remains outside all moral law, beyond any decision for good or evil. Such redemption is rooted in a wholly different world, in a wholly different region from that of spiritual renewal.

That which elevates the Christian to an essential superiority over the non-Christian is therefore not a higher level of morality as such. The decisive difference is to be found in baptism, where the miracle becomes effective. The sacrament gives everything and leads to everything. The preaching of Paul proclaims, not a new ethic, but a new salvation, a miracle which creates immortal men. And the same is true of the doctrine of those who preached the faith after Paul. What is decisive according to their teaching is not a better and different commandment, but "water, bread, and wine"; through these man is given the grace which guarantees redemption. In Luther's words: "the nourishment of Christ does it."[33]

The Pauline religion is thus a religion of redemption through sacraments. To describe it, as has sometimes been done, as an ethical religion of redemption, constitutes a perversion of fact and a denial of its very essence. Everything here depends on the liberating

---

33. Erlangen edition, 48, 63: "What are the Ten Commandments to me? Why should I require the Law or good works for blessedness? When the nourishment of Christ does it, I am not permitted to do any good works to attain eternal life."

miracle; ethical achievement adds nothing to it. Any belief in the vital validity of such achievement would be unbelief and submission to the old yoke of the Law. The question, "What is my task? What does God demand of me?" is beside the point. The miracle redeems, and nothing else. Thus the romantic faith as such is utterly amoral; precisely this is its essence. However high the moral stature of some human beings who had this faith may have been, they achieved this stature not on account of the faith but, one might almost say, more likely in spite of it. Tolstoy's remark sounds perhaps like an exaggeration, but when applied to the faith it does bring out the crux of the matter: "One does what one likes and allows oneself to be redeemed."

All religious hope and reflection thus points to the single question: Have I been redeemed? When and how shall I be redeemed? What is here preached is the doctrine of the salvation of the self and the upward glance of receptivity. Everything revolves around the yearning to be saved; the self is central in the meaning of religion. The hope of becoming eternal dominates and decides everything. Religion becomes the pledge of life, the guarantee of eternity; the baptized are those who receive it, and the Church becomes the institution which grants this surety. The romantic faith in redemption is the pious faith of self-centeredness; in the religious sphere, as elsewhere, the self with its aspirations is foremost. Augustine put it correctly: "God and the soul and nothing more" is the content of man's religion; our fellow men do not absolutely belong to it, they are dispensable. In the human sphere, romantic passivity requires only itself. The pious man exults in his own eternal happiness; he remains within the circle of his self.

278

Even the idea of sacrifice could in this connection receive an egoistic meaning. For romantic faith develops a peculiar kind of asceticism and a special kind of sacrifice—the sacrifice which a man makes for his own sake. Asceticism as such is not romantic; it is found everywhere in many different forms, ranging all the way from the most impressive heights down to the abysses of quaintness. It can have profound religious significance and be entirely genuine; in fact, no religious seriousness can completely dispense with it, as it trains the power of resistance and the steadfastness of the will. But in romanticism, the nature of asceticism is changed entirely and it is often no longer part of education but belongs far more in the sphere of selfishness. Even so, it assumes many different forms. But all of them have something in common: in Catholicism there has sometimes been a tendency toward phantastic self-mortification, while in Protestantism a certain sentimental brooding on sin has often been cultivated; but a self-centeredness that wallows in itself is always there—that "voluptuousness" which distinguishes romanticism. The self serves only the self.

The hermit who is exclusively preoccupied with himself, and whose experience of activity in the human sphere is confined solely to the things which a man does for himself, can therefore be regarded here as the great representative of sacrifice and hence as a saint. He is truly the egoist of piety: he lives for himself without doing any work for others and is therefore able to be wholly an object; he is in a position to devote himself entirely to the feeling of absolute dependence and to the experience of the bliss of redemption. He knows only himself and his God and hence exemplifies the purest piety—in the romantic sense of that term. Every such religion of redemption creates its hermits since it leads man back to himself. The neo-Platonic religion did so, and Buddhism has its hermits no less than Christianity.

Here is one point where Luther, who generally sought to reawaken the romanticism of faith in its full purity, turned his back on it. He expelled monasticism from his Church, and he rigorously repudiated celibacy which had created, and had been intended to create, a class of quasi-hermits. On the other hand, Luther had no sufficient knowledge of genuine ethical asceticism and gave up much of the real strength of genuine restraint; and this is a decisive shortcoming of Protestantism.

The banished child of romanticism, moreover, soon found another door of admission. By making the sense of sin a dominant feeling in his faith, Luther opened the door again to romantic asceticism. In Protestantism, too, the pious, who submerge themselves again and again in the consciousness of their sinfulness, are primarily interested in themselves. Such preoccupation of the sinful ego with itself is one of the prime characteristics of Lutheranism; it is a trait which has also been associated with its revivals, in the early days of Pietism no less than in the nineteenth century. Above all, however, it is the very core of this pious egoism that survives in Protestantism: the principle of faith alone. For to this faith which is held to be everything there belongs essentially only the ego which wants to receive from God and possess, and thus egoism dwells in the very heart of this religion.

Such has ever been the nature of romantic faith when it has remained true to its essence. It is merely a last, logical step for romanticism finally to carry egoism into the conception of the deity itself and claim that it is of the essence of God that he seek his own redemption. That is what a romantic philosophy taught. But do we not really find the same idea in the ancient mystery religions and, basically, also in the Pauline faith? Resurrection which was the central fact of the ancient mystery cults is essentially nothing other than the self-redemption of God. To this Paul added the old Jewish ideas of sacrifice and atonement, the idea of devotion; but the other conception still remains clearly visible underneath. It was entirely consistent to proceed from the egoistic doctrine of redemption, preached by romanticism, to the idea that the divine ego revolves around itself.

This was not the only decisive trait within the Church. As has been pointed out a number of times already, the Pauline faith contained, from the very beginning, some elements of legalism which had been derived from the Old Testament without having been overcome. In the course of the history of the Pauline faith these elements came to the surface time and again and were responsible for the other major tendency—that which is opposed to all egoism. This is most evident in the history of monasticism, in the development that leads from the solitary and self-seeking anchorites, who lived in the desert and desired only their own salvation, to the brothers and sisters of mercy and love who knew how to sacrifice themselves for their fellow men. They became the pride and glory primarily of the Catholic Church, but also of some of the other Churches.

It was not in vain that the Church possessed the Old Testament and the old Gospel which belonged with it. But whenever the romantic faith reflected on itself and tried to recover an awareness of its distinctive essence, it experienced and manifested itself again as the religion of pure egoism. The higher it ascended and the more tender and ecstatic it became, the more egoistic it became. Its distinctive character has always shown itself in this manner.

Another trait characterizes such a doctrine of salvation. Eudaemonism finds a place in it; but any connection between eudaemonism and ethical achievement, from which it derived its original justification as well as its limitations, is completely dissolved. It was like "the cunning of the idea."[34] Pure romanticism had rejected eudaemonism along with the moral law. Now the idea of salvation provided it with a new and ample sphere. Happiness, or bliss, became the one and only meaning and purpose of existence and the quintessence of fulfillment. It was no longer something that attends and follows ethical action, it was no longer the warmth of the pious mind; it became merely the gift of grace in which everything is granted and which means everything; and man himself could do nothing to attain it. The content and dignity of existence consisted, in this instance, too, in that which was received without effort: the good man is he that receives. The happiness which is granted as a gift is everything.

Another conception would hardly be possible in this faith. For here life is not supposed to be a task set by God as in classical religion, nor is it negated as in Buddhism; hence the bliss which is granted remains the only value. Sometimes this bliss has been understood in more sensuous terms, sometimes more spiritually. But it is not decisive whether the longing for it is primarily sentimental and aesthetic or whether it drowns in the rapture of an ecstatic trance; whether it spends itself in the fervent enjoyment of the sacra-

34. An allusion to Hegel's posthumously published lectures on the Philosophy of History, Introduction. *Tr.*

ments or in the voluptuous brooding on sinfulness;
whether it wallows in the images of one's own para-
disiac delights or those of the hellish tortures of another: in any case, everything revolves around the self
and its possessions and enjoyment. Faith has become
desire: an appetite for happiness.

This egoism of bliss is then rounded out by the anxiety and concern whether salvation has really been
secured; and this anxiety colors the mood of the life
which is supposed to receive everything from the supernatural realm. All and nothing seem to confront each
other, while man himself is characterized only by impotence with its agonizing question. Despair is often
the first and truest psychic expression of absolute dependence; and Tertullian's words are justified: *timor
fundamentum salutis,* being afraid is the foundation of
salvation. This was also the motivation of the young
Luther when he reached out for the faith that meant
everything to him and became his salvation. In terror
and anguish that the promises of the Church might
grant only hope and no more, he clung to the desire to
live in the full certainty and security of faith. In his
Catholic faith he had felt uncertain, as if in suspense,
fretful and fearful. There were the two realms of the
works that were demanded and of the grace that had
been proclaimed, the realm in which one had to prove
oneself and the realm in which one simply received.
The first is not omnipotent and the second does not
always grant man's hope: so he could never know if his
salvation was certain. Only if he reached out wholly
and entirely for the goal, prompted by sheer despair,
grasping for salvation, without first searching for a
way to it, he could feel the peace of salvation. Thus
Luther attained his faith out of the fear of his soul.

Such anxiety has nothing in common with the old

biblical fear of God except its name. It is worlds removed from the ancient reverential awe of the sublime. Only the religion of the ethical will creates that
reverence for God which characterizes the religious
consciousness of those who perceive the commandment,
those who consider themselves created and nevertheless
also subjects, because God addresses commandments to
them. In romantic religion we find anxiety in the face
of God—the fainthearted feeling of those who want to
be objects only. Where everything depends on the fate
of grace, nothing else could possibly dwell in the mind,
alongside the believer's waiting and longing, except
this agonizing anxiety and trembling. The vacillation
between these two states is characteristic of egoistic
piety. These ups and downs, this alternation of elation
and discouragement, are among the most distinctive
features of the romantic and make up his ego feelings.
They should be sharply distinguished from that feeling
of hesitancy which overcomes men when they consider
the distance of their ideals, and from that concern over
the length of man's road which seizes the man of classical religion. These attitudes are as opposed to each
other as are fleeing and seeking.

THE MESSIANIC IDEA

The romantic faith in salvation also furnishes us with
the very opposite of the ancient messianic idea which
was still the idea of Jesus, too: the idea of the days to
come, the idea of the promised kingdom. Such confidence in the meaning of man's exertions is clearly the
opposite of the desire for the possession of the promise
as a gift. In Paul these two ideas had still contended
against each other: the Old Testament on the one side,
romanticism on the other. He was full of his new faith

and yet also still full of his Jewish heritage; and this
inner conflict had introduced a split into the world of
his ideas. The contradiction here was the same as that
which the question of the Law had introduced into his
thought. Those who later went beyond him, the Gnostics, lacked in this respect, too, the experience of that
which had still checked and determined his course;
hence they were able to give the pure romantic answer,
void of the tension of the "time to come."

Even then, however, this pressing thought of the
future could not be completely silenced. That which had
confronted Paul as his Jewish legacy, the old Bible,
had been accepted as part of the Holy Scriptures of
the new faith; and once this had been done, the messianic heritage could never disappear entirely. Again
and again, and often quite suddenly, it emerged, especially as the doctrine of the "eternal gospel" of which
John had spoken in his Apocalypse. But in the end, it
never came to more than a heroic episode. The whole
spirit of the Church was altogether too deeply opposed
to this heritage and always rejected it as soon as possible, disposing of it as the voice of phantastic vision-
aries. Luther in particular, as a decided romantic, bade
it be silent; in the Augsburg Confession[35] it is specifically condemned as a "Jewish doctrine."[36] It has had

35. The confession of the faith of the Lutheran church, written
by Melanchthon to be read at the Diet of Augsburg in 1530. *Tr.*
36. XVII, 5, ed. Tschackert, p. 14: *Damnant et alios, qui nunc
spargunt judaicas opiniones, quod ante resurrectionem mor-
tuorum pii regnum mundi occupaturi sint, ubique oppressis im-
piis.* The German version reads: *Item, hie werden verworfen
auch etliche jüdische Lehren, die sich jetzt auch eräugen, dass
vor der Auferstehung der Toten eitel Heilige, Fromme ein welt-
lich Reich haben und alle Gottlosen vertilgen werden.* In English:
"Here we also repudiate various Jewish doctrines which are now
being spread to the effect that the pious will have a worldly
kingdom before the resurrection of the dead and destroy the
impious."

a certain effect only among the Calvinists and Baptists who stood outside the main stream of strict romanticism. In all the other Churches the pure doctrine of salvation remained predominant. This has been one of the most significant or, if one prefers to put it that way, one of the most fateful spiritual consequences of the triumph of romanticism in the Church: the messianic idea out of which Christianity had developed and from which it had received its name was now pushed back more and more and eventually annulled historically. The place of the kingdom of God on earth, the ancient biblical ideal, was taken over by the kingdom of the Church, the romantic *civitas Dei.*

The tremendous missionary activity developed by the Church may seem to contradict these assertions. For it is after all the meaning of missionary work that one goes out for the sake of one's fellow men to save them and to show them the way of salvation in order that all men may eventually be as one in a single kingdom of salvation—*ut omnes unum.* Yet this desire to convert grew originally, no less than all other messianic hopes, out of strong roots in the Old Testament which remained part of the new Christian community. It was taken over from Judaism almost as a matter of course and continued to be active, and was further strengthened by the feeling that one was proclaiming a new truth. The form of Christian missionary preaching, especially insofar as it was addressed to the educated, was, to begin with, in no way essentially different from the manner of the old Jewish apostles who had proclaimed the one God, His commandment, and His judgment. A change set in only during the second and third century, the decisive period in the development of the Church when dogma and authority prevailed: then the distinctive character of the Church which set it off from

Judaism asserted itself in its propaganda. And here it may be mentioned in passing that this is what happened quite generally: as the Church developed, the changeful history of its faith consisted quite often in this—that one contended and wrestled, consciously or unconsciously, about the space to be left to the ideas of the Old Testament. Consider the issues which, after changing fortunes, eventually were decided formally at the Council of Nicaea:[37] not a few of them were, at bottom, not fights for or against Jewish Christianity, as was supposed at one time—for this Jewish Christianity had had a very brief history which scarcely extended beyond the destruction of the temple—but for or against the Jewish elements in Paulinism itself. For these elements still drew strength from their ancient tradition and still aspired to be effective. In later centuries, too, this dispute was renewed not infrequently.

The missions developed in their own way once the edifice of the Church had been built. Not only the preaching changed, but the whole character of the missions, their motivation and the nature of their successes became something completely different. The Church was now a powerful kingdom of this world, and it began to follow the pressures and the laws of its power. To be sure, the Church did not at any time lack men who wanted to convert others out of promptings of deep love; but any such heartfelt wish to save souls was bound to recede considerably before the domineering aspiration to extend and expand the sphere of dominion. The power of the sword and the art of politics spoke more frequently and urgently than the language

37. The first oecumenical council, held in 325, at which the position of Arius was condemned and the so-called Nicene Creed adopted. *Tr.*

of the heart. It was combat and conquest that issued in the great triumphs. It was the decisive age of the egoistic and really vigorous missions that really created the world-wide church.

The "Catholic" motive, to be sure, did its share and contributed to this development; that is, the now evident and then again unconscious desire to see one's own faith confirmed by the agreement or the subjection of others and to see the principle demonstrated as far as possible: "everywhere and by everybody." This strong Catholic tendency and the God-fearing desire to lead men into the light were easily fused in the mind of the believers. Both are inspired by the image of the one herd led by the One Shepherd, and this is only too easily transmuted into the compelling idea of the world-wide empire wanted by God, the "city of God" to which all must belong who wish to claim any right to existence on earth. *Coge intrare!*[38] Thus in the end everything culminates in the striving for ecclesiastical power. When romanticism turns toward this world, it always arrives eventually at the idea of dominion and authority which, in turn, wants subordinates. The missions, too, are in the end a demand for universal obedience; here, too, the concept of man is discarded in favor of the concept of the obedient subordinate.

That the pious desire to convert men is altogether derived from the sphere of the Old Testament is shown time and again by history. And the course of its further development amply illustrates this origin. The purely religious missions continued where the Jewish heritage was preserved at least within limits. The fate of this Jewish heritage has always been the same as the fate

38. Luke 14.23: "compel (them) to enter"—often interpreted as here. *Tr.*

of the purely religious missions. Hence there is no place
for such missions in the Greek Orthodox Church which
has, for the most part, preserved very little of the Old
Testament legacy, while the wish for redemption and
deification is most prominent in it. The opposite is true
of Roman Catholicism. Here there has always been a
tendency to agree with the ancient Jewish demand
which extolled the value of man's task and man's work.
In spite of all purely ecclesiastical aspirations, the
heartfelt and unselfish desire to convert has never lost
its place entirely in the Catholic Church, but remained
as a way of martyrdom. And it emerged still more
freely in the Baptist sects, that is, in those churches
which accepted more than any of the others the legal
tradition and Old Testament elements. Among these the
call to seek and save souls for God's sake was heard
often.

Lutheranism as such, on the other hand, knows little
or nothing of religious missions; it is something that
has been grafted onto it only relatively late. Its characteristic and original fire spends itself in the interior
affairs of the Church, in the care for the authority of
the word, for the pure doctrine in preaching and instruction. Nor does Pietism refute this, though it did
indeed feel the urge to send out apostles of its faith.
For while it is certainly part of Protestantism, it took
over the motif of the missions, and the decision and
feeling associated with it, not from Lutheranism but
entirely from the Calvinistic, Baptist churches. The
forms in which this desire to make conversions has
manifested itself are manifold indeed, but throughout
an inner connection with the survival of Jewish elements is quite evident. The romantic idea of salvation
could only produce the demand for unlimited ecclesiastic power and the missions that relied on coercion.

What we find in the end are once again external authority, instituted power, and obedient subordinates with
their dazzling poetry and their gloomy prose.

Thus the circle is closed. Feeling is supposed to mean
everything: this is the quintessence of romanticism. It
can be the strength of romanticism that it is capable
of immersing itself and of drawing on powerful feeling; and it is the tenderness of romanticism that it
knows the experience of that which flows and floats.
The romantic may indeed have the gift of which
Schleiermacher spoke in his eulogy on the deceased
Novalis: "everything which his spirit touched became
art, and his whole world view immediately became a
great poem." Romanticism is the contradiction and the
opposition, often so necessary, against that shallow
reasonableness which would dispose of everything,
against that enlightenment which has knowledge of and
answers to everything, and against that activism which
would take care of and execute everything.

Its danger, however, which it cannot escape is this:
the all-important feeling culminates eventually in vacu-
ity or in substitutes, or it freezes and becomes rigid.
And before this happens, it always follows a course
which takes it either into sentimentality or into the
phantastic; it dodges all reality, particularly that of the
commandment, and takes refuge in passivity when confronted with the ethical task of the day. Empathy
makes up for much and gives a freedom which is really
freedom from decision and independence from any inner obligation. All the aesthetic airs and all the irony
that give romanticism its attractive appearance merely
secure for the few pre-eminent that presumption which

reduces religion to the religion of the *beaux-esprits* or the skeptics. And for the many who either do not belong or are not supposed to belong to this élite, strong and strict authority, coercive statutes have been erected and serve at the same time as a great bulwark against that anarchy in which the few are wallowing. Nothing remains unaffected by this development which seizes, in turn, faith and symbol, history and culture, truth and justice, commandment and ideal.

It is not by any means true that romanticism is characterized by some subtle apprehension and knowledge of the irrational. On the contrary, this is no less characteristic of classicism, and above all classical religion which is something altogether different from rationalism or "enlightenment." But for classical religion the irrational is not an ocean in which the ego, swelled with feeling, drowns. Classical religion finds in the irrational the revelation of the existent which summons the self; the revelation of that which is actual and commanding; of that in which everything is rooted that is and shall be; of that in which creature and Creator meet. In classical religion, the irrational is the profound truth of life and therefore also the profound source of the Law, the profound guarantee of certainty, the "arm of eternity" which embraces everything. In classical religion, the irrational appears as the holy, the covenant between the Eternal and man.

The longing which surpasses all mere reason is probably also one of the ingredients of romanticism and its religion. One of its representatives, Augustine, spoke the moving words of the heart that is restless until it rests in God. But there is yet a decisive difference: in romanticism, longing always in the end returns to the self and remains at the level of a mere mood. In clas-